Network
Television
and the
Public
Interest

Network Television and the Public Interest

A Preliminary Inquiry

Edited by
Michael Botein
David M. Rice
New York Law School

LexingtonBooks
D.C. Heath and Company
Lexington, Massachusetts
Toronto

Library of Congress Cataloging in Publication Data

Main entry under title:
    Network television and the public interest.

    Consists chiefly of edited papers presented at a conference held on October 19-20, 1978, and sponsored by the New York Law School and the Edison Electric Institute.
    Includes bibliographical references and index.
    1. Television broadcasting—United States—Addresses, essays, lectures. 2. Television broadcasting and state—United States—Addresses, essays, lectures. 3. Television advertising—United States—Addresses, essays, lectures. I. Botein, Michael. II. Rice, David, 1942-   III. New York Law School, New York. IV. Edison Electric Institute.
    HE8700.8.N365   384.55'4'0973   79-1751
    ISBN 0-669-02927-0

International Standard Book Number: 0-669-02927-0

Library of Congress Catalog Card Number: 79-1751

Contents

Contents

List of Figure
and Tables

Acknowledgments

The editors gratefully acknowledge the invaluable assistance of Ms. Janel Radtke, assistant director of the Communications Media Center, in the research and preparation of this volume. Thanks are also due to Mr. Andrew Laschuk, Ms. Madeleine Nichols, Mr. Howard Simms, Ms. Sherri Reiss, and Mr. Steven Weissman, students at New York Law School, for their research.

Introduction

Michael Botein

Ever since the latest flurry of activity concerning the television networks began at the Federal Communications Commission (FCC) in 1976,[1] my colleagues at the Communications Media Center and I had been thinking about presenting a conference to discuss some of the issues. We should not have been as surprised as we were to find out that some friends at the Edison Electric Institute—the national trade association of electric utilities—had many of the same concerns about network television as did media-reform groups. As an official of the institute later wrote about its attempts to place issue advertising on network television, "we found ourselves somewhere between that croquet game in *Alice in Wonderland*, where the wickets got up and moved around, and the most frustrating trial in Kafka."[2]

New York Law School and the institute thus jointly sponsored a conference at the law school, "Network Television and the Public Interest: A Preliminary Inquiry," on 19-20 October 1978. (Even the timing appeared to be propitious; on 19 October 1978 the FCC issued a new and expanded document in its Network Inquiry.[3]) We called on the expertise of five principal speakers and sixteen panelists to discuss the legal, economic, and operational aspects of network television. The results (edited to reflect subsequent developments and augmented by a chapter by David M. Rice, associate director of the Communications Media Center) appear in this volume.

Some interest groups' concerns about network television are fairly specific—for example, inadequate children's programming. But the narrow nature of many of these concerns led us to ask another question—that is, why people were so interested in network television in the first place. As is common with complex regulatory issues, no one answer emerges; rather, a variety of factors seems relevant.

Concern about network television is hardly new and may even be somewhat cyclical in nature. For example, the FCC's 1941 Chain Broadcasting Rules were prompted largely by a popular perception that CBS and NBC controlled most of a comparatively small number of radio stations through affiliation agreements.[4] Each generation thus seems to have its own distinct set of problems and motivations.

There appear to be at least three moving forces behind today's call for close scrutiny of the television networks. First, U.S. society increasingly distrusts private concentrations of economic power. One manifestation of this attitude has resulted in amendment of the antitrust laws to impose stricter penalties and in the Justice Department's inclination to seek criminal prosecutions. The three commercial networks conveniently fit the traditional image in the United States of economic villains. Their profits are generally high,[5] and they openly assert first amendment and other rights to be free from government supervision.[6]

Second, citizens' groups have become increasingly aware of and concerned about the power of the electronic media. Indeed, the number of media-reform organizations has grown dramatically during the last decade.[7] To a large extent this change in attitudes is probably a result of the role that the electronic media—particularly network television—played in bringing the Vietnam War into the living rooms of the United States. A recent study of audience attitudes thus found that most viewers were content with television programming, but that an increasingly large number favored close government scrutiny of the media.[8] Once again, network television is the most visible medium and thus perhaps the most convenient target.

Third, many observers today seem to believe that television has a quasimystical power to grab—and thus manipulate—a viewer's attention. To a certain extent, this is just a regurgitation of the teachings of now-discarded gurus like Marshall McLuhan.[9] More recent history, however, has witnessed institutions ranging from the American Civil Liberties Union[10] to the Supreme Court of the United States[11] talking about the "impact" or "power" of television. If the television mystique actually exists, its primary beneficiary naturally would be the networks, which reach more people than any other electronic medium.[12]

This new level of consciousness about the media leads different groups to focus on different problems that concern them. These issues cover a wide variety of economic, social, and legal areas.

In terms of economics, there appear to be three basic problems: advertisers' inability to buy time on network programs; the price of advertising time; and the impact of the networks' dominant positions in the advertising market on competing media. (Parts I, II, and III discuss the economic and business policies of the networks.) Groups as dissimilar as the Mobil Oil Company and the Democratic National Committee perceive unfairness in the networks' refusal to accept editorial advertisements on controversial issues.[13] They feel that it is somewhat anomalous for the networks to sell them time to advertise their products but to deny them time to air issue-oriented messages. Second, many advertisers believe that the price of network advertising time is unduly high, because of the oligopolistic structure of network television and the limited amount of advertising time; indeed, the Justice Department's antitrust suit against the National Association of Broadcasters' Television Code claims that restrictions on the amount of advertising time have driven up the price of commercials.[14] Third, independent program producers and owners of independent stations or other media argue that the networks have used their large audience shares and political resources to prevent the development of new programming and distribution systems. For example, the cable-television industry has claimed for a decade that the networks are largely responsible for regulatory restrictions on its growth.[15]

Network television also has been held responsible for many of the nation's social ills. Some of these complaints clearly relate to program content—for example, too much violence in children's programming and too little news coverage of minority groups.[16] Just as the business community wants more commercial minutes at lower prices, citizens' groups want the ability to place their messages on network television. Part V discusses the regulatory and constitutional aspects of this situation.

Finally, the federal government has its own vested interest in regulation of network television, as parts I and IV explain. On the congressional level, the networks have a substantial impact on the political fortunes of all representatives and senators through coverage of them and their campaigns. On an equally immediate level, hundreds of employees of the FCC and other federal agencies make their livings from regulating the networks—regardless of the policy directions in which the regulatory winds blow at any given time. For this subgovernment, regulation of the networks is not only a way of life but also a justification of their very existence.

The networks have aroused intense public interest and scrutiny for more than two generations. On the one hand, the networks have no inclination to relinquish their large shares of the viewing audience. On the other hand, many inherent pressures are pushing the regulatory regime in precisely this direction. This book thus attempts to examine economic, operational, and regulatory developments in network television.

Notes

1. *See* S. Robb, *infra* at 83-86.
2. Young, *Network Television and the Public Interest*, 79/2 Electric Perspectives 2, 3 (1979).
3. Further Notice of Inquiry, Docket No. 21049, 69 F.C.C.2d 1524 (1978).
4. *See* S. Robb, *infra* at 76-77.
5. *See* A. Pearce, *infra* at 12-14.
6. *See* R. Jencks, *infra* at 51-52.
7. *See* Schneyer, *An Overview of Public Interest Law Activity in the Communications Field*, 1977 Wis. L. Rev. 619.
8. The Roper Organization, Inc., Public Perceptions of Television and Other Mass Media: A Twenty-Year Review 1959-1978 (1979).
9. *E.g.*, M. McLuhan & Q. Fiore, The Medium is the Massage (1967).
10. American Civil Liberties Union, Policy No. 19 (March 5, 1978).
11. FCC v. Pacifica Foundation, 438 U.S. 726 (1978). *See also* O. Chase, *infra* at 140.

12. *See* S. Robb, *infra* at 73.

13. *See* R. Jencks, *infra* at 50-52.

14. United States v. National Ass'n of Broadcasters, Civ. No. 79-1549 (D. D.C., complaint filed June 14, 1979).

15. *See* P. Gross, *infra* at 176-177.

16. *See* A. Schwartzman, *infra* at 64-65.

Part I
The Business of
Network Television

1

The Economic and Political Strength of the Television Networks

Alan Pearce

Introduction

Broadcasting in America is both politically and economically powerful. It probably wields more political influence and economic clout than any other industry.

Broadcasting is politically important because every representative and senator has one or more broadcasting stations in his or her home district or state, and relies on those stations for coverage that is essential in a reelection campaign. This simple fact of life gives the broadcasting stations a great deal of influence or power over politicians. In addition, the president, congressional leaders, cabinet members, and the heads of the federal departments and agencies rely heavily on the broadcasting industry—and in particular the television networks—to "inform and educate" the general public via national and local news programs as well as by on-the-spot coverage of press conferences and other "media events."

The industry is economically important because it provides an audience for the advertising industry, which many observers believe to be an integral part of the current prosperity and future growth of the country. Broadcast advertising provides a vital link between manufacturers and consumers. It is perhaps the most effective way for advertisers to reach a vast nationwide audience at relatively low cost.

The three commercial-television networks—American Broadcasting Companies, Inc. (ABC); CBS Inc. (CBS); and National Broadcasting Company (NBC)—are by far the most powerful entities in American broadcasting. They dominate broadcasting and thus wield a great deal of political, social, and economic power. Whatever people think of them, the television networks are major forces in our daily lives.

Seven days a week, year round, the networks offer programming during most of the day to their local affiliates in more than two hundred statistically defined *television markets* throught the country. The networks buy or produce programming and sell commercial minutes within this programming, which is then aired by the local affiliates. In return, the local affiliates receive *station compensation*. This is usually only about one-third of the gross advertising receipts that they would have received if they had

3

taken the risk of buying or producing their own program material, a choice that, however, would have involved far greater expenses. Network affiliates also are allowed to sell short segments of time within the network programming, known as *station breaks* or *adjacencies*, which are often very valuable because of the high rating levels of many network shows.

Although this system at first seems rather complex, it is actually quite simple. And it has led to extremely high profits for the networks, their parent corporations, their other broadcasting properties, and their affiliates. This formula has become so successful, in fact, that the American broadcasting industry is regarded by many as recession-proof.

Industry Structure

Not only are the three commercial networks a triopoly in the purchase, production, and distribution of television programming nationally, they also own the three most powerful and profitable groups of television stations. Each network has five owned-and-operated (O&O) stations. All three own stations in New York, Los Angeles, and Chicago—the first-, second-, and third-largest markets in the United States, accounting for about 18 percent of total television households.[1] Each network has access to between 21 and 23 percent of the total television households through its O&O VHF (channels 2-13) stations.[2] It also should be borne in mind that national television-advertising revenue—the amount of advertising dollars spent by the major advertisers—is disproportionately high in the major markets where the networks have their O&O stations. They thus compete directly—and very successfully—with the non-network-affiliated "independent" stations in these markets.[3] The structure of the television-broadcasting industry is shown schematically in table 1-1.

The dominant parent company in broadcasting is the RCA Corporation (originally called the Radio Corporation of America), which was founded just after World War I.[4] The activities of this conglomerate are divided into four major groups:

1. Broadcasting: the National Broadcasting Company (NBC).
2. Electronics: consumer electronics (color television sets, radios, videocassette recorders, and so on); SelectaVision videodiscs; solid-state components, picture tubes, distributor and special products; government and commercial systems; and RCA Service Company.
3. Communications: RCA Global Communications, an international cable- and radio-communications service; Random House, a major book publisher; and RCA Records.

4. Diversified businesses: Banquet Foods; Coronet Industries, a carpet and home-furnishings manufacturer; Cushman and Wakefield, a real-estate concern; Hertz, the leading automobile renter; and Oriel Foods.[5]

CBS Inc. was the most profitable broadcasting company for twenty years, until it recently lost its ratings lead to ABC.[6] CBS Inc. owns a number of businesses in leisure and consumer fields, all of which involve communications:

1. CBS Broadcast Group: the company's broadcasting interests.
2. CBS Records Group: domestic and international record production and sales.
3. CBS Columbia Group: toy manufacturing and distributing, and a musical-instruments division.
4. CBS Publishing Group: Holt, Rinehart, and Winston, a major U.S. publisher; and other publishing interests.
5. "Other" group: This is a mixed bag that includes a number of business projects that CBS Inc. is attempting to dispose of or is in the process of reorganizing. They include CBS Laboratories Division; Cinema Center Films (which owns the blockbuster movie "My Fair Lady," among others); a number of Canadian cable-television investments; and certain proprietary schools.[7]

American Broadcasting Companies, Inc. resulted from a merger between the American Broadcasting Company and United Paramount Theatres Corporation in 1953,[8] although the ABC broadcasting network was begun in the 1940s.[9] ABC is dominated by three major groups:

1. ABC Broadcasting Group: broadcasting operations.
2. ABC Publishing Group: Word, Inc., a diversified religious-communications company; ABC Farm Publications; ABC Leisure Magazines; *Los Angeles* magazine; and various other book and specialty-periodical publishing enterprises.
3. ABC Leisure Group: ABC Entertainment Center, and ABC Scenic and Wildlife Attractions.[10]

Until recently ABC also owned ABC Records; ABC Record and Tape Sales; and ABC Theatres (formerly United Paramount Theatres), which operated a total of 278 theatres.[11]

Banks have a keen interest in the networks. According to a 1973 report by the Senate Subcommittees on Intergovernmental Relations and Budgeting, Management, and Expenditures, eleven banks owned 38.1 percent of the total shares of CBS Inc., eight banks owned 34.8 percent of

Table 1-1
The Television Broadcasting Industry as of 31 December 1978

	ABC	CBS	NBC	Commercial Independent Stations
Parent Company	American Broadcasting Companies, Inc.	CBS Inc.	RCA Corporation	—
Subsidiary or Division	American Broadcasting Company	CBS Broadcast Group	National Broadcasting Company	—
Network	ABC television network	CBS television network	NBC television network	—

Network Owned-and-Operated (*) and Affiliated Stations (all VHF)

Largest thirteen Markets (ranked by size)	ABC	CBS	NBC	Number of Commercial Independent Stations VHF	UHF
1. New York	*WABC-TV	*WCBS-TV	*WNBC-TV	3	4
2. Los Angeles	*KABC-TV	*KNXT(TV)	*KNCB(TV)	4	7
3. Chicago	*WLS-TV	*WBBM-TV	*WMAQ-TV	1	4
4. Philadelphia	WPVI-TV	*WCAU-TV	KYW-TV	0	4
5. San Francisco/Oakland	*KGO-TV	KPIX(TV)	KRON-TV	1	5
6. Boston	WCVB-TV	WNAC-TV	WBZ-TV	0	3
7. Detroit	*WXYZ-TV	WJBK-TV	WDIV(TV)	0	3
8. Washington, D.C.	WJLA-TV	WDVM-TV	*WRC-TV	1	1
9. Cleveland	WEWS(TV)	WJKW-TV	*WKYC-TV	0	1
10. Dallas/Ft. Worth	WFAA-TV	KDFW-TV	KXAS-TV	1	1
11. Pittsburgh	WTAE-TV	KDKA-TV	WIIC-TV	0	2
12. Houston	KTRK-TV	KHOU-TV	KPRC-TV	0	2
13. St. Louis	KTVI(TV)	*KMOX-TV	KSD-TV	1	1

All U.S. Markets	Number of Network-Affiliated Stations			Number of Commercial Independent Stations
VHF (508)	140	169	164	35
UHF (207)	53	32	42	80
Total (715)	193	201	206	115

Sources: FCC, *TV Broadcast Financial Data—1978*; *Broadcasting Yearbook 1979.*

Note: Each network's total number of affiliates includes its owned-and-operated stations and those nonowned stations that are "primarily" affiliated with it. Over fifty stations located in smaller markets are also "secondarily" affiliated with one or both of the other networks, but these secondary affiliations are not reflected in the table.

American Broadcasting Companies, Inc., and three banks owned 6.7 percent of RCA Corporation.[12]

The top executives at the networks are among the highest paid corporate executives in the United States. Leonard H. Goldenson and Elton H. Rule, chairman and president respectively of ABC, were each paid over $1 million in 1978.[13] William S. Paley, the founder of CBS, usually receives in excess of $750,000, and was paid over $1 million in 1978.[14] Robert W. Sarnoff, who headed RCA from 1968 until 1975, received $483,000 in compensation during 1974.[15] Fred Silverman, who became NBC's new president in 1978, reportedly earns almost $1 million dollars a year.[16] Top network officials earn considerably more than high executives in corporations of similar size.

The Economics of Network Programming

The television networks basically were organized to do two things: (1) to acquire programs of high technical quality and great expense (for example, national-news, sports, drama, comedy, and variety shows) which, in turn, are transmitted to affiliates, including network O&O stations; and (2) to sell commercial time within these programs to national sponsors. In the last twenty years, network programming time has expanded considerably. About two-thirds of affiliate programming (and usually quite a bit more on weekends) is now network-supplied.[17]

Program Costs and Profits

Network affiliates naturally present some locally originated programming, mostly news and public affairs, or off-network syndicated reruns. But the networks are responsible for the bulk of the daily programming for several reasons.

First, with their central programming, sales, promotion, service, and station-distribution facilities, and the weight of their O&O stations, the networks have the resources to afford the cost of popular entertainment shows. This entertainment programming includes: movies from theatrical release that can cost anywhere from $800,000 for two plays of a "B" movie or a made-for-TV two-hour movie, to as much as $15 million for one showing of a blockbuster like "The Godfather"; situation comedies like "Happy Days" or "All in the Family" that cost more than $250,000 for two showings of each half-hour segment; and sixty- or ninety-minute dramas costing from $350,000 to $850,000 for two plays, depending on the length and on talent costs.[18] In addition, all three networks do costly daily news programming, occasional documentaries, and a lot of sports; the three networks, for example, are paying the National Football League (NFL) member clubs $162 million a year for the rights to broadcast games beginning in the 1978 season.[19]

Second, network television is also the most effective system of national advertising. For a relatively small distribution cost, it reaches vast numbers of homes that are tuned in to nightly television programs. In the broadcasting business, of course, ratings determine revenues; the larger a network's audience, the more it can charge for the time it sells to advertisers.

From an advertiser's point of view, the key factor is the size of the audience watching the program and, more importantly, the commercial minutes. The rating points express the absolute number of television homes tuned in to a particular program; in effect, they are the only way for broadcasters to price their merchandise, which is the time the public spends watching television.

Audience-measurement ratings equate with circulation or readership in the print media—that is, copies of newspapers or magazines in the print media, and numbers of homes tuned in to a program in broadcasting. But there is an important economic difference since marginal unit costs for print media differ significantly from those for broadcast media. For example, suppose that a newspaper operation costs $1 million a day with a daily circulation of 1 million copies and advertising revenue at $500,000; the publisher must sell each newspaper for 50 cents in order to break even. If circulation were to double to 2 million copies a day and, as a result, advertising revenue were also to double to $1 million dollars, the publisher still might have to charge nearly 50 cents per copy because some of the costs would increase. The publisher might need more presses, more metal for type, more ink, more pages to carry the advertising (which means higher newsprint costs), and possibly more vehicles and workers to handle distribution of the product. In fact, if a newspaper or magazine becomes very popular and if advertising revenue does not keep pace because the readership is not attractive to advertisers, per-unit costs might actually begin to rise—which could lead to uneconomic publishing.

On the other hand, network broadcasting is not beset by the threat of increases in per-unit costs. Indeed, the reverse is true: As more people watch a program, the per-unit costs fall quite dramatically. If a program costs $1 million dollars to produce and the program has an audience of 1 million TV households, the program costs the broadcaster $1.00 for each household in the audience; the broadcaster thus attempts to fix the rates for the commercial minutes accordingly. If the audience for the show doubles, the unit cost becomes only 50 cents, and so on. The broadcaster, like the newspaper or magazine owner, can charge more for commercial minutes because of the larger audience offered. Unlike the competitors in print, however, the broadcaster's per-unit costs always fall sharply as audience size increases.

(This is not to say, of course, that absolute costs decline; in fact, overall production costs on most television shows have been rising at an average of at least 10 percent a year.[20]

This is a simplistic example, of course, but it does show why the broadcasting industry can make a lot of money when audience size increases. The bigger the audience in broadcasting, the higher the advertising rates, the smaller the per-unit costs, and the larger the profit per program. This explains why the broadcasting business is tied very much to numbers— numbers of homes with television sets turned on and numbers of people watching.

In more scientific terms, two factors become relevant:

1. *Volatility*: A small percentage increase in price (resulting from or following an improvement in ratings) leads to a large percentage improvement in profits. This profit is usually around 85 cents on every incremental dollar, with 15 cents being paid to advertising agencies as a commission.
2. *Profit effect*: After the break-even point has been reached, 85 percent of the additional revenue falls to the bottom line as profit. Conversely, to the extent that the break-even point is not achieved, 100 percent of the revenue shortage is reflected in a bottom-line loss.

In other words, the broadcasting industry presents great profit opportunities if a program earns ratings popularity; but it can result in great losses if a program is unpopular and does not reach the break-even point. This is expressed graphically in figure 1-1.

Program Costs and Revenues

Network-television programming is expensive, but it generates substantial advertising revenues. In 1977, the three networks' program costs totalled about $1.33 billion, excluding network administrative and general-operating expenses and the line charges that the networks pay for feeding the programs to their affiliates.[21] This programming produced gross revenues for the networks of $3.35 billion.[22] There are two important deductions from these gross-revenue figures: advertising-agency commissions and station compensation, which together amount to about 20 percent of gross revenues, leaving net revenues of $2.58 billion for 1977.[23] Of course, these revenues are in addition to the more than $500 million that the networks' O&O television stations gross annually.[24]

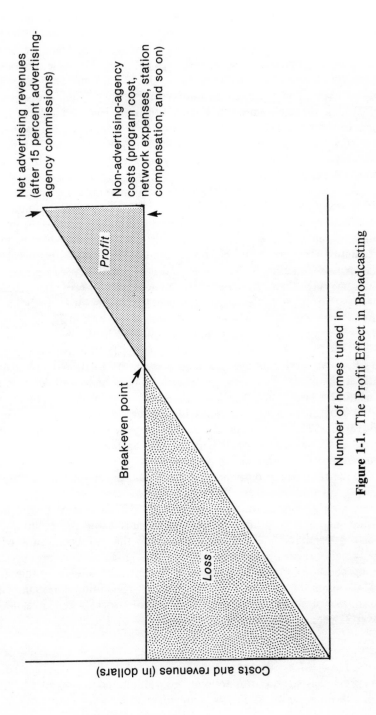

Figure 1-1. The Profit Effect in Broadcasting

Investments in different types of programming result in widely different advertising revenue—and ultimately profit—figures. For example, news and sports programming, almost all of which is network-produced, generates little advertising revenue above its very high costs. In 1977 these program costs were some $400 million, with gross revenues of $527 million.[25] After factoring in station compensation and advertising-agency commissions, this programming was barely a break-even proposition. Even aside from the very high broadcast-rights payments to the sports leagues, program costs in news and sports are high; in addition, very little programming can be repeated as can a situation comedy or a movie. Consequently, news and sports programming has never been regarded as a profit center.

Although prime-time entertainment programming generates high advertising revenues—about $1.25 billion in 1977 against approximately $700 million in program costs[26]—station compensation for prime-time programming is greater than for other types of programming. The prime-time programming schedule also receives a great amount of administrative attention and expense, resulting in a lower overall profit on this type of programming than one might expect. Nonetheless, some of the hit programs return high profits. Consider, for example, the two ABC situation-comedy hits from the 1977-1978 season, "Happy Days" and "Laverne and Shirley." In 1977, the average price of a one-minute commercial in these shows was about $160,000 for "Happy Days" and $143,000 for "Laverne and Shirley." Both shows carried an average of four minutes of national advertising per half-hour show. As a result, "Happy Days" generated an average of $640,000 a week in advertising revenues; it cost the network roughly $140,000 for each of two plays in the season. "Laverne and Shirley" averaged $572,000 in gross advertising every week with slightly lower program costs. ABC thus made hefty profits on both of these shows, which helped to offset losses on less-popular shows.

Entertainment programming outside the prime-time period produces even greater revenues per dollar of program cost. In 1977, daytime programming grossed about $575 million on $155 million of program costs, while late-night programming, which cost only about $35 million, grossed some $90 million in revenues.[27] Relatively the most profitable of all is children's programming, most of which is independently produced: Program costs of about $35 million in 1977 generated four times that amount ($140 million) in gross revenues.[28] In all, non-prime-time entertainment programming accounts for under 17 percent of program costs, yet produces over 31 percent of advertising revenues.

Profits

As previously stated, programming costs amounted to roughly $1.33 billion for the three networks in 1977, out of total broadcast expenses of $2.18

billion.[29] Since net revenues amounted to $2.58 billion, the three networks were left with total pretax profits of $406.1 million in 1977.[30]

Using the *TV Broadcast Financial Data* of the Federal Communications Commission (FCC) for the years 1966 to 1977, it is possible to trace the profits of the networks and their owned-and-operated television stations during a thirteen-year period. In analyzing these data, set forth in table 1-2, it should be borne in mind that the ABC television network lost money quite heavily from 1963 through 1971. In these nine years, ABC lost $113 million on its television network.[31] (During this period some of its critics referred to it as the "half network.") ABC's O&O stations, however, have always made money.[32] In addition, it can be seen that profits fluctuated somewhat during the late 1960s and early 1970s, but have gone from strength to strength since 1972, with the three television networks performing more strongly then their owned-and-operated stations. In 1977, the average television network made a pretax profit of over $135 million—a very handsome 16 percent return on gross revenues, or a 20 percent return on net revenues. And the number-one network, ABC, obviously made substantially more than the average pretax profit.

In 1977, the average network O&O station made a pretax profit of about $10 million, or a 30 percent return on gross revenues. This compares very favorably with the average pretax profit for the remaining 474 VHF commercial-television stations—$1.6 million.[33] The average pretax profit for the 181 commercial UHF stations was $392,000.[34] The substantially lower average profit for UHF stations is a result of the so-called "UHF handicap"—low-quality reception by most viewers. In addition, fewer of the UHF stations are affiliated with a network. This profit gap between the

Table 1-2
Pretax Profits of the Networks and Their Fifteen Owned-and-Operated Stations
(millions of dollars)

Year	Total Profits	Three Networks	Fifteen O&O Television Stations
1966	187.0	79.0	108.0
1967	163.0	56.0	107.0
1968	178.8	56.4	122.4
1969	226.0	93.0	133.0
1970	167.4	50.1	117.3
1971	144.9	53.7	91.2
1972	213.4	110.9	102.5
1973	287.7	184.9	102.8
1974	330.8	225.1	105.7 -
1975	314.2	208.5	105.7
1976	454.6	295.6	159.0
1977	555.4	406.1	149.3

Source: FCC, *TV Broadcast Financial Data* (1966-1977).

O&O stations and those that are not network-owned is sure to persist because of the location of the O&Os in the nation's largest markets.

Financial Arrangements between Networks and Affiliates

Since the networks and their O&O stations dominate the airwaves, the government has made several attempts to stem the power of the networks and to encourage the affiliates to do more of their own programming. However, most of these attempts have failed.

Theoretically, any network affiliate can choose to "clear"—that is, broadcast—or not to clear any network-supplied program that is fed to it.[35] In exchange for their broadcasting network programs with network commercials, the network pays station compensation to its affiliates. The individual affiliate does not have to bill the advertiser, but receives a monthly check from the network for doing virtually nothing other than carrying network programming. Thus the affiliate's risks are reduced and its rewards increased. The rewards depend on the salability of the commercial positions—station breaks—within and following network programs. An affiliate's decision to clear a program depends, in large part, on whether or not the network's guaranteed compensation exceeds or falls short of the estimated profit on a local or syndicated program. Another very important factor in this decision is the impact the selected program has on the value of station breaks.

Within this general framework, affiliates have the discretion not to carry certain network programs on their stations. When an affiliate chooses not to clear a network program, this decision is known as a preemption, and the preempted programs naturally have usually been the less-popular network-originated programs. Preemptions are comparatively rare, however, because network affiliates are generally not particularly innovative.

Amount of Advertising

One of the most frequent complaints directed at broadcasters concerns the amount of commercialization. Generally speaking, the networks' O&O and affiliated stations adhere to the National Association of Broadcasters (NAB) Television Code.[36] Despite this, the Justice Department has commenced an antitrust suit against the NAB, alleging that the Code illegally restrains competition and has driven the prices of the commercials to artificially high levels.[37]

All three networks follow the NAB Code requirement on children's programming between the hours of 7 A.M. and 2 P.M. on Saturday and Sunday. This states that there be no more than nine minutes and thirty seconds of nonprogram material in any sixty-minute period.[38] Weekday children's programming may have a maximum of twelve minutes of nonprogram material per hour.[39]

The Advertisers

Over 550 national advertisers compete vigorously with each other to buy "time" in the popular network-television shows. They spend hundreds of millions of dollars every year in order to speak to network television's vast audiences. Some buy spots only in prime-time shows, but the vast majority advertise in all segments of the programming day. Proctor and Gamble, the nation's biggest television advertiser, sells its soap, detergents, toilet paper, and other household goods via television from first thing in the morning until last thing at night. Over 90 percent of its total advertising expenditure goes to television.[40]

Other top advertisers, ranked according to the amount they spend on network television, are: General Foods, Bristol-Myers, American Home Products, General Motors, General Mills, Sears Roebuck, Lever Brothers, Ford Motor, Nabisco, Warner-Lambert, Colgate-Palmolive, Ralston Purina, Sterling Drug, Johnson & Johnson, Gillette, Kellogg, Pillsbury, McDonald's, and Nestle.[41]

If advertisers are classified by product category, some interesting trends emerge. The top five product categories in terms of advertising expenditures—food products; toiletries and toilet goods; automobiles and accessories; over-the-counter drugs; and soaps, cleaners, and polishes—account for more than half of all advertising on television.[42] The next five—household equipment; confectionery and soft drinks; beer and wine; sporting goods and toys; and records, tapes, radios, and television sets—account for another 21 percent of all national television advertising.[43]

As in many business relationships between buyers and sellers, the networks and the advertisers often have differences of opinion. The advertisers believe that the networks have too much control over both the amount and content of advertising. They also believe that the networks can increase the prices of advertising arbitrarily, because more than 150 advertisers want to buy what only 3 networks sell. For their part, the networks claim that unless they control advertising standards, the major advertisers would attempt to sell objectionable products—such as hard liquor, contraceptives, and vaginal sprays—during daytime, prime-time, and perhaps even children's programs.

Generally speaking, the networks have won the battles against the advertisers; attempts by advertisers, including some big advertisers, to start a "fourth network" in order to increase the amount of advertising time, have failed miserably.[44] Thus, along with other broadcasters and the National Association of Broadcasters, the networks currently regulate the quantity and quality of advertising as they see fit. The recent Justice Department antitrust suit against the NAB has obviously created some turmoil, but it is generally expected to be unsuccessful. After all, not only the industry (which promulgated the Code) but also the public, politicians, and regulators at the FCC favor industry-imposed restrictions on advertising.[45]

Some advertisers would like to play a much more active role in the process, but they usually just sit back and pay their bills. They argue that commercial broadcasting would collapse without them, and some of them believe that they should be able to choose much of the network programming, since they are expected to pay for it. Occasionally they can do so, as in the "Hallmark Hall of Fame" series, and at least one network has been talking about giving advertisers a greater say.[46]

For their part, the public-interest groups want the government to regulate both the amount and the types of advertising. Over-the-counter-drug advertising[47] and commercials aimed at children[48] are particularly sore points for many groups. The FCC has, for the most part, been content to accept industry self-regulation in lieu of direct Commission control over advertising.[49] There has been speculation, however, that if self-regulation is upset as a result of the Justice Department's suit, the FCC, and perhaps the Federal Trade Commission (FTC) as well, would act to impose such direct regulation.[50]

In response to pressure from public-interest groups, in 1978 both the FCC[51] and the FTC[52] instituted inquiries into advertising directed toward children. So far, the only governmental interference with broadcast advertising has been the congressionally imposed ban on cigarette advertising,[53] enacted after the surgeon general had determined that cigarettes were a cause of cancer.

Network Power

As we have seen, the network triopoly is the single most powerful force in television broadcasting today. As the brokers for roughly 600 of the 700 or so local commercial stations' time, the networks control the crucial bottleneck through which virtually all national programs must pass. They also own the most lucrative television stations and can exert a life-or-death influence over both the program-production industry and the syndication business. In addition, they control the vital link between advertisers and consumers.

When threatened by changing technology, the networks have either attempted to stifle the development of new systems, as in the case of cable television, or sought control over its development and ownership, as in the case of domestic satellites.

Politicians, government officials, minority groups, and public-interest organizations generally regard the three networks as all-powerful and thus have initiated a number of attempts to reduce this power.

Three separate investigations were launched in the mid-1950s to study economic concentration and other problems related to network operations: one by the FCC,[54] one by the Senate Commerce Committee,[55] and one by the House Committee on the Judiciary.[56] While an enormous amount of testimony was gathered and many critical reports written, no new legislation was passed. The FCC investigation, however, was an ongoing one. The Office of Network Study, created in 1957, conducted further investigations and hearings, culminating in the mid-1960s when the Commission began a rule making concerning the program procurement, production, and scheduling practices of the networks.[57] As a result of that proceeding, the Commission eventually forced the networks to divest themselves of their syndication rights and financial interests in independent television-program production,[58] and adopted the Prime Time Access Rule (PTAR), which restricted the amount of entertainment programming that the networks could supply to their affiliates to three hours a night during the prime-time hours between 7 P.M. and 11 P.M.[59] The half-hour network news programs were always exempted,[60] and after the fall of 1975 children's programming as well as public-affairs and documentary programming were also exempted from PTAR.[61]

There has also been talk at the FCC from time to time of making the networks sell some or all of their owned stations and of getting the networks out of program production almost entirely. Indeed, the Justice Department filed suit against all three networks in the early 1970s in an attempt to restrict their program-production functions.[62] Its theory is that a distributor of programming should not also produce that programming, since this gives the distributor or the network an upper hand in any negotiations with other program producers—for example, the major Hollywood producers such as Twentieth Century Fox, Columbia, Paramount, Warner, Disney, United Artists, and so on—as well as with the many smaller companies—like M-T-M, Tandem, Q-M, and Spelling—that sometimes claim that they are "urged" to produce their programs in network-owned studios.[63]

The networks, their owned stations, and most affiliates belong to the National Association of Broadcasters (NAB), one of the most power lobbying groups in Washington. Aside from the NAB, the networks themselves have powerful Washington representation and have managed to fight effectively most plans to curtail the power of the broadcasting industry or to aid new competition. Indeed, the networks, particularly ABC, claimed credit for putting congressional pressure on FCC Chairman Dean Burch early in 1974, when the FCC was about to adopt rules encouraging the development of pay cable television.[64] Broadcast-industry and network lobbying also resulted in a policy statement on children's programming in October of 1974,[65] instead of threatened and more serious rules.[66] It is also widely believed that people are unlikely to be named as members of the FCC unless they have network and broadcast-industry approval.[67]

The last three FCC chairmen—Dean Burch, Richard Wiley, and Charles Ferris—have all attempted to conduct public inquiries into the networks' power. Dean Burch's proposed inquiry was voted down by a majority of the other commissioners after intensive network lobbying in late 1973.[68] Richard Wiley's inquiry was approved by the Commission in early 1977,[69] but was halted by Senator Ernest Hollings, chairman of the Senate Communications Subcommittee; his explanation was that if a network inquiry was needed, it should be tackled by the new Democratic chairman, not the old Republican chairman.[70] Chairman Ferris's inquiry is now underway;[71] it is expected to last until at least 1981, and the networks are lobbying vigorously against the FCC's taking any action.

The networks, however, scored significant victories on Capitol Hill in 1977 and 1978. In 1977, the House Communications Subcommittee, under Chairman Lionel Van Deerlin, threatened to publish a report on television violence after a series of hearings in Denver, Los Angeles, and Washington, D.C.[72] The report was critical of the networks, saying that they were primarily responsible for the amount of violence on television, and that violence on television was partially the result of the structure of broadcasting in the United States.[73] The report also criticized parents who allowed their children to watch as much television as they pleased.[74] As a result of intensive network lobbying, the report was not released until that fall, although it was ready for publication in May.[75] In September of 1977 the subcommittee adopted a much weaker, far less critical report.[76] A majority of the young Democratic members of the subcommittee disagreed with the final report, describing it as a "whitewash" of network practices.[77]

The broadcasters had a second success before the Senate in the spring and summer of 1977. The Food and Drug Administration (FDA) had determined that saccharin caused cancer in some laboratory tests on animals. Senator Ernest Hollings, chairman of the Senate Subcommittee on Communications, wanted to make sure that saccharin advertisements on television contained some kind of cancer warning. He believed he had a comfortable majority behind him, but when the issue came up for a vote it was heavily defeated.[78] A surprised Senator Hollings later said that broadcast-industry lobbying had made the vote the equivalent of confronting a "fixed jury."[79]

In 1978 the networks and the broadcasters won another victory, again before Representative Van Deerlin's House Subcommittee on Communications. Chairman Van Deerlin had announced two years previously that he was going to "rewrite" the Communications Act of 1934 in order to bring it up to date, not only to incorporate new technology but also to encourage further technological development.[80] He made statements that the broadcast industry, and the networks in particular, believed were critical.[81] Indeed, the networks feared that a new Communications Act might allow the FCC to regulate them directly. (Under current law the networks are not regulated, although their O&O stations and, of course, their affiliates are.)When the draft rewrite bill[82] was released in June of 1978, the broadcasters and the networks were ecstatic. There was no threat—in fact no hint—of network regulation, and broadcasters were virtually promised their licenses in perpetuity. The public-interest groups, who had long opposed the powerful broadcast industry, felt betrayed by the new bill. Dr. Everett Parker, director of the Office of Communication of the United Church of Christ, described the Van Deerlin bill as a "bigger giveaway . . . than Teapot Dome."[83]

After the congressional session had ended with the rewrite still in subcommittee, Chairman Van Deerlin introduced a revised rewrite bill in 1979,[84] but not until two bills to amend the Communications Act had been introduced by Senators Hollings[85] and Goldwater.[86] Following hearings in the spring of 1979 at which objections to the rewrite were voiced by both broadcasters and public-interest groups,[87] its broadcasting provisions died in subcommittee, the victim of "intense pressure . . . from both sides of the fence."[88] The fate of the House rewrite makes the prospect for passage of the broadcasting provisions of either Senate bill rather slim.

The broadcasting industry, including the networks, ultimately turned against the rewrite for a number of reasons. Foremost among them was the proposed imposition on licensees of a substantial "spectrum resource fee,"[89] which Chairman Van Deerlin refused to drop from the bill despite industry pressure.[90] The quick success of the broadcasters' opposition further demonstrates their political power.

Another Capitol Hill success came in the spring and summer of 1978, when a coalition of the broadcast industry and major advertisers, including sugar manufacturers, fought to curtail the FTC inquiry seeking to ban certain television advertising directed toward children.[91] As a result of the pressure, at one point it appeared that the FTC's appropriation would include a prohibition on its taking any action eliminating any category of product advertising directed at children unless the FDA decided that such advertising would be hazardous to the health of young viewers.[92] This was subsequently struck down, and the FTC was instead warned by Congress of potential constitutional problems in its proposed restrictions on advertising.[93]

Nonetheless, the overall inquiry into the issue of children's advertising was slowed down, and at one period completely halted. And, FTC Chairman Michael Pertschuk was disqualified from further participation in the proceeding—a result later upset on appeal—for having prejudged the issues, a victory for the broadcasters as well as for the advertisers who had sued to secure the disqualification.[94]

Conclusion

In spite of the attacks on them, the networks remain sound politically and economically. In fact, they appear to go from strength to strength—financially and politically—as the attacks on them increase.

Notes

1. *See* Broadcasting Yearbook 1979, at B-77.

2. *See id.*

3. *See* Comments of NAACP et al., filed in FCC BC Docket No. 78-101 (Aug. 7, 1978), at C-1 to C-5.

4. Federal Communications Commission, Report on Chain Broadcasting 9 (1941); E. Barnouw, A Tower in Babel 59 (1966).

5. This grouping is the author's, and does not necessarily correspond to the internal corporate structure of RCA. *See generally* RCA Corporation, Annual Report 1978.

6. *See* D. Halberstam, The Powers That Be 417 (1979); W. Paley, As It Happened 268 (1979).

7. *See generally* 1978 Annual Report to the Shareholders of CBS Inc.

8. S. Quinlan, Inside ABC 46-47 (1979).

9. *Id.* at 19-21; E. Barnouw, The Golden Web 187-90 (1968).

10. This grouping is the author's, and does not necessarily correspond to the internal corporate structure of ABC. *See generally* American Broadcasting Companies, Inc., Annual Report 1978.

11. *Id.* at 2.

12. Subcommittees on Intergovernmental Relations and Budgeting, Management and Expenditures, Senate Comm. on Government Operations, 93rd Cong., 1st Sess., Disclosure of Corporate Ownership 169-70, 175 (Comm. Print 1973).

13. Broadcasting, April 16, 1979, at 29.

14. Broadcasting, March 26, 1979, at 32; Broadcasting, March 20, 1978, at 28.

15. Broadcasting, March 15, 1976, at 97.

16. Broadcasting, Jan. 30, 1978, at 34.

17. Petition for Inquiry, Rule Making and Immediate Temporary Relief (RM-2749), filed by Westinghouse Broadcasting Company, Inc. (Sept. 3, 1976), at 13.

18. The costs of the various types of entertainment programs have been estimated by the author, based on conversations with persons in the broadcasting and program-production industries, as well as on published estimates, *e.g.*, Broadcasting, Sept. 4, 1978, at 22; Variety, Nov. 16, 1977, at 55.

19. Broadcasting, Oct. 17, 1977, at 24.

20. *See* Broadcasting, Sept. 4, 1978, at 22.

21. Total program costs have been estimated by the author, based on FCC, TV Broadcast Financial Data—1977, Release No. 3686 (Aug. 14, 1978), table 10 (reporting combined program and technical expenses of $1.88 billion), and on conversations with persons in the broadcasting and program-production industries.

22. FCC, TV Broadcast Financial Data—1977, Release No. 3686 (Aug. 14, 1978), table 6.

23. *Id.*

24. *Id.* table 2.

25. Program costs and revenues for each type of programming have been estimated by the author, based on FCC, TV Broadcast Financial Data—1977, Release No. 3686 (Aug. 14, 1978); Broadcast Advertisers Reports; and conversations with persons in the broadcasting and program-production industries.

26. *See* note 25 *supra*.

27. *See* note 25 *supra*.

28. *See* note 25 *supra*.

29. FCC, TV Broadcast Financial Data—1977, Release No. 3686 (Aug. 14, 1978), table 10.

30. *Id* table 2.

31. *See* A. Pearce, The Economics of Prime-Time Access 29 (1973).

32. Even in 1970, when the ABC television network was still mired in third place behind NBC and CBS, its O&O stations earned over one-third of the total profits of the fifteen network-owned stations; and this share increased to over 50 percent by 1978, when ABC had taken over first place from its two rival networks. *See* S. Quinlan, Inside ABC 166, 170 (1979).

33. *See* FCC, TV Broadcast Financial Data—1977, Release No. 3686 (Aug. 14, 1978), table 2.

34. *See id.*

35. 47 C.F.R. §73.658(e) (1979).

36. National Association of Broadcasters, Television Code (20th ed. 1978).

37. United States v. National Ass'n of Broadcasters, Civ. No. 79-1549 (D.D.C., complaint filed June 14, 1979).

38 National Association of Broadcasters, Television Code §XIV(2)(C) (20th ed. 1978).

39. *Id.*

40. Television Bureau of Advertising, Inc., Top 100 National Advertisers—1977.

41. *Id.*

42. *See* Television Bureau of Advertising, Inc., TVB News, Report No. 78-18 (Apr. 10, 1978).

43. *See id.*

44. *See, e.g.*, Broadcasting, March 14, 1977, at 54.

45. *See* Broadcasting, June 25, 1979, at 29-30; Brown, *Antitrust Action on TV Commercials: Industry and Admen Fear an Exercise in Futility*, The N.Y. Times, June 16, 1979, at 46, col. 1.

46. Remarks of Fred Silverman at Young & Rubicam Dinner Forum (Sept. 14, 1978); Broadcasting, Sept. 18, 1978, at 29-30.

47. *See, e.g.*, Broadcasting, March 1, 1976, at 20.

48. *See, e.g.*, Broadcasting, Feb. 27, 1978, at 27-28; Broadcasting, March 6, 1978, at 94-96. *See generally* B. Cole & M. Oettinger, Reluctant Regulators 243-88 (1978).

49. *E.g.*, Children's Television Report and Policy Statement, 50 F.C.C.2d 1, 13 (1974).

50 *See* Broadcasting, June 18, 1979, at 27; Brown, *supra* note 45. Indeed, the National Citizens Committee for Broadcasting has already petitioned the FCC to impose time limitations on television advertising. *See* Broadcasting, Aug. 13, 1979, at 26.

51. Second Notice of Inquiry, Docket No. 19142, 68 F.C.C.2d 1344 (1978).

52. Notice of Proposed Rulemaking, FTC File No. 215-60, 43 Fed. Reg. 17967 (1978).

53. Public Health Cigarette Smoking Act of 1969, 15 U.S.C. §§1331-1340 (1976).

54. FCC Delegation Order No. 10 (July 22, 1955), *reprinted in* House Comm. on Interstate and Foreign Commerce, Network Broadcasting, H.R. Rep. No. 1297, 85th Cong., 2d Sess. 667 (1958).

55. *See* Senate Comm. on Interstate and Foreign Commerce, Television Inquiry, 8 volumes, 84th Cong., 2d Sess. (1956).

56. *See* House Comm. on the Judiciary, The Television Broadcasting Industry, H.R. Rep. No. 607, 85th Cong., 1st Sess. (1957); House Comm. on the Judiciary, Hearings on Monopoly Problems in Regulated Industries, Part 2, Television, 4 volumes, 84th Cong., 2d Sess. (1956).

57. Notice of Proposed Rule Making, Docket No. 12782, 45 F.C.C. 2146 (1956).

58. Report and Order, Docket No. 12782, 23 F.C.C.2d 382, 397-99 (1970) [hereinafter cited as PTAR I], *modified,* 25 F.C.C.2d 318, *aff'd*

sub nom. Mt. Mansfield Television, Inc. v. FCC, 442 F.2d 470 (2d Cir. 1970). The current rule is codified in 47 C.F.R. §73.658(j) (1979).

59. PTAR I, *supra* note 58, at 384. The Prime Time Access Rule, as amended, is codified in 47 C.F.R. §73.658(k) (1979). In the Central and Mountain time zones the prime-time hours are from 6 P.M. to 10 P.M. *Id.*

60. PTAR I, *supra* note 58, at 395 n. 36, codified in 47 C.F.R. §73.658(k)(3) (1979).

61. Second Report and Order, Docket No. 19622, 50 F.C.C.2d 829 (1975), *aff'd sub nom.* National Ass'n of Independent Television Producers & Distribs. v. FCC, 516 F.2d 526 (2d Cir. 1975), codified in 47 C.F.R. §73.658(k)(1) (1979).

62. United States v. ABC, Civ. No. 74-3600-RJK (C.D. Cal., complaint filed Dec. 10, 1974); United States v. CBS Inc., Civ. No. 74-3599-RJK (C.D. Cal., complaint filed Dec. 10, 1974); United States v. NBC, Civ. No. 74-3601-RJK (C.D. Cal., complaint filed Dec. 10, 1974). The Justice Department had originally sued the networks in 1972, but those suits were dismissed without prejudice, following which the 1974 complaints were filed. The *NBC* case was settled, United States v. NBC, 449 F. Supp. 1127 (C.D. Cal. 1978)(order approving consent judgment), over the objections of ABC and CBS, *id.* at 1138-40, against whom the litigation is still pending.

63. *See* Notice of Inquiry, Docket No. 21049, 62 F.C.C. 2d. 548, 557 (1977); A. Pearce, The Economics of Prime Time Access 89-125 & Apps. IIA-IIC (1973).

64. *See* Home Box Office, Inc. v. FCC, 567 F.2d 9, 52-53 (D.C. Cir.), *cert. denied*, 434 U.S. 829 (1977); B. Cole and M. Oettinger, Reluctant Regulators 45-46 (1978); Pearce, *The TV Networks: A Primer*, J. Com., Autumn 1976, at 54.

65. Children's Television Report and Policy Statement, 50 F.C.C.2d 1 (1974).

66. *See* B. Cole and M. Oettinger, Reluctant Regulators 276-80 (1978).

67. *See id.* at 5-6.

68. *See id.* at 61-62. (The reference there to "1972" is a typographical error.)

69. Notice of Inquiry, Docket No. 21049, 62 F.C.C.2d 548 (1977).

70. *Broadcasting*, July 4, 1977, at 23; Schuessler, *FCC Regulation of the Network Television Program Procurement Process: An Attempt to Regulate the Laws of Economics?*, 73 Nw. U. L. Rev. 227, 230 n. 9 (1978).

71. *See* Broadcasting, June 19, 1978, at 34. On 19 October 1978 the Commission issued a Further Notice of Inquiry, Docket No. 21049, 69 F.C.C.2d 1524 (1978).

72. *See* Broadcasting, July 25, 1977, at 19-23; Broadcasting, March 7, 1977, at 52-56.

73. Broadcasting, July 25, 1977, at 19-23; Broadcasting, Oct. 24, 1977, at 49-50.

74. Broadcasting, July 25, 1977, at 19-23.

75. *See id.*; Broadcasting, Aug. 1, 1977, at 23.

76. Subcommittee on Communications, House Comm. on Interstate and Foreign Commerce, 95th Cong., 1st Sess., Violence on Television (Comm. Print 1977). *See* Broadcasting, Oct. 3, 1977, at 29-30.

77. Subcommittee on Communications, House Comm. on Interstate and Foreign Commerce, 95th Cong., 1st Sess., Violence on Television (Comm. Print 1977) (dissenting views of Representatives Henry A. Waxman, Timothy E. Wirth, Barbara A. Mikulski, John M. Murphy, Edward J. Markey, and Albert Gore, Jr., at 17-26). *See* Broadcasting, Oct. 3, 1977, at 29-30; Broadcasting, Oct. 24, 1977, at 49-50.

78. Broadcasting, Aug. 1, 1977, at 19-20.

79. Arieff, *Members' Need for Broadcast Exposure Cited as Basis for Industry's Lobbying Clout*, 36 Cong. Q. Weekly Rep. 1548 (1978). *See* Broadcasting, July 11, 1977, at 14; Broadcasting, July 25, 1977, at 81-82; Broadcasting, Aug. 1, 1977, at 19-20.

80. Broadcasting, Oct. 11, 1976, at 30-32.

81. *See, e.g.*, Broadcasting, Feb. 13, 1978, at 30-34.

82. H.R. 13015, 95th Cong., 2d Sess. (1978).

83. Broadcasting, June 12, 1978, at 41.

84. H.R. 3333, 96th Cong., 1st Sess. (1979).

85. S. 611, 96th Cong., 1st Sess. (1979). The Hollings bill would increase television license terms to five years, *id.* §301(a).

86. S. 622, 96th Cong., 1st Sess. (1979). The Goldwater bill would increase television license terms in all but the top twenty-five markets to four or five years, *id.* §301, and looks toward ultimate deregulation of television as well as of other broadcasting services, *id.*

87. *See, e.g.*, Broadcasting, May 28, 1979, at 67-70; Broadcasting, June 11, 1979, at 26-34.

88. Broadcasting, July 16, 1979, at 24.

89. H.R. 3333, 96th Cong., 1st Sess. §414 (1979).

90. Broadcasting, June 18, 1979, at 31-34.

91. Notice of Proposed Rulemaking, FTC File No. 215-60, 43 Fed. Reg. 17967 (1978). *See* Broadcasting, March 13, 1978, at 23; Broadcasting, May 22, 1978, at 30.

92. *See* Broadcasting, May 8, 1978, at 27; Broadcasting, May 29, 1978, at 36-37.

93. *See* Broadcasting, Sept. 18, 1978, at 59.

94. Association of National Advertisers, Inc. v. FTC, 460 F. Supp. 996 (D.D.C. 1978), *rev'd*, ____ F.2d ____, No. 79-1117 (D.C. Cir. Dec. 27, 1979).

2

The Many Sources of Television Power

David Blank

Pearce's discussion, although impressive as always, is unfortunately vastly oversimplified and, more importantly, vastly distorted. This distortion is evident in the way he evaluates the success or failure of the broadcasting industry in general, and of the networks in particular, in their continual jousting in Washington. In his view, when the broadcasters or the networks win one of these jousts, that victory is a result of network power; but if the broadcasters or the networks lose, it is because of the facts.

An alternative view of the situation might be that in recent years the regulators and supervisors of broadcasting have run rampant, but that occasionally one of their proposals is so blatantly illogical that it falls of its own weight. My own views conform more closely to this latter interpretation.

Pearce's basic message is that the networks are all-powerful politically and economically. The networks, however, are not the only source of power that affects the operation and performance of American television.

First, in presenting evidence to support his view that the networks wield great political power, Pearce makes at least two fundamental errors. One error lies in his failure to distinguish sharply between the social influence of the networks and that of their programming. The latter is in my view an entirely separate and unresolved question, because communications researchers are unclear on how to evaluate precisely the influence of those programs on our society. Pearce does not distinguish at all between the impact of network programs on our society and the political influence of the networks in Washington in defending their economic interests, two issues that are almost totally unrelated.

Second, Pearce errs in glossing over the distinction between the networks and their affiliates. To the degree to which there is any political power inherent in the broadcasting industry, that political power largely resides with the individual affiliates who provide, or don't provide, opportunities for congressmen to get on the air in their local communities. Anyone acquainted with Washington knows, as Pearce must know, that in the real crunch the networks must turn to their affiliates for political support because their own power is so modest.

Finally, in listing the three FCC chairmen who have been trying to set aside the networks' dominant status, Pearce suggests that the failures of the first two were somehow related to network power. But it would be hard to find anyone who would believe that the deferring of the Network Inquiry[1] from the sponsorship of Chairman Wiley to that of Chairman Ferris[2] occurred under duress from the networks.

In his discussion of the networks' economic power, Pearce again leaves a false impression of power unrestrained by other influences. Without dwelling on this, let me point out that at one end of the marketplace for the television networks their adversaries in fact are the customers—the advertisers. And the television-network market is fairly simple—an auction market with a limited and fixed amount of supply. Given those two facts, any economist knows what determines price levels, gross revenues, and to some degree profits—demand. In years when advertising budgets are rising rapidly, this pressure begins to raise the prices rapidly. In other years, when advertising demands are not rising so rapidly, the networks cannot do anything about raising their prices because of the nature of the auction market. Fortunately for the networks and for all other advertising media, the last few years have been extraordinarily good ones in the advertising market. But during the last two recessions and during the period immediately after cigarette advertising was lost to the broadcasting industry,[3] things were quite different. It is important to remember that today's economic status was not necessarily yesterday's, nor will it necessarily be tomorrow's.

At the other end of the marketplace is the cost to the networks of the programs that they buy. Again, the networks are faced with a marketplace in at least some major areas of which their influence is small and their exposure is great. Powerful unions control the input of craft and artistic talent into the network-television business but do not deal with the television networks in determining their wage rates. The program producers, with whom they do deal, are prone to acceding quickly to the unions' demands. Several years ago, a twenty-four-hour negotiation with craft unions resulted in a 54 percent increase in wage rates over a three-year period;[4] this was a fairly steep rise in wage rates even in the current inflationary environment. This has a heavy impact on the networks, although they did not even participate in the negotiations. This, along with the foregoing examples, indicates that within the television marketplace there are various sources of power that have an impact on the profitability of the television networks.

As Pearce has pointed out, the profits of the networks are indeed directly dependent on audience size.[5] It is therefore in the networks' self-interest to pursue every possible idea for attracting a potential audience. The competition among the networks for audience means that the public has the power to make the ultimate programming choices, so that network programming generally mirrors public tastes. Thus over the past twenty years we have witnessed the most radical set of changes in popular tastes seen in any medium in such a short period of time in the nation's history. This was not created, designed, or planned by anyone; it simply happened. It happened in the process by which new ideas and new types of programming competed for public acceptance, and the public either bought them or did not buy them. For example, at one time motion pictures did poorly on television; nevertheless, someone tried motion pictures again, with much greater success, so that now motion pictures are on the air only two years after being shown in the theaters. In just this way, television programming has undergone extraordinary changes.

Audience selection takes place every hour on the television set, and as a result of that selection programs stay on or go off the air. Anyone has the privilege of liking a different type of program. But I am surprised at those who criticize television programming by saying that minority tastes are neglected while only the tastes of a large population are catered to. There is an institution in the United States that attempts to cater to minority tastes—the public-television system, which covers over 80 percent of the country[6] and has many programs dealing with a number of minority interests. And these programs get very small ratings.[7] It is unclear to me why there is any great virtue in having a marvelous program on the air that nobody watches. If Yevtushenko were on television reading his poetry in Russian, it might be a wonderful experience for the few people who know Russian; but if nobody watches the program, it would seem to be of little value to society. It should not be a source of embarrassment that the television industry, like any other private industry, is attempting to further its own self-interest, because in general it does so by trying to please the most people—something I consider a very good thing.

Since network-programming decisions depend on audience size, it is necessary to have a reliable measure of the numbers of people who watch each program. Unlike industries that can measure public acceptance of their products and services directly in dollars or other units sold (such as theater tickets), television viewing must be measured by a statistical process utilizing sampling techniques, a method not unlike that used by the government to measure such things as the unemployment rate.

Broadcast ratings have been subjected to much criticism, some of it valid, but most of it simply based on either misinformation or misunderstanding. The ratings do not, for example, sample only affluent viewers; an enormous amount of effort and expense goes into preparing and testing the national ratings to ensure their statistical validity. In the more local measures, where the samples are smaller, the margin of error is naturally greater; and of course there are more problems at the fringes of the marketplace.

The ratings are far from perfect, and errors have been found in them over time. But this does not mean, as some critics have charged, that the ratings are "phony." To the contrary, they are probably the best reports available today on the American public's views on the products of a commercial enterprise.

A former chairman of the FCC once proposed that the networks work together to program opposite types of shows, so that instead of fighting for the audience they could agree to split it up at different hours by offering programming of different sorts.[8] This would have required an exemption under the antitrust laws. If such an exemption was ever applied for, it was certainly never granted. I know of no one who is now actively pursuing that approach, although similar proposals are made from time to time.[9] The possibility of this kind of approach to programming raises the question of whether any of us can or should undertake to decide what is best for everyone.

When I was young, everybody knew what standards were. You "knew" that Dickens was great and you "knew" that Shakespeare was greater. I didn't happen to like Shakespeare, and I loved Dickens, and I knew that it was my fault, that it was an inadequacy on my part that I didn't appreciate Shakespeare and higher standards. I don't think there are standards like that today, and I don't know any more what is "better" or "worse" in art and entertainment. I know what *I* think is better or worse, but my opinion differs so much from that of the American public these days that I am not sure I should impose my standards on them; nor am I willing to let them impose their standards on me.

Notes

1. Notice of Inquiry, Docket No. 21049, 62 F.C.C. 2d. 548 (1977).
2. *See* Broadcasting, July 4, 1977, at 23.
3. *See* Public Health Cigarette Smoking Act of 1969, 15 U.S.C. §§1331-1340 (1976).
4. *See* Variety, Sept. 10, 1975, at 3, col. 1.
5. A. Pearce, *supra* at 8-10.
6. Carnegie Commission on the Future of Public Broadcasting, A Public Trust 53, 235 (Bantam ed. 1979).
7. *Id.* at 330.
8. *See* Broadcasting, Jan. 18, 1960, at 46.
9. *E.g.*, W. Paley, As It Happened 275-76 (1979).

3 Assessing the Networks' Lobbying Power

David M. Rubin

Pearce has expressed concern about the networks' power, particularly their lobbying power and their ability to get what they want in Washington. He concludes that this power is almost unlimited and suggests that the networks' exercise of power has been contrary to the public interest. His analysis appears to be flawed in several respects.

First, Pearce fails to say anything at all about the courts. While judges certainly read newspapers and are aware of political climates, the courts are nevertheless greatly insulated from lobbying pressure. Even assuming that the networks and the broadcasting industry have the best and strongest lobbying effort in the country, as Pearce claims,[1] this seems unlikely to be helpful to them when decisions are being made by the courts. And it is in the courts that many of the most significant decisions shaping the nature of the broadcast system in this country are being made.

Examples of such decisions include the *Red Lion*[2] case and the recent *National Citizens Committee for Broadcasting* (*NCCB*) decision on cross-media ownership and divestiture.[3] Both these cases, while not speaking directly to the networks, affect them as station owners, as well as affecting their affiliates in many major markets—and affect them in ways that they probably do not like. A recent decision in the D.C. Circuit concerning licensing has also certainly made the networks and their affiliates unhappy, since it threatens to upset the way in which a station can demonstrate that it has done a good job in its community in order to get its license renewed.[4]

Thus much of the real action is going on in the courts, where the question of lobbying is simply irrelevant. By not addressing this issue, Pearce has overstated the extent of the networks' power.

Second, I would disagree with Pearce's implicit suggestion that most of the networks' lobbying efforts are evil—that they are aimed at stopping things that ought to go forward. I often find that the broadcasters are fighting to stop things that I would also oppose, for strong first amendment reasons.

As one example, I support the networks' lobbying efforts to keep Congress and other bodies from interfering in the area of programming content in the name of controlling violence, sex, or anything else. Broadcasters should have complete freedom, insofar as possible, to broadcast whatever they wish. Anyone who does not like it does not have to watch. But under the first amendment, the government should not dictate what television content should or should not be. Thus I disagree with Pearce's criticism of the networks' conduct during the House Communications Subcommittee's 1977 investigation of violence on television.[5]

In the area of advertising, similarly, it seems to me that Congress made a mistake in banning cigarette advertising on television.[6] Cigarettes are a legal product, and if they are as dangerous as is claimed, the FDA ought to ban them. If, indeed, there are products that children ought not to be ingesting, then there should be ways to deal with that problem other than by making the broadcast industry the scapegoat. This issue raises serious first amendment questions (particularly in view of the increasing blurring of commercial speech and political speech[7]) about whether or not advertising aimed at children should be banned, limited, or more highly regulated. I have never been particularly impressed by the evidence produced to indicate the damage that is being done to children by television advertising.[8] I am pleased, however, that the broadcast lobby has fought back,[9] because all our first amendment interests are at stake.

This does not mean, however, that all the networks' lobbying is salutary. For example, their massive efforts to cripple cable television and other technological innovations that would undercut the networks' market[10] may well be contrary to the public interest. It is understandable why the networks do this, however; it makes perfect economic sense for them and has helped them tremendously. In discussing the rewrite of the Communications Act,[11] one of the crucial issues is whether cable television should be federally regulated, completely deregulated, or left to be regulated by the cities and states. On this issue we can expect the lobbying activities of the broadcasters to continue. I would note that this lobbying campaign, which Pearce mentions only in passing,[12] is probably the most significant such effort the broadcasters have mounted.

Finally, one could hardly dispute Pearce's claim that the networks are powerful both economically and politically. In this chapter, however, I have attempted to show that they are not always powerful nor are they the most powerful group in contention.

Notes

1. A. Pearce, *supra* at 17-18.
2. Red Lion Broadcasting Co. v. FCC, 395 U.S. 367 (1969).
3. FCC v. National Citizens Committee for Broadcasting, 436 U.S. 775 (1978).
4. Central Florida Enterprises, Inc. v. FCC, 598 F.2d 37 (D.C. Cir. 1978), *cert. dismissed*, _____ U.S. _____, 99 S.Ct. 2189 (1979).

5. A. Pearce, *supra* at 18.

6. Public Health Cigarette Smoking Act of 1969, 15 U.S.C. §§1331-1340 (1976).

7. *See, e.g.*, First National Bank of Boston v. Bellotti, 435 U.S. 765 (1978).

8. *See, e.g.*, Broadcasting, Feb. 28, 1977, at 20.

9. *See, e.g.*, Broadcasting, May 2, 1977, at 57-58; Broadcasting, March 7, 1977, at 52-56.

10. *See, e.g.*, Home Box Office, Inc. v. FCC, 567 F.2d 9, 52-53 (D.C. Cir.), *cert. denied*, 434 U.S. 829 (1977).

11. H.R. 3333, 96th Cong., 1st Sess. (1979).

12. A. Pearce, *supra* at 18.

4 A Persistent Question

Aaron Kahn

In 1972 the Justice Department filed antitrust suits against each of the three networks, alleging that they used their control over access to broadcasting time to obtain a competitive advantage over other producers and distributors of television programming.[1] Although the case against NBC has been settled,[2] the litigation with the other two networks is still going on.

Underlying these antitrust cases is a fundamental question: Who shall choose what programs the public will see—the networks, advertisers, the government, or others? This question is a persistent one that has been addressed by the FCC over and over again—in the old Chain Broadcasting Report,[3] in the Barrow Study,[4] and most likely in the Network Inquiry that is going on now.[5]

The thrust of both the Justice Department suits and the various FCC investigations has been that programming choices should be made as pluralistically as possible, not by a few powerful entities. Nevertheless, the fact remains that we have three networks, and with the current allocation of television stations the prospects for the creation of an additional network seem dim. Therefore, the crucial question becomes whether there are going to be new competitive forces outside of the networks that will provide alternatives for advertisers and for viewers who wish to see things not now available on television.

At the present time, cable television appears to be the most promising alternative and competitive force. It is not surprising that the networks have tried hard to prevent cable from reaching its potential,[6] since it is in their economic self-interest to do so. If that effort were to succeed, however, it would have serious economic and social consequences. Although FCC regulations have slowed the development of cable in the past,[7] present indications both at the FCC and in Congress are that these regulatory barriers may soon be lifted.[8]

Nevertheless, the networks can be expected to continue to wield their considerable political power to protect their strong economic position. As Blank states, the affiliates probably have more political power than the networks themselves;[9] perhaps the outcome of the current Network Inquiry will demonstrate whether or not this is true. However, since for most purposes the interests of the networks and their affiliates coincide, their lobbying power is applied in a concerted fashion.

Notes

1. The 1972 cases were dismissed without prejudice and refiled in 1974. *See* United States v. NBC, 449 F.Supp. 1127, 1129 (C.D. Cal. 1978).

2. United States v. NBC, 449 F.Supp. 1127 (C.D. Cal. 1978)(order approving consent judgment).

3. Federal Communications Commission, Report on Chain Broadcasting (1941).

4. House Comm. on Interstate and Foreign Commerce, Network Broadcasting, H.R. Rep. No. 1297, 85th Cong., 2d Sess. (1958).

5. *See* Notice of Inquiry, Docket No. 21049, 62 F.C.C.2d 548 (1977); Further Notice of Inquiry, Docket No. 21049, 69 F.C.C.2d 1524 (1978).

6. *See, e.g.*, Home Box Office, Inc. v. FCC, 567 F.2d 9, 52-53 (D.C. Cir.), *cert. denied*, 434 U.S. 829 (1977).

7. *See* Botein, *CATV Regulation: A Jumble of Jurisdictions*, 45 N.Y.U. L. Rev. 816, 826-39 (1970).

8. *See, e.g.*, Broadcasting, May 28, 1979, at 36-37; H.R. 3333, 96th Cong., 1st Sess. §453(b)(1979); S. 622, 96th Cong., 1st Sess. §301 (1979).

9 D. Blank, *supra* at 25.

Part II
The Networks and
Programming

5 How Network Television Program Decisions Are Made

Richard W. Jencks

Introduction

During the entire history of network radio entertainment, and during the first decade of network television, program decisions were largely made, not by the networks themselves, but by advertisers and their agencies.

They decided on the format and nature of the programs, selected the stars and supporting players, supervised day to day production, and monitored the programs for taste and propriety. Sometimes, indeed, an advertising agency had its own in-house production unit which directly produced the program. Even the task of scheduling was one primarily for the advertiser and its agency, for they decided to which network they would offer it and negotiated with the network for the specific time periods in which it would be shown and which stations would be included in the network lineup.

The networks, during this period, were primarily in the business of selling airtime, and selling it in accordance with the terms of published rate cards, just as a print publisher sells space. They acquired this airtime by purchasing it wholesale through affiliation contracts with stations. Their profit was the amount by which the network time charges paid by advertising agencies exceeded the total of the amounts paid to the stations, the charges for telephone company interconnection of the network, and the cost of the network's own organization.

I have said that program decisions were *largely* made by advertisers and their agencies because, of course, it was plain almost from the beginning that the commodity that the networks were selling, broadcast time, would be relatively more valuable if the programs carried on it were popular, and that the popularity of any given program would be enhanced if it were preceded and followed by other popular programs.

The negotiations between the networks and the advertising agencies concerning the purchase of airtime came to reflect the logic of this situation. An agency that wished to buy time for a program known to be weak would be apt to have difficulty finding a desirable time period, and might end by having to place it in an undesirable position or on a weaker network. On the

---

The numbered footnotes to Mr. Jencks's paper have been supplied by the editors of this volume.

other hand, an agency wishing to buy time for a program known to be highly popular, or predicted to be such, could insist on the most attractive time period, as well as on other inducements. These might include specially tailored station lineups or a so-called "program contribution" from the network, which meant, very simply, that the network was helping to pay for the cost of the program by giving up a portion of its time charges.

The stronger a network became through the process of attracting placement by advertisers of popular programs, the more it was in a position to be picky about new programs offered by advertisers and the more, therefore, that it could be said to be making program decisions itself. As networks grew stronger, they sometimes directly acquired the rights to certain popular programs or stars, so as to be able to present some attractions whose permanence on the network was not subject to advertiser inconstancy.[1]

Nevertheless, the influence of the advertiser all through this period remained dominant, and those in government, in academia, and in the intellectual community generally were united in believing that the shortcomings of network programming—first in radio, and then in television—were primarily due to advertiser control. (Then as now they tended to accept as a given that the programming was indeed unsatisfactory, and to be rather vague about the criteria by which this primarily aesthetic judgment was being made.)

In its famous 1946 Report on Public Service Responsibilities of Broadcast Licensees, which came to be known as the "Blue Book,"[2] the Federal Communications Commission (FCC) vigorously asserted its view that advertiser influence was responsible for deficiencies in network program offerings.

"The concept of a well-rounded structure," said the Commission, "can obviously not be maintained if the decision is left wholly or preponderantly in the hands of advertisers in search of a market, each concerned with his particular half hour, rather than in the hands of stations and networks responsible under the statute for overall program balance in the public interest."[3]

With the arrival of commercial network television, in the late 1940s, the pattern that had been established in radio continued for a time with little change. Many of the program series themselves were simply adaptations of their radio counterparts.

But by the mid-1950s economics and technology began to force changes in the pattern of advertiser dominance. Television production was, from the start, immensely more expensive than radio, even when, like radio, it was done on a live basis in a broadcast studio. Live television broadcasts could not reach the network as a whole in their live form; recordings had to be made by delayed broadcast over some affiliates, and these recordings—or "kinescopes"—made by filming the televised image, were inferior in quality; they were not suitable for repeated broadcast use. The live television unions early established reuse payment patterns, in the interest of maintaining high employment, which made a reuse virtually as expensive as the initial use.

The answer was television production on film, made as motion pictures are made, infinitely reusable, and having the benefit of union terms which made reuse economical. Since the initial cost of film was high it had to be amortized by being rerun on the network, at first in a pattern of thirty-nine new programs and thirteen repeats. Its advantages over live production were such that by the late 1950s over 80 percent of entertainment programming in prime time was by means of film.[4]

But a film series was becoming too expensive for a single advertiser to bankroll, so sponsorship had to be shared with others. Even cosponsorship became too expensive, as well as too cumbersome. Moreover, advertisers found that they no longer wanted to spend all their money on a single program series, as had been commonly the case in radio. The money outlay having become so huge, the risk of program failure became unacceptable.

At the same time, rating data were becoming more sophisticated. The old idea that advertisers were buying viewer gratitude was giving way in the face of new demographic knowledge about the television audience. Advertisers now knew that they were buying circulation, and that to spread their risk and heighten their prospects they ought to try to more accurately and efficiently reach their target audience.

These tendencies, encouraged by the FCC and by critics generally, gave promise that programs would no longer be shaped to serve merely as vehicles for commercial messages. They made possible Pat Weaver's vision of a so-called "magazine format" in which editorial and entertainment content would be utterly separated—as, allegedly, in magazines—from paid advertisements. The quiz scandals of the late 1950s served to further emphasize the need for networks to be masters in their own houses, and to assume full responsibility for what they presented.[5]

The term "sponsor" remained, but it was no longer apt. The advertiser no longer presented the program in any real sense—although the concept survives today for certain specials such as the "Hallmark Hall of Fame." The network was presenting the program. The advertiser was no longer buying thirty minutes or an hour; he was buying advertising minutes in which to place his messages. And he was not buying minutes according to some prepared printed schedule of rates and charges. He was buying minutes on the basis of a continuous auction—what the traffic would bear. A single purchase on his part might involve fifty or one hundred minutes, spread among two or three prime time series, as well as daytime programming, sports, or news.

The larger audience accruing to a very popular program became an economic advantage not of the advertising agency and sponsor, but of the network, which was in firm control. (The networks even sought to keep actual production in their own hands. This was, to a great extent, frustrated, first by the desire of major stars for tax and other reasons to form their own production companies—Lucille Ball leading the way with Desilu Productions—and later by the growing insistence of the FCC[6] and of the Anti-trust Division of the Department of Justice that network domination over the production process be curbed in various ways.) Thus, the presentation of entertainment programming on television came to involve the judgments of the three networks.

Now that advertisers were mostly out of the program selection process it was not clear to everyone that what had replaced them was an improvement. Program producers had had many customers to whom to present their wares. Now they had three. Advertisers and agencies had sometimes been driven by different motives than merely to maximize audience—pride, tradition, intuitive feelings, what the sponsor's wife liked.

Networks could make program choices almost totally responsive to ratings and demographic information. Networks could also, it is fair to say, be much more flexible in scheduling news and entertainment specials than they could be in the day when advertisers owned time period franchises.

In general, however, although the program schedules might be better balanced, and the programs themselves more popular, or even markedly superior, the number of program decision makers was less diverse and pluralistic than it had been.

Program Development

The process by which networks select what the American people will see culminates, for each network, in a meeting of top executives in late February or early March, in a room that has been kept as secure as any war plans headquarters.[a]

At CBS the Committee which so meets is called the Program Board, perhaps because the principal feature of the room in which it meets is a large portable bulletin-board-like structure, perhaps eight by five feet, supported at the end by standards, divided vertically by columns representing the days of the week, and horizontally by columns representing the half hours of the prime time period.

In the space representing each half-hour time period is room enough for three plaques to be placed side by side—blue for CBS, red for NBC, white

---

[a]Author's note: In the ensuing discussion reference is made to prime time only. Daytime, sports, specials, late night, and children's programming, not involving regular scheduling in prime time, are not subject to Program Board decision. News, of course, is entirely separate.

for ABC—each bearing the name of a program series. The plaques are so made that they adhere easily to the magnetized board, and can be removed with equal ease.

In my time the members of the Program Board were the chairman of CBS Inc. (then and now, William S. Paley), the president of CBS Inc. (then Frank Stanton), the president of the CBS Broadcast Group (myself), the president of the CBS Television Network (then Robert D. Wood), and the vice president in charge of programs (then Fred Silverman). Present also at most meetings were the vice president in charge of sales, the vice president in charge of programs, Hollywood, the vice president in charge of research, and the director of program research.

The board that the committee is facing contains the then current prime time broadcast schedules of the three networks. The meeting is turned over to the vice president in charge of programs. Deftly—he and his associates in the Program Department have been gaming the schedule among themselves for weeks—he removes from the board the programs that on the basis of his best information he believes the other networks are cancelling. Quickly he adds to the board plaques for new series that the other networks are believed to be adding, changing time periods of existing programs to reflect rescheduling moves. His information is gleaned from talent agents, production studios, tradepaper reports, and private sources. The information usually proves to be quite accurate.

The new schedules of the competition having been completed on the board, the program vice president addresses himself to the CBS schedule. Casually, somewhat brutally, he pulls from the board the plaques for the CBS series that he is recommending be cancelled. Then, night by night, he analyzes for the group the strength of the competition, the rearrangements of existing CBS series that he recommends to meet that strength, and the new CBS series that he believes should be added to the program mix. Only when he has completed his presentation do questions and discussions begin.

The Program Board meeting which I have been describing, and to which I will return, is the culmination of an elaborate and costly effort of program development that began at least twelve months before-hand—that is to say, eighteen or twenty months prior to the commencement of the broadcast season for which the developed programs are intended.

Program development is in the hands of a staff headed by a vice president of program development located in Hollywood. Into his office flows a stream of new program ideas from many sources and in many forms. They come from the public, from writing and producing talent, from literary agents on behalf of published books or stories, from talent agents on behalf of their clients, from production companies that have existing programs on the network, and from producers and writers on the network's own payroll.

The number of such program ideas accumulated and reviewed in a single development season ranges between 200 and 300. Most often they come in the form of a written precis of a program format, describing at length the characters of a series, the era and locale in which they are placed, their interrelationships and the kinds of story involvements which will typify the series. If a program package is being proposed, or complete production, the names of the creative team will be given, together with their past credits and accomplishments.

If the package comes from an agency or production company the prospective star will likely be named, and other casting will be indicated. Sometimes script outlines are provided, or even an entire sample script.

At the other end of the spectrum, however, the so-called idea may be described no more elaborately than as a "comedy series starring" an established personality and with an established creative team. In programming, as in dining out, it is usually better to choose a restaurant than a menu.

By summertime the program development staff has sifted through the various proposals and reduced their number to thirty or forty. If you were to ask members of a program development team what their main objective is they would probably say that it is to find "new program forms." Critics of television who find most of its fare hopelessly imitative and banal may find that hard to believe. In any event, as is well known, there are no new stories or plots under the sun, and few demonstrably new characters.

Nevertheless, there are new forms in the sense that there are new combinations of series elements capable of creating interest and excitement in the mass audience; it is these new combinations that create the big hits, and that make possible the growth of the medium.

So, while in the short range it often seems that television changes little or not at all, in the longer view—the view that any anthropologist would take of human characteristics—change has been constant. We are different, and television is different, from the era of the 1950s and 1960s, and the difference is critical. As Martin Mayer has written, "Television drama is often stupid; but it is profound."[7]

Think, if you will, of the difference between two Westerns—the comic book panache of the "Lone Ranger" and the acerbic understatement of "Gunsmoke." Or, among family shows, the differences in and approach between "My Three Sons" and "The Waltons."

"Dragnet," when it was introduced, was a new format in that it emphasized, as a main theme, the hard-slogging work behind police activity, and a principal character with stoic endurance of that work. It carried an implicit understanding that police work was both effective and important to society. Compare, for example, "Charlie's Angels" which, if it tells us anything, tells us that the characters are merely playing at arresting and investigating criminals, and implicitly informs us that the detection, arrest, and imprisonment of criminals is useless, ineffectual. Hence the cardboard girlie show.

The new comedic idea of exploiting relationships in the workplace, among the work "family," seems simple enough, but until "The Mary Tyler Moore Show" no one had successfully brought it off, nor had they considered the appeal of a female Charlie Brown.

And, of course, "All in the Family" and its many spinoffs brought a new form—several new forms, really—to television comedy, including an interest in vulgar lower class life previously explored only in the brilliant Jackie Gleason "Honeymooners" series, and yet strikingly different from what Gleason had done, in that it is married to a contemporary media consciousness about modern social conflicts—abortion, racial discrimination, religion, the welfare state—and animated by a tone of unremitting hostility.

I could go on, but the point is that there is something happening behind that television screen, and program development is at the heart of it.

From the reduced group of program ideas, story outlines and scripts are ordered. By early fall a decision has to be made as to which of the scripts will be produced as pilot programs. Not all, of course, need go this route. The new vehicle of an established star, with a proven production team, may be definitely tagged for the first opening in the schedule without further consideration, as may a spinoff of an existing series.

The remaining prospects are canvassed by the program vice president and the network president, and, depending on programming needs, a decision is made to "go to pilot" on a number of properties which may be as few as eight or ten—say four dramas and four comedies—or may run to fifteen or twenty. Obviously a network in a trailing position, as CBS has been of late, will produce more pilots than one with a solid schedule.

Costs are enormous. A half hour comedy pilot, these days, may cost as much as $300,000. A one hour action drama may cost $750,000 or more. CBS was reported to have spent over $12 million for the pilots produced for the 1977-1978 season.[8]

The pilots are completed in late fall or early winter. Before being viewed by executives other than those in the program department itself they must first be submitted to the so-called "program analyzer."

The terms for this process vary among the networks, but essentially it amounts to this; that the pilots are each screened in a private network screening room before members of the general public, the room so arranged that at every seat there are "like" and "dislike" buttons by which the viewer can instantaneously register his reaction to what he sees and hears. This produces data making possible an exact comparison of viewer attraction or repulsion—capable of being graphed—during each discrete moment of the production. In addition, the viewers are interviewed after the screening so that the network research department may understand why they reacted as they did.

A great deal of derision has been directed over the years to the program analyzer process, it is instinctively repugnant to those who regard even television entertainment as, primarily, an art form, and the creator's self-expression as solitary and sacred. But popular entertainment is a communal art form, many hands are involved in it, and the program analyzer has its counterparts in the tryout of Broadway plays in New Haven and Boston, and in the sneak preview screenings of theatrical films.

It seems slapdash at best. The participants in the screening are not scientifically chosen, but are tourists gathered up off New York streets. Furthermore, since three out of four new television series turn out to be failures, a system that predicted *all* would be failures would be correct 75 percent of the time. The program analyzer's predictions are somewhat more reliable than that, but its greatest strength is in gauging audience acceptability of a star or featured player. If the program analyzer rejects the performer, great weight is attached to it, and a series, even if chosen, is not infrequently recast as a result of this information.

The researchers who supervise the program analyzer believe that results would be better if producers and program executives paid more attention to them. But they acknowledge that its greatest weakness is in determining audience acceptance of a new form—a series with a mix of elements not theretofore familiar to the general audience. People are innately conservative; they react favorably to the familiar and reject the strange. "All in the Family," for example, had one of the lowest all time scores on the program analyzer. When a network decides, regardless, to go ahead with such a series, it must place great emphasis on on-air promotion as well as to the scheduling of the series in a position that will assure audience sampling.

When the process is completed the pilot films are made available in New York for screening by members of the program board. The screening takes place during January and February at odd times, suited to individual convenience. All of which brings us back to the meeting of the program board, which may occupy several sessions of several hours each.

After the head of programming has made his presentation, the questions are many. Is a show recommended for cancellation really weak or merely badly hurt by its position in the schedule? Will a new series, recommended for inclusion in the schedule on the basis of a pilot film with dazzling production and a meticulously crafted script, be attractive when it has to be produced week after week on a very much lower budget? Should a highly popular existing series not recommended for cancellation be cancelled, nevertheless, because its large audience is concentrated in rural areas and small cities, whereas its reception is only lukewarm in the big cities?

Will the deletion of a particular series result in program imbalance? Is a proposed new series suitable for viewing in early prime time, in the light of violence or sexual allusions, or should it be broadcast at all?

As in any complex comparative selection process, the first exclusions and inclusions are the easiest. The approach is to build the schedule night by night, one night at a time. The atmosphere of the group is give and take. There are few arbitrary opinions. Everyone realizes how chancy the business of selecting popular entertainment is, and how foolish purely subjective impressions may seem to be after the event.

The most difficult questions are not necessarily those of determining the overall program mix, but those involved in the precise scheduling of programs with respect to their network competition.

Fundamental is the concept of counter programming, namely the strategy of placing opposite a strong program of the opposition a different program type, appealing to a substantially different audience. This, for example, was the principle underlying the scheduling of the low key family drama, "The Waltons," opposite NBC's then number 1 hit, Flip Wilson's manic variety show, or scheduling a movie night of films chosen for their appeal to women opposite prime time professional football.

Another principle has to do with using one's strongest existing programs to create traffic for new programs which need audience sampling. Thus the creation of so-called "hammock positions," where a new untried program is placed in the schedule between two strong programs. Then, in a succeeding year, when the new program is strong enough to stand on its own legs, the strong programs which nurtured it can again be used to prop up a new entry somewhere else in the schedule. Always the effort is to build a strong harmonious nighttime lineup on as many nights of the week as program strength permits.

Shows that are well thought of, but which do not make the fall schedule, are often slated by the program board to be available for midseason replacement, in case any of the chosen programs falter.

In weighing the existing popularity of programs in the schedule careful attention is given to demographic information. For, although advertisers no longer dominate programming, the medium's dependence upon advertising has a crucial role: it encourages programmers to prefer audiences that are young or female to those that are old or male, and to prefer city people to rural people. To that extent, advertiser supported television is undemocratic; one viewer's preference for a program is not necessarily as important as that of another viewer. In 1969 Robert D. Wood, then president of the CBS Television Network, inherited from his predecessor a schedule that was the most popular, in terms of raw rating points, in the history of television. But it was an aging schedule, not as popular with younger women, or with big city dwellers, as were its network competitors' schedules. Within the next two seasons Wood replaced the heart of the schedule—Red Skelton, Ed Sullivan, Danny Thomas, "Hee Haw," and others—with progams appealing more to the young and to urban viewers.

In May the schedule is presented to the network's affiliates at their annual convention, and the new program series are screened for them. They also receive presentations on daytime, sports, news, and special programs. Affiliates, after viewing the pilot program of a new series, may indicate that they will fail to clear it on their stations, either because they do not believe it will be a success or because they think it will be offensive to their local audiences, or, most common, because they have definite plans to preempt network programming in a certain time period so as to present local or syndicated programming of their own choice.

Meanwhile, when the schedule has been set and announced, the network's salesmen go to the street with it, and the major advertisers—who for prestige and marketing reasons need to plan their campaigns with the greatest lead time—place early orders.

It cannot be emphasized too often that for the networks the name of the game is programming. Well over 80 percent of network revenues go for the acquisition of programs.[9] There is no avoiding the fact that there *is* a strong tendency toward uniformity and homogeneity of product. The financial pressures in this direction are enormous. The reason: there is no correlation between audience size and program cost.[10] Once a network is committed to the production of a given number of episodes of a series it can do little to adjust to the fact of a lower than expected audience. And, it is important to stress, such a series' loss of audience is not confined to its time period, but extends to the programs immediately preceding and following the unpopular program. Indeed, an unpopular program infects the whole prime time schedule for that night, and the viewers who leave for another network may not return, even when the unpopular program is ultimately replaced. Small wonder, then, that proven formulas greatly outnumber innovative programs.

In this competition, as in many others, success breeds success. The most promising new programs tend to be offered first to the leading network. It is that network, after all, whose schedule is such that the new program has the best chance of being massively sampled.

Program Acceptability

The fundamental aspect of program acceptability is a program's conformance to the Television Code of the National Association of Broadcasters.[11] The networks are members of the Code and, like most of their affiliates, have included in their station renewal applications agreements to observe its provisions.

The Code's guidelines are broad, and are interpreted and administered by each network for its own programming. It is rare that a series in its inception will signal any clear violation of the Code—that is to say, it is rare that a series format or characters *inherently* present a Code problem. "All in the Family" was one such, with the open racial bigotry of its principal character, which was at the very heart of the show's concept. Similarly, "Bridget and Bernie," with its irreverent treatment of an interfaith marriage, might be said to have presented a Code problem. Both were placed in the schedule, although "Bridget and Bernie" was ultimately cancelled under circumstances that led some to believe that its offensiveness on religious grounds had contributed to its demise.

Probably the most common aspect of the Code which is involved in program selection is its stricture against gratuitous violence.[12] Again, however, even if a pilot program is excessively violent, a series based on it can be accepted provided that subsequent episodes can be kept within bounds. Often, however, it is clear that a series will be nothing without a good deal of action—an industry euphemism for violence—in which case it will either be omitted from the schedule or, if it is deemed permissible as part of the overall program mix, scheduled during later prime time hours. Judgments are often subtle ones. Even the most energetic of antiviolence crusaders rarely objected to "Gunsmoke." On the other hand, "Wild Wild West," almost a burlesque of a Western, a cartoon series ahead of its time, was widely cited as violent, and was in fact dropped by CBS from its schedule on that ground.

Another aspect of program policy has to do with the intrusion of views on controversial issues into the content of entertainment programming. Despite Sam Goldwyn's famous preference for Western Union, the fact is that most entertainment does convey messages, explicit or implicit, of one kind or another. Some, like concern over alcoholism or kindness toward animals, are consensus points of view and cause no problem. The turmoil of recent years has, however, greatly increased the number of issues now deemed to be controversial.

The position of CBS and, I believe, of the other networks is that the presentation of controversial issues in entertainment programming is acceptable so long as it is integral to the story and characters and not gratuitous. In other words, if it grows naturally and inevitably out of the characters and plot—like the "Maude" episode dealing with abortion—it is unexceptionable even though, as in that case, it represented and advanced strongly the views of the producer of the program.

Again, this question rarely arises at the inception of a program series. As the series progresses its individual scripts are reviewed by the program practices department, which is charged with enforcing this and other Code related policies. Thus, we at CBS deemed the Smothers Brothers' espousal of drug use to be controversial and gratuitous, as well as raising serious questions of licensee responsibility.

Always in the background of network concern with the intrusion of controversial issues into entertainment programming is the fear that the FCC's fairness doctrine[13] might someday be applied so as to weigh in the balance positions on such issues advanced in such programming. There is nothing in the doctrine which confines its reach to informational programming. Moreover, there is a principled position, especially strongly held at CBS, that controversial issues ought to be discussed and explored in news and public affairs programs produced under the auspices of its news professionals, and not by entertainers in program repartee or by advertisers in thirty-second advertisements.

This position, which is inextricably related to the underlying philosophy of the fairness doctrine, led CBS to the adoption of three important policies having to do with the integrity of its role as a news medium. The other networks have somewhat similar policies.[14] The CBS policies are:

1. a policy of not accepting outside produced informational programs dealing with controversial public issues;
2. a policy of not accepting advertising that explicitly addresses such issues;
3. a policy of not selling time to proponents of views on such issues except, during election campaigns only, to political candidates and to spokesmen for and against ballot issues.

Because of the importance of these policies let us pause to discuss them in some detail.

Outside Produced Informational Programs

Documentaries, for CBS, are a form of journalism; they are not, primarily, a form of art or of artistic self-expression; they must meet journalistic standards of truth, pertinence, and fairness of presentation. Film—or tape—is a medium easily capable of abuse, and since it is a powerful medium, abuses are both resented and found out.

In dealing with controversial issues CBS has found that only the most rigorous supervision of every stage of reportage and filming can insure adherence to journalistic standards. Even with such supervision, as such productions as "Hunger in America" and "The Selling of the Pentagon" have demonstrated, improper practices can occur out of the zeal of reporters and producers to obtain visually arresting images and striking confrontations.

Almost invariably, when CBS has in the past accepted outside produced documentaries, serious violations of journalistic standards are found to have occurred. Thus, for example, in a documentary about Wall Street broadcast some years ago, CBS found after the event that the production had been submitted for approval to the principal subject of the documentary and had been shaped so as to promote him and his undertakings.

It is to be noted that CBS is prepared to take such risks if the documentary does not deal with currently controversial public issues, that is to say, if the documentary does not come within the reach of the FCC's fairness doctrine. If the documentary is historical in nature—as were the Teddy White documentaries on "The Making of the President"—the policy permits their acceptance. But CBS insists that documentaries dealing with current controversy be done by CBS personnel only.

This is a rule which might well be followed by any large journalistic organization without regard to government policies. *Time* or *Newsweek* or *The New York Times* would hardly devote their columns to the unexamined product of another journalistic organization, let alone to producers who acknowledge no journalistic obligation. But given the sensitive regulated status of broadcasting, the application of the fairness doctrine, and the gravity of FCC charges of news "staging,"[15] the policy is an imperative one for a broadcast news organization to follow.

The fairness doctrine enters into the policy from another standpoint as well, that having to do with the choice of public issues to be presented, which the doctrine vests in the licensee. The amount of airtime available for informational programming is limited. By keeping control of such programming in its own shop a network can maintain balance in the subject matters chosen, as well as in the views presented. This must be done in the light of its hard news presentation of the same or related issues, as well as such presentation in interview formats and in CBS news specials. Outside producers do not and cannot have these considerations in mind, and the agenda of public discussion in network documentaries cannot be made to depend on chance, or on the particular interests of outside filmmakers.

An internal operational problem also bears on the matter. The news functions of the networks represent an enormous investment in personnel and facilities that now must approach $100 million a year for each network.[16] To attract and keep talented personnel a network needs to do more than merely undertake to compensate them in money; it needs to be able to assure them that their work will find a place in the schedule. It cannot fulfill this assurance and at the same time provide a ready market for outside produced material.

Needless to say, the network policy on outside produced informational programming is bitterly resented by outside producers, many of whom banded together in September 1978 to file an antitrust suit against the three networks, charging them with restraint of trade and monopolization of news and public affairs programming.[17]

But most people will agree, I believe, that from Murrow on the record of CBS and the other networks in presenting news and information has been one of the brightest pages of American broadcasting. In large part this has been the result of the building of strong journalistic organizations, and the application to these organizations of disciplined standards of performance. It could not have happened if the function of a network were merely to be a conduit of informational film produced by others.

Advertising that Addresses Controversial Issues

CBS policy, and that of the other networks, in refusing to accept advertising that explicitly addresses controversial issues, is likewise aimed at protecting the integrity of the journalistic process, though it also involves protecting the viewer from offensive and jarring intrusions into both entertainment and news programming. Again, consideration must be given to the power of the medium and its unique characteristics.

It is true that an advertiser can plead his cause in a page purchased in the *Wall Street Journal* or *The New York Times*. Some advertisers, like Mobil, do an able and vigorous job of presenting views on important subjects of current controversy. But such advertisements in newspapers or magazines allow the reader, without putting aside the publication entirely, to make his own choice as to whether to read the material.

In television, on the other hand, the advertiser's messages are inserted into other content, not clearly separated from it. They come uninvited upon the viewer who has chosen to look at drama or comedy or sports or news and who, for the period of the advertisement, is to some extent a captive of the advertiser. In the case of ordinary commercial messages, devoted to the sale of a product, this intrusion—if sometimes resented—is nevertheless understood and accepted as part of the price a viewer must pay for advertiser-supported free television. The intrusion of explicit argument on controversial issues would not be so understood and accepted.[18]

Most important, there would be an essential unfairness in allowing the agenda and content of public discussion on television to be dominated, as it might well be, by the financial power of advertisers.

It is argued that the networks could balance advertisers' messages by making available other short time periods for the presentation of opposing views.[19] Mobil, for example, has even offered to pay for the presentation of such views.[20] But this complicates the matter without solving it. Most advertisers are not so willing.

More important, even with such a regimen, the advertiser would then have taken over from the network the job of determining the agenda of public discussion.[21] Issues in which advertisers were interested would receive such discussion in heightened form. Other issues would not.

Finally, it is the view of CBS and of the other networks that the trading of thirty- or sixty-second messages by partisans on important public issues is not an adequate substitute for good journalism, nor even for effective partisan debate.

This is not to say that network policy is without problems of its own. It forbids the acceptance of explicit advertiser messages on controversial issues and in this respect is consistent with an FCC ruling that it is only explicit messages which would trigger the application of its fairness doctrine.[22]

But the line between explicit messages and implicit ones—which are not subject to fairness doctrine treatment—is not always easy to draw. In practice, all advertisements are reviewed at CBS by the program practices department and, in difficult cases, referred to the legal department.

Editorial Advertising by Issue Partisans

In refusing to accept so-called "editorial advertising"—other than that done, during political campaigns, on behalf of candidates or ballot issues—the networks are again concerned about the advantage that would be accorded to the wealthiest partisans, as well as the imposition upon the public of one-sided propagandistic materials that the public cannot easily opt not to view.

The latter consideration is exacerbated by the virulence of many contemporary controversies and the difficulty that would attend any network effort to moderate or otherwise edit particular messages. Who would view, with equanimity, the intrusion into a "Waltons" episode of a "pro-life" message illustrated with graphic pictures of dead fetuses?

As in the case of explicit issue advertising, the acceptance of such messages would make it almost impossible to achieve balance in the presentation of public issues. At its most objectionable it could force networks—in order to comply with the fairness doctrine—into the ridiculous position of altering their own news and informational output in order to achieve such balance.

CBS policy with respect to the nonacceptance of editorial advertising was upheld by the U.S. Supreme Court in the case of *CBS Inc.* v. *Democratic National Committee*.[23] The committee had sought to buy time for editorial spot announcements from CBS other than during an election campaign, and argued a first amendment right of access. CBS responded that to force a broadcaster to accept and broadcast certain matter was itself a violation of the first amendment and that, in addition, a mandatory right of access would be inconsistent with the fairness doctrine as embodied in the Communications Act. The Court held that the asserted right of access would be inconsistent with the obligation imposed on licensees by virtue of the fairness doctrine. Justice Douglas took the view that the asserted right of access, by mandating acceptance of the Democratic National Committee's message, would in any event violate the first amendment.

Few issues have been more strongly argued than those revolving about an asserted right of access, and the arguments for such access are not without appeal. Yet, so long as broadcasters are treated under the Communications Act as trustees for the public interest it seems untenable to allow the agenda of public discussion to be determined, on the one hand, by advertisers or wealthy partisans who can afford the immense costs involved, or by those who have gained access to a camera and microphone through the exercise of entertainment talent. It is the licensee which must determine the agenda of public discussion, and it is the licensee that is obligated to search out and present the principal opposing views on the issues he determines to address.

Reforms of the Network Programming Process

Over the years there have been many proposals, some of them implemented, for the reform of the network programming process by alteration of the structural relationships involved.

Perhaps the earliest idea was that embodied in the FCC's Chain Broadcasting Rules of 1941,[24] which were predicated on the proposition that the deficiencies of network radio broadcasting would be corrected if the hold that networks had over their affiliates could be loosened. It was, with no discernible effect on programming.

Then came the notion, already adverted to in my previous discussion, that the villain was the commercial sponsor, and that better programs and better program balance depended on confining the advertiser to a non-programming role. As we have seen, this change in fact came about, though it was not primarily of the FCC's doing. The change did remove the worst excesses of advertiser influence over program content, and left networks freer to achieve a balanced schedule. But in so doing it decreased the number of program decision makers while, in the view of some, liberating television from advertisers only to enslave it to ratings.

In 1967, in its proposed so-called "50-50" rule,[25] the FCC did a startling about face from its Blue Book conclusion, twenty-one years earlier, that the trouble lay in the sponsor.[26] The rule would have required that, for at least 50 percent of its schedule, a network would have to return to the role of merely selling time to advertisers and others for the placement of programs over which the network would have no control. Whatever its merits, this proposal came too late, for advertisers were no longer willing or able to return to the high risk business of obtaining their advertising circulation by bankrolling individual programs.

In 1969 the FCC adopted the so-called Prime Time Access Rule,[27] which was intended, for four hours a week of the prime time schedule on each network, to shift programming responsibility from networks to affiliates. It would do this by prohibiting affiliates during those four hours from accepting network programs. This, it was thought, would open up a market among network affiliates for the production, through other than network auspices, of network quality programming chosen directly by affiliates, and not by those "three men" in New York. The rule had unintended consequences. By creating a shortage of network minutes it made the ABC network competitive for the first time, and increased the profits of all three networks. It also enhanced the audiences and profitability of independent stations, and even of network affiliates. But the programming it stimulated was not remotely of the calibre of network programming.

At the same time as the Prime Time Access Rule the FCC also moved to restrict network power over program producers, by barring networks from obtaining profit sharing or syndication rights from program producers, and prohibiting networks from engaging in the busines of program syndication.[28] Since that time the Department of Justice has commenced legal action, still pending, to bar networks from any direct production of programs altogether.[29]

It is to be noted that these moves—aimed at weakening network power over programming by changing the structure of network/affiliate, network/advertiser, and network/producer relationships—are none of them explicitly concerned with improving the quality of network programs per se, with the sole exception of the antiadvertiser position asserted by the FCC in its 1946 Blue Book.[30]

Rather, they speak in terms of traditional economic regulation and their hallmark is to restore diversity and pluralism in the network program market by seeking to force more competition or, perhaps more accurately, to make other competitors more vigorous by eliminating some of the economic roles that networks had assumed.

But even their most ardent proponents agree that these moves to limit network power have been relatively ineffective, and, in some cases, even counterproductive.

The Quality of Television Programming

It seems to me highly unlikely that any structural change will have any qualitative impact on network programming, except to worsen it. The problem, such as it is, with the quality of network programming has to do with the inherent nature of television and of an advertiser supported mass medium. It has also to do with our culture as a whole.

The most obvious deficiencies of network television are its general inattention to what might be called "high culture," its inability to do meaningful programming for minority groups among its audience—including most particularly, programming for separate child age groups—and its persistent tendency to pander to the mass taste for violence in programming. These deficiencies are hardly likely to be more responsibly dealt with by advertisers, by individual stations, or by program producers. At the same time, the strength of the network position in entertainment programming permits them to do what most observers regard as a superior job in their vital role of presenting news and information.

Encouragement, more substantial support, and further development of the public television system provide one answer to the problem of programming diversity and the satisfaction of minority tastes. Pay cable television and the video cassette offer promise as well, though perhaps only to the relatively affluent. And a fourth commercial network, when economic conditions justify it, is bound to offer important program choices in various programming areas.

It is my view that the hustle and bustle of academic and government activity aimed at tinkering with the networks vastly misapprehends and trivializes the real problems posed by the presence of television at the center of our way of life.

There is no reason to believe that network television entertainment falls below the standard of any other popular medium. And there is a good deal of evidence—particularly in the enthusiastic use of popular American television programs by the BBC and by European governmental broadcasting systems generally—that it is deservedly the most popular entertainment being produced in the world today.

At its best, there has been high achievement. And beyond its value as pure entertainment it is really our only remaining mass medium that provides a common cultural base and a sense of national community for everyone. It is hard to imagine the major social revolutions of the past twenty-five years without television—the civil rights revolution, the fight for equal opportunity, the rise of consumerism, the drive for the equal treatment of women. Entertainment and informational programming have shared in this role. Parenthetically, the very linearity of television—that makes it so difficult to attend to minority interests and drives it to seek the largest possible audiences—operates to produce news and informational audiences that are truly mass in nature, a phenomenon that has never happened either in the print media or in theaters.

In truth, the disaffection with network programming is the disaffection of the few. Sir Robert Fraser of the BBC put it well when he said:

> Every person of common sense knows that people of superior mental constitutions are bound to find much of television intellectually beneath them. If such innately fortunate people cannot realize this gently and with good manners, if in their hearts they despise popular pleasures and interests, then of course they will be angrily dissatisfied with television. But it is not really television with which they are dissatisfied. It is people.

At the same time, no conceivable structural change or possible qualitative upgrading of television offers a real answer to those critics who are concerned, not with the quality of television programming in any specific sense, but with television itself.

For those who decry the effects of television as an enveloping semantic system, for those who are concerned that it is a Pied Piper beckoning children away from the traditional transmission of their parents' cultural values, for those who are concerned that it steals time away from their ability to relate to their peers, for those who believe that it has shattered the wholeness and sweetness of the family unit, for those who believe that it has made us a nation of compulsive consumers, for those who are profoundly concerned that the medium must inevitably teach the false and dangerous message that it is reasonable for men and women to be entertained all the time—for all of these, McLuhan's insight was right when he concluded that it is after all the medium, not the message, that is the problem.[31]

Changing its content will have only a marginal effect upon the person, child or adult, who spends 2,000 hours or more a year in front of the set. To correct that, we need either authoritarian intervention—which we will not tolerate and should not—or a genuine popular movement of a spiritual nature. That may be a dour and unsatisfying conclusion for those who believe that in government there is an easy fix to social problems, but there has never been any real reason to believe that the twentieth or twenty-first centuries would be any freer of agonizing predicaments than any other era of man's time on earth.

Notes

1. For another, more detailed view of this era, *see* E. Barnouw, The Sponsor: Notes on a Modern Potentate 32-58 (1978).
2. FCC, Public Service Responsibility of Broadcast Licensees (1946).

3. *Id.* at 13.

4. For a discussion of the transition from live production to film, *see* M. Mayer, About Television 80-85 (1972).

5. *See* E. Barnouw, *supra* note 1, at 55-57.

6. *See, e.g.*, House Comm. on Interstate and Foreign Commerce, Network Broadcasting, H.R. Rep. No. 1297, 85th Cong., 2d Sess. (1958) (the "Barrow Report").

7. M. Mayer, *supra* note 4, at 96.

8. For discussions of the costs of program development and pilot production, *see* R. Wiley, *infra* at 113; S. Robb, Television/Radio Age Communications Coursebook 2-24, 2-34 (1978).

9. FCC, TV Broadcast Financial Data—1978, Release No. 19540 (July 30, 1979), table 6.

10. *See* A. Pearce, *supra* at 9-10.

11. National Association of Broadcasters, Television Code (20th ed. 1978).

12. *Id.* §IV(1)(A).

13. *See* the discussions of the fairness doctrine in R. Wiley, *infra* at 110, and O. Chase, *infra* at 138-39, 144-49.

14. *See* FCC, Second Interim Report (Part II) by the Office of Network Study, Television Network Program Procurement 331-32 (1965).

15. *See, e.g.*, Hunger in America, 20 F.C.C.2d 143, 151 (1969); Letter to Mrs. J.R. Paul, 26 F.C.C.2d 591 (1969).

16. FCC, TV Broadcast Financial Data—1978, Release No. 19540 (July 30, 1979), table 5 n. 5.

17. *See* Broadcasting, Sept. 11, 1978, at 30; Broadcasting, Sept. 18, 1978, at 78-80. *See also* Neubauer, *The Networks' Policy Against Freelance Documentaries: A Proposal for Commission Action*, 30 Fed. Com. L.J. 117 (1978).

18. *See* CBS Inc. v. Democratic National Committee, 412 U.S. 94, 128 (1973).

19. *See* A. Schwartzman, *infra* at 64.

20. E. Barnouw, *supra* note 1, at 88.

21. *See* CBS Inc. v. Democratic National Committee, 412 U.S. 94, 123 (1973).

22. Fairness Report, 48 F.C.C.2d 1, 22-28 (1974), *reconsideration denied*, 58 F.C.C.2d 691 (1976), *aff'd in part and rev'd in part on other grounds sub nom.* National Citizens Committee for Broadcasting v. FCC, 567 F.2d 1095 (D.C. Cir. 1977), *cert. denied*, 436 U.S. 926 (1978).

23. 412 U.S. 94 (1973).

24. FCC, Report on Chain Broadcasting (1941).

25. Notice of Proposed Rulemaking, Docket No. 12782, 45 F.C C. 2146, 2164 (1965).

26. FCC, Public Service Responsibility of Broadcast Licensees 54-56 (1946).

27. Report and Order, Docket No. 12782, 23 F.C.C.2d 382, 384, *modified*, 25 F.C.C.2d 318, *aff'd sub nom*. Mt. Mansfield Television, Inc. v. FCC, 442 F.2d 470 (2d Cir. 1970).

28. *Id.*, 23 F.C.C.2d at 397-99, 25 F.C.C.2d at 330-33, 336-37.

29. United States v. ABC, Civ. No. 74-3600-RJK (C.D. Cal., complaint filed Dec. 10, 1974); United States v. CBS Inc., No. 74-3599-RJK (C.D. Cal., complaint filed Dec. 10, 1974); United States v. NBC, Civ. No. 74-3601-RJK (C.D. Cal., complaint filed Dec. 10, 1974).

30. *See* note 26 *supra*.

31. *See generally* M. McLuhan & Q. Fiore, The Medium is the Massage (1967).

6 Some Reflections on Network Programming

Howard Eaton

Many of the participants in the Network Television Conference have expressed the thought that regulation of the networks is necessary in order to redress the power they control because of the scarcity of available air time. This concept of scarcity is at the heart of regulatory thinking. I would propose, however, that this is a false concept at a time when technical innovation is creating an abundance of channels through cable—many more channels than we will know how to use. Rather than limiting the power of the networks, as is now fashionable, public policy should focus on how to use that power to speed up the development of multichannel reception. The networks should be allowed to get back into the cable business;[1] it is ridiculous to exclude them if we believe that it is in the public interest to have cable, two-way, multichannel, and so forth.

Although on the one hand I believe that the television industry should expand its power for the public good, on the other hand I fail to understand the irresponsibility to the public demonstrated by its recent actions in expanding the amount of allowable nonprogram time by 30 seconds, from 9.5 to 10 minutes per hour.[2] That 10 minutes consists of commercials and other nonprogram elements. The reason for doing this has more to do with the promotional announcements that the networks run for themselves than with commercials, although the networks can always substitute commercials for promotions for economic reasons. It is hard to understand how the networks can justify their action in simply, with the stroke of a pen, taking 30 seconds out of the public's time. It is even more difficult to understand the Justice Department's antitrust suit attacking the NAB's Television Code for limiting the amount of commercial time at all.[3]

Much criticism has been leveled at the prevalence of violence and sex in network programming. At one point 62 percent of prime time was composed of "action-adventure" programs—and "action-adventure" equals violence. Whenever such a high percentage of prime-time programming is composed of any single program form, there is bound to be a public reaction—in this case, not so much to the amount of actual blood and gore as to the lack of diversity in nightly programming. In the case of sex, the advertising agencies are quite concerned because public-pressure groups do present problems for them. At a meeting of the American Association of Advertising Agencies Broadcast

Committee, I asked the committee members whether they saw a *current* problem; their answer was: "Not yet," although they are a little nervous about future developments.

Jencks talked about how programming changes over the years.[4] But there is truth in the old adage that there really is nothing new in show business. "Wagon Train" in 1958 was basically no different from "How the West Was Won" in 1978. Likewise, "My Three Sons" in 1960 was the same as "The Brady Bunch" in 1973, and "Dragnet" in 1955 was the same as "Police Story" in 1975.

Jencks also discussed the difficult subject of program research.[5] The real problem is that a pilot really only tests the pilot itself; the producer cannot guarantee that the twenty-five other episodes he will make later on will maintain the quality of the pilot. A bad pilot is likely to lead to a bad series. But a good pilot will lead to a good series only if the creative elements that made that pilot—and the time and the money that went into it—will still be available when the series is produced. Nevertheless, program research is better than no research at all. Furthermore, those who criticize the ratings system are often absurdly ignorant of how it works. The system is used by advertisers and networks to make business decisions and has been entirely satisfactory for that purpose.

Hollywood is a very imitative place: If someone has just made a million dollars from a show, that kind of show will be repeated. If "Star Wars" is a success, we will have "Battlestar Galactica" on television, and if that works we will have many more science-fiction shows. It is an imitative process that leads to a flood of programming of a certain type. One show is successful, and perhaps also a second and a third of the same type. The fourth version may be less successful and the fifth and sixth total failures. Eventually there are so many of them that they self-destruct.

The process by which programs are selected and scheduled reveals some truths about the creative process itself. Art does imitate life, especially what is interesting in life. For example, why was "Paper Chase" a ratings failure? "Paper Chase" was a cerebral program concerned with the standards of teaching at the Harvard Law School, and this is simply not a subject that will make for a hit show. The things that are really interesting in life are death, crime, pain, marriage, family, love, and sex. And these are the bases of shows such as "Medical Center," "Eight is Enough," "Family," the cops-and-robbers shows, and even the soap operas.

The stuff of life is of interest to creators and writers, who are looking for a unique character, situation, or story. Archie Bunker, Sergeant Bilko, and Jack Benny were unique characters, as is Mork of the current show "Mork and Mindy." "The Fugitive," "The Love Boat," "Fantasy Island," and to some extent "Perry Mason" are all examples of shows based on unique situations, as are westerns and science-fiction shows.

"Mission Impossible" told very complex, even overwritten, stories. The same was true of "Perry Mason"; the viewer had to try hard to follow each twist of the plot.

In a recent issue of *TV Guide*, twelve series were listed that had an episode based on love or sex; fourteen with episodes based on crime (including eight murders); two based on family, two on status, three on death, two on avarice, one simply on thrills, and only one on work. That is why many critics dislike much of what they see.

Jencks's discussion raises the question of whom the networks are programming for.[6] People who have spent four years at college have different viewing preferences than does the general population. Their viewing time is about 16 percent lower than the national average in prime time. "Laverne and Shirley," "Charlie's Angels," and "Happy Days" are rated by better-educated viewers about 30 percent lower than in the nation as a whole, while "Starsky and Hutch" receives ratings among well-educated men that are about half the show's national ratings. On the other hand, "M*A*S*H" and "60 Minutes" come out about 10 percent above their national ratings in viewing by the better-educated.

If we look at the same figures for PBS, the "Dick Cavett" show was 38 percent above its national rating, and "Masterpiece Theatre" (the "Poldark" episode) was 85 percent above its national rating in viewing by highly educated people. For "MacNeil-Lehrer" the figure was 58 percent above, for "Evening at Pops" 45 percent, and so on. Of course, PBS's total ratings are low.[7] The average network rating is about 18, while 5 is considered high for PBS. But the public system does offer service to the more highly educated, and as soon as PBS can overcome its political difficulties and obtain adequate funding, there will be a genuine alternative to "Laverne and Shirley."

Notes

1. This is now forbidden by 47 C.F.R. §76.501(a)(1) (1979).

2. National Ass'n of Broadcasters, Television Code §XIV(2)(A)(2) (20th ed. 1978, as amended eff. Jan. 1, 1979). *See* Broadcasting, Oct. 16, 1978, at 25-26.

3. United States v. National Ass'n of Broadcasters, Civ. No. 79-1549 (D.D.C., complaint filed June 14, 1979).

4. R. Jencks, *supra* at 42-43.

5. *Id.* at 43-44.

6. *See id.* at 45-46, 53-55.

7. Carnegie Commission on the Future of Public Broadcasting, A Public Trust 330 (Bantam ed. 1979).

7 The Need for Access to Network Television

Andrew Jay Schwartzman

The influence of sponsors on entertainment programming, although it is an extremely important subject, will not be addressed in this chapter. Jencks made some important points about the history of broadcasting, including the change from advertising agencies to networks as the primary production entities.[1] A new book by Erik Barnouw, the preeminent historian of broadcasting, contributes greatly to the understanding of this phenomenon.[2] The essence of Barnouw's thesis is that it is no longer necessary for advertisers to produce programs themselves. Network broadcasters serve the interests of the sponsors, and direct sponsor control is unnecessary because the networks anticipate and fulfill every wish and need of the sponsors. Hence the situation today is functionally no different than it was thirty years ago when advertisers themselves were producing the programming.

Jencks's defense of the need for networks to have complete control over the content of nonentertainment programming is eloquent.[3] His reasons—although he expressed an ambivalence in some areas—are persuasive, but I think they are incorrect. Nor do they necessarily represent the views and motives of many other people employed by the networks, who have other reasons for maintaining careful control of nonentertainment programming. But the result, regardless of the reasons, is the stifling of diversity.

One of the finest things that television and radio can do is to let people get on the air and express their own views in their own words. The policy of keeping the entire presentation of nonentertainment programming in the hands of the networks is ultimately elitist. First, networks control the selection of the issues. Second, they control the way in which the issues are explained and the force with which they are presented.

In the last two decades, the civil-rights movement and the antiwar movement both tried hard to get their viewpoints across to the general population. They were largely frustrated and succeeded only in obtaining belated, often second-hand summaries of their positions. A strong argument can be made that had antiwar activists been able to buy air time—the subject of the *CBS* v. *Democratic National Committee* case[4]—the persuasive impact of that programming might have increased antiwar sentiment and thus led to a situation that would have ended the war in Vietnam a little earlier. The point is that the decision by the networks to run their own nonentertainment-programming operations, with no provision for outsiders ever to appear, can cut off meaningful discussion and have a significant societal impact.

Treatment of corporate issue advertising is largely similar. Edison Electric Institute wants to broadcast issue advertising.[5] In doing so they will make a stronger, more powerful case than CBS could, even in a special documentary on energy. In this case the fairness doctrine is important, particularly the so-called *Cullman* corollary.[6] If the Edison Electric Institute wants to buy some time, it can, but the network must somehow present opposing viewpoints. It is true, as Jencks says, that it is not so good for the network's news department to present those views.[7] But the answer is simple: Give some time to responsible opposing spokespersons. Broadcasters could air these persons' views as public service announcements (PSAs) and even get some credit from the FCC. The Public Media Center in San Francisco produces such PSAs. I agree with Eaton in deploring recent network decisions to expand nonprogram time.[8] But since PSAs are not included in the program categories, networks could run more PSAs and fewer promotional announcements. In the course of a two-hour network movie there may be numerous promotions for one upcoming network program. One of these could certainly be replaced by a PSA responding to an advertisement from the Edison Institute or some other entity.

The usual objection is that this might cost money, and it might. But one thing we have learned in the last few years, through CBS's patience with "60 Minutes," is that responsible programming can be both interesting and profitable.

There is nothing wrong with a little controversy. Some people think viewers will be disturbed if a presentation against abortion is shown in the middle of "The Waltons."[9] This may be true, but the issue of taste is separate from that of substantive content. Broadcasters lag far behind the print media in accepting new voices. Howard Jarvis, for example, had some important things to say to the American people, but he could not get those views on network television. Ten years ago he was regarded as an eccentric. Likewise, people who opposed the use of aerosol propellants were regarded as eccentrics several years ago and could not get on the air. Yet their views turned out to be substantially correct, and manufacturers are now eliminating fluorocarbon propellants.

Jencks's arguments about the problems of keeping the network newspeople on staff are also persuasive.[10] But these claims are not the real motives for exclusion, nor are they Jencks's motives. In a document recently filed by CBS, commenting on a so-called "access proposal" made in connection with an FCC reevaluation of the fairness doctrine, the network describes the people who might be seeking access for their viewpoints on the air as bigots and quacks:

> If the Commission is to adopt the COM [Committee for Open Media] pro-
> posal, it must be prepared to respond daily to frantic calls for on-the-spot
> guidance from licensees who have Nazis, Klansman [sic], lay hypnotists, or
> conventional lunatics at the head of their access lines.[11]

Metromedia, one of the larger group owners, expressed fear that "community misfits and malcontents of every description [would] monopolize
the airwaves with personal diatribe."[12] These views are examples of the
elitism with which the people at the networks view the public. It was their
view of Howard Jarvis and of people who opposed the Vietnam War, and it
is their view of people today who oppose abortion. There is a tremendous
arrogation of responsibility in not letting such people on the air to make
first-person presentations.

A final issue is the nonprogram, nonentertainment question that Eaton
has already raised.[13] About 25 to 30 percent of daily television programming
is neither entertainment nor nonentertainment. It consists of commercials,
PSAs (early in the morning or late at night), and, especially, promotional
announcements. We spend 95 percent of our time talking about 70 percent
of the programming, and only 5 percent of our time talking about the other
30 percent. The opportunity exists to use nonprogram time for spot presentations on controversial issues by persons other than the networks. And the
major source of the trouble is the Advertising Council, Inc. Despite all their
claims about keeping programming entirely within their control, the networks have handed over the responsibility for deciding what is going to be
done with limited PSA time to the advertising industry. And that group, the
networks' major customer, treats this as a kind of rebate. Through the
Advertising Council, it produces bland, quiet, noncontroversial, and often
nonessential public-service announcements.[14] This is a great waste of an important opportunity.

There is a proceeding underway at the FCC where, on behalf of the
Public Media Center, the Media Access Project is trying to do something
about this.[15] We want to see requirements for public-service announcements
during all times of the broadcast day, and we want to see some minimum requirements and some encouragement of controversial issue advertising and
controversial PSAs, because that is what broadcasting ought to be all
about.

Finally, I want to mention the Prime Time Access Rule.[16] This must be
regarded as a lost opportunity—not a case of oppressive government regulations, but rather a case of the networks convincing the FCC to water down a
sound proposal so that it never had a chance. The moment that the networks realized that it would be all right to run off-network programming on
their O&O stations for the first few years of PTAR, they sentenced us to an
endless tide of game shows. Without criticizing game shows per se, one can
nevertheless maintain that viewers want more than that. Only now, seven

or eight years after the advent of the Prime Time Access Rule, are broadcasters learning that they can make money with informational programs like "60 Minutes" and with other innovative programs in the prime-time access period. "The Muppet Show," for example, should have been there seven years ago, and the same is true for the new magazine shows. Broadcasters can make a lot of money this way, and this is the kind of innovation that PTAR should have fostered.

Notes

1. R. Jencks, *supra* at 37-40.

2. E. Barnouw, The Sponsor: Notes on a Modern Potentate (1978).

3. R. Jencks, *supra* at 48-52.

4. CBS Inc. v. Democratic National Committee, 412 U.S. 94 (1973).

5. *See* Young, *Network Television and the Public Interest*, 79/2 Electric Perspectives 2 (1979).

6. Cullman Broadcasting Co., 40 F.C.C. 576 (1963).

7. R. Jencks, *supra* at 51.

8. H. Eaton, *supra* at 59.

9. *See* R. Jencks, *supra* at 51.

10. *Id.* at 49.

11. Comments of CBS Inc., BC Docket No. 78-60 (Sept. 5, 1978), at 24.

12. Comments of Metromedia, Inc., BC Docket No. 78-60 (Sept. 5, 1978), at 2.

13. H. Eaton, *supra*, at 59.

14. *See* E. Barnouw, *supra* note 2, at 140-46.

15. See Memorandum Opinion and Order and Notice of Inquiry, BC Docket No. 78-251, FCC 78-602, 43 Fed. Reg. 37725 (1978).

16. 47 C.F.R. §73.658(k) (1979).

8 Entertainment Law and Network Television

Melvin Simensky

The focus of the Network Television Conference is on television as a regulated medium of communications or, one might say, television as an "output" vehicle. My major interest, however, is on television as an "input" vehicle, that is, the regulation of those human contributors whose services actually create the programs aired—performers, writers, producers, and so on. In other words, I am concerned with the regulation of television's content, not its airwaves.

In this chapter I present my view of the relationship between performers and producers on the one hand and television on the other, and the means of regulating the business conduct between these entities. The conduct among these entities falls generally into three parts: considerations of compensation, considerations of credit, and considerations of artistic control. The fabric that connects all these considerations is money, both in terms of what gets on the air and in terms of what services are offered to the networks and syndicators and by whom.

Each of these three considerations can actually be expressed in dollars. *Compensation* is easy to understand; it is payment for services rendered. *Credit* means the screen credit at the end of a program, which goes into a performer's portfolio and has an enormous value in negotiating that performer's next entertainment contract. The performer's credit is associated with a certain dollar level that provides a base from which he or she will then try to negotiate the next deal. *Artistic control* involves the maintenance of a performer's artistic reputation. This is a means by which the performer protects his earning ability, because only through the protection of his artistic reputation will a performer be guaranteed reemployment.

One place to start in regulating business conduct in television is with the various entertainment unions, called guilds, such as the Screen Actors Guild, the Directors Guild of America, and the Writers Guild of America. These guilds establish minimum requirements over such matters as credit attribution and compensation, which networks and producers for networks must satisfy if they wish to employ union members. However, there are limitations on the applicability of these guild requirements, and therefore on their impact on regulated conduct. The guilds only establish minimums, and once negotiations for a performer begin, minimums cease to apply. An established performer can demand top dollar, regardless of the guilds' minimums. Also, guild agreements do not always require the resolution of disputes under the auspices of a guild or another entity, such as the American Arbitration Association. Thus if there is a breach of contract, one must go to court. As a result one must take into account the intrusion of judges who may not understand the entertainment industry but who are empowered to regulate business conduct in that industry. This makes entertainment law a fascinating, complex field, in which judicial decisions may have a definite effect on the parties involved and the actions taken in the entertainment industry.

For example, in one important recent case, *Broadcast Music, Inc. (BMI)* v. *CBS*, the U.S. Supreme Court held that the issuance by BMI and the American Society of Composers, Authors, and Publishers (ASCAP) of blanket licenses for the right to perform any and all musical compositions in their repertoires, as opposed to a per-use license for each musical composition, was not a per se violation of the antitrust laws.[1] This reversed the Second Circuit's ruling that BMI and ASCAP, as a condition to continuing their blanket licensing of music to the networks, had to issue per-use licenses as well. Should the lower courts, upon remand, find an antitrust violation under a different legal analysis, there undoubtedly will be a demonstrable effect on the sale of music to network television.

A 1977 Supreme Court case, *Zacchini* v. *Scripps-Howard Broadcasting Company*, found that the broadcast by a television station of the entirety of a celebrity's performance (the performer was shot out of a cannon, and the broadcast lasted only fifteen seconds) exceeded ordinary news reporting and constituted the appropriation of the performer's property interest in his performance, in violation of his right of publicity.[2] This decision has concerned many broadcasters. It involves the conflict between the first amendment and what has only recently come to be recognized as the right of publicity—that someone has a commercial interest in the public likeness and characterization that he promotes as a performer. What questions does *Zacchini* pose for broadcasters? Would it have been proper to broadcast seven seconds of Zacchini's performance, or one-quarter of it? Can a television news show broadcast a film of Marcel Marceau in performance, and if so, for how long a period of time?

Other cases deal specifically with the three areas of concern previously mentioned: compensation, credit, and artistic control. Let us first examine how performers are compensated and review some of the questions pertaining to such compensation.

It is easy to say that if someone does not get paid for his or her services, he or she should sue the network, the producer, or the syndicator. But what about the situation in which the performer is being compensated on a contingent basis in terms of a royalty, a percentage of the proceeds that the film or program produces? What if the program is not aired? What if the program is a failure and does not run as long as expected? Does the performer have the right to sue for specific performance requiring the broadcaster to air the program because that is the only way that the performer can be compensated by means of the royalty?

In other words, since a program must be aired so that a royalty can be earned, and since that is one of the reasons the performer entered into the agreement, does the failure to show the program constitute a failure of consideration? Can the performer whose series is cancelled get an injunction to enforce the continuation of the broadcasts? These questions, as the case law indicates, are not so far-fetched.

For example, *Reback* v. *Story Productions, Inc.*, a 1958 case in the New York State Supreme Court, addresses some of these questions.[3] The court in this case had to determine whether there was merely a promise to exercise best efforts to produce the film in question, or a requirement that the producer actually produce the film and cause it to be broadcast. The court held on a motion to dismiss that it was unable to make that determination, ruling that such a determination would be better made at a trial of the matter.

In the area of screen credit, a recent decision made new law in the federal courts. In *Perin Film Enterprises, Ltd.* v. *TWG Productions, Inc.*, an independent producer sued a national television syndicator because he was not given a credit as "executive producer" for the program, while someone else received an undeserved and confusingly similar credit as "executive in charge of production."[4] On a motion to dismiss plaintiff's claim for failure to state a cause of action, the court denied the motion, holding, in an unreported decision, that plaintiff's claim constituted a good cause of action for unfair competition under a federal statute called the Lanham Act.[5] Thereafter, a settlement was reached. This was the first time the Lanham Act was ever used in connection with a matter of credit to require the correct attribution of the credit. This decision gives performers another tool for protecting their rights.

Another example of an artistic control issue was the case of *Gilliam* v. *ABC*, the so-called "Monty Python" case, in which the comedy group known as Monty Python sued the ABC television network for cutting into a Monty Python performance for the insertion of commercials.[6] The defense argued that Monty Python should have known that ABC was going to do this. Monty Python claimed that the extent of ABC's commercial interruptions had so mutilated its product that it constituted a gross distortion of its performance. In my view, Monty Python correctly feared the damage that could have resulted from the distortion of its performance. An adverse impact on the group's artistic reputation might result if viewers did not find Monty Python as funny as if they had seen the performance intact and therefore did not wish to see future Monty Python performances. The court agreed and sustained Monty Python's claims.

Notes

1.Broadcast Music, Inc. v. CBS Inc., 441 U.S. 1 (1979), *rev'g* CBS Inc. v. American Soc'y of Composers, Authors & Publishers, 562 F.2d 130 (2d. Cir. 1977).

2. 433 U.S. 562 (1977).

3. 15 Misc.2d 681, 181 N.Y.S.2d 980 (Sup.Ct. N.Y. Co. 1958), *aff'd*, 9 App. Div. 2d 880, 193 N.Y.S.2d 520 (1st Dep't 1959).

4. 400 Pat. T.M. & Copyright J. (BNA) A-13 (S.D.N.Y. Sept. 13, 1978).

5. 15 U.S.C. §1125(a) (1976).

6. Gilliam v. ABC, 538 F.2d 14 (2d Cir. 1976).

Part III
Distribution of Network Programming

9

Network-Station Business Relationships: The Affiliation Process

Scott H. Robb

Introduction

In large part, broadcasting in the United States is a creature of three conglomerate companies—CBS, ABC, and NBC. The networks own radio and television stations, have facilities for the production of programming, operate extensive news-gathering and sports-production divisions, and provide network programming to both radio and television stations. While the ownership of broadcast properties in key cities throughout the country provides the networks with a tremendous financial base, the network organization allows each company to become a primary program-supply source to broadcast stations and accounts for its unparalleled power and influence.

Indeed, network affiliates number well over 75 percent of all U.S. commercial television outlets (approximately 600 out of slightly more than 700 stations).[1] Outside major population centers, in fact, most stations are network affiliates. In order to serve this vast market, networks currently provide over 60 percent of the programs broadcast by affiliated stations.[2] And networks play a key function in the development, acquisition, selection, and distribution of television-programming material.

This chapter will explore the fundamental commercial relationships that define the affiliation process by which stations become members of the network "family." The focus of the study will be on the television-network operations, which account for the networks' primary revenues and commitment of resources. While each network company operates at least one radio network, the great diversity of almost 8,000 radio outlets has over the years substantially lessened the importance of networks in the industry. Since radio gave birth to the network organization, however, it is useful to explore some elements of the historical development of radio networks in order to understand the current status of the network companies.

Historical Background

The mid-1920s witnessed a basic industrial realignment that set the pattern for the development of the fledgling radio industry. This reorganization involved the removal of the American Telephone and Telegraph Company (AT&T) from broadcasting; AT&T agreed to concentrate on common carrier functions such as telephone service and the joining of radio stations through long-line facilities.[3] As part of the agreement, the Radio Corporation of America (RCA) emerged as the dominant broadcast company in the United States.[4] RCA formed a new broadcasting company, the National Broadcasting Company, which was to provide a programming service to stations interconnected by AT&T lines.[5]

The concept of network operation—called *chain broadcasting* in the early days of radio—was actually pioneered by AT&T; in 1924 it joined together some eighteen radio stations to carry coverage of the Republican and Democratic National Conventions.[6] And in 1925 the company linked twenty-two stations together to carry the inaugural address of President Calvin Coolidge.[7]

It was not until 15 November 1926, however, that the inaugural broadcast of the newly formed National Broadcasting Company took place over a network of twenty-six stations stretching from Maine to Washington, D.C. to Kansas City.[8] As a reflection of its great power as the country's first truly national news and entertainment service, NBC appointed an advisory council that included a former presidential candidate, John W. Davis; the head of the American Federation of Labor (AFL), William Green; and a prominent jurist, Elihu Root.[9]

NBC expanded swiftly as it became the key programming source for radio stations. In fact, the demand for service was so great that in early 1927 NBC announced the formation of two networks, the Red and the Blue networks.[10] These names were derived from the color designations used by NBC engineers in outlining the interconnection of affiliates.[11] Cultural programs dominated the Blue network, while the Red network's schedule included a number of early radio's commercial hits.

Although NBC's position certainly was dominant, it did have competition from a new network formed in January of 1927. In 1928 William S. Paley bought control of this network, which was experiencing financial and organizational problems; the network was renamed the Columbia Broadcasting System.[12]

As the only supplier of national program material, in its early days NBC could dictate the commercial terms by which stations would be permitted to become affiliates. With the entry of CBS, however, the picture changed, as the two network companies began to contest for affiliates; after all, at that time only about 700 stations existed in the country.[13] One of CBS's chief strategies was a revision of the basic affiliation agreement. CBS agreed to provide its affiliates with ten to twelve hours of free ("sustaining") programming daily, in return for the right to use any part of the time available on the affiliate for sponsored programming.[14] Sponsors paid CBS established rates based on station costs; the network and the stations divided the total receipts under a negotiated formula, with the larger share—generally 70 percent or more—going to the network.[15] The payment to affiliates was called *station compensation*.

NBC was forced to alter its basic affiliation terms to meet CBS's competitive challenge. NBC affiliates received station compensation for programs broadcast.[16] At the same time, however, the new NBC contract included a vital provision that defined certain time periods on each station as *network optional time*, not under control of the station.[17] This shift of control of option time later became the subject of regulatory action by the federal government, which eventually prohibited the practice.[18]

The basic commercial relationship under radio affiliation agreements was quite simple. As a middleman, the network sought to sell commercials to national sponsors through advertising agencies. The networks sold time periods only; the advertiser had the responsibility for supplying programming. From gross revenues (after discounts), the network retained about 50 percent to cover costs of operations, including telephone-line charges; each station received about 35 percent of each sales dollar as compensation for carrying the program; and the remaining 15 percent constituted a commission for the advertising agency making the purchase.[19]

While the allocation of compensation was based on per-program carriage of network material, station-compensation payments were made in accordance with an elaborate and complicated payment formula; this took into account station payments for telephone interconnection as well as a reverse-sliding-scale payment schedule that gave the station more compensation when greater numbers of hours of network programming were carried each month.[20] The overall effect of the station-compensation formula was to pay the station about 30 to 35 percent of its established rate-card price for its broadcast time.

It might be asked why a broadcast station would accept a commercial arrangement that paid it only about one-third of the revenue it could normally expect to earn if it retained control over all sales dollars. The critical factors are basically simple, and they continue to govern affiliate relationships in the television industry to this day.

A continuous supply of network programming is the key concern of an affiliate. Network programming brings audience popularity and local sales revenues to an affiliate. This service includes entertainment, news, and public-affairs programs. And of course all the programming is free of charge to a local station. While the affiliate is compensated at rates substantially below its own price structures, it should be remembered that station collections often fall short of 100 percent of the rate-card price. Finally, station compensation carries no additional administrative expense at the local level and therefore constitutes a direct source of revenue against general-operating expenses.

The radio-network organizations thus became vital to the broadcast industry as a main source of programming material and a key source of revenue. Indeed, by the late 1930s the four radio networks (the two NBC networks, CBS, and later the Mutual Broadcasting System) had affiliation agreements with nearly 350 of the 660 radio stations licensed throughout the country.[21] More significantly, this group of network affiliates represented nearly all radio stations authorized to operate during the nighttime hours.[22] As a national entertainment and advertising medium, radio was based on interlocking contractual arrangements. The station entered into an affiliation agreement with the network covering its sale of time; and the network in turn sold commercial time to national advertisers through their advertising agencies, which supplied programming for presentation over the networks.

Early Regulation

In the late 1930s the expansion of network influence became the subject of extensive hearings by the FCC, and in 1941 an extensive set of regulations (the Chain Broadcasting Rules) was adopted by the Commission.[23] The Commission's main concern was the fact that under the Communications Act it licensed stations—not networks—to broadcast in the public interest, convenience, and necessity.[24] As the industry developed, however, stations largely abdicated control over their schedules to the network companies as the price of an affiliation agreement. As a result, the network programming departments—not the local stations—determined the composition of program schedules.[25]

A prime example of the constraints on network affiliates occurred in 1939, when the Mutual network secured the rights to broadcast the World Series. As the smallest of the four networks then in operation, Mutual had been unable to secure affiliated stations in many areas throughout the country. When Mutual sought to contract with NBC and CBS affiliates to expand its station lineup for the World Series coverage, it found it could not clear time on these stations; the NBC and CBS affiliation contracts prohibited the stations from carrying any other network's programming.[26]

The Chain Broadcasting Rules sought to alter the networks' power. Since the FCC lacked statutory authority to regulate the networks directly, it accomplished its goal indirectly by adopting extensive new rules for affiliated stations. Under the new regulations no radio station could enter into an affiliation agreement that prohibited the station from "broadcasting the programs of any other network organization."[27] The aim of the rule was to end the exclusivity provisions in network contracts and to restore power to local stations to determine the content of their programming schedules.

The rules also guaranteed stations an unconditional right to reject network programs, a provision also aimed at returning power to the station operator.[28] The former practice under affiliation agreements had been to place the burden on the station to prove that any program it wished to substitute for a network offering met a higher public-interest standard than the network program.[29]

Finally, the Commission adopted a rule prohibiting stations from entering into affiliation agreements with any network operating more than one network.[30] This rule resulted in NBC divesting the Blue network, which became the basis for the American Broadcasting Company.[31]

The networks naturally predicted the doom of networking because of the strict new regulations.[32] Judicial review of the rules went to the U.S. Supreme Court, which found that the rules represented a proper exercise of the Commission's powers to fashion a regulatory framework in the public interest.[33] Despite all the dire predictions, the operation of radio networks changed very little because the stations still needed the programming material and sales dollars provided by the networks. And although the Chain Broadcasting Rules were designed to increase the stations' freedom to determine their schedules, most stations had little interest in the new flexibility but preferred to rely on network scheduling determinations. No real changes took place until television arrived as the nation's primary home-entertainment medium and caused radio to develop a new role as a music-news-information service medium.

Television Networks

With the arrival of television, the pattern of network organization followed the early radio experience. By the beginning of 1952, over a hundred television stations had been established in sixty-four major metropolitan centers, with some fifteen million television sets already in use.[34] NBC and CBS were early entrants in the television race, followed by ABC and Dumont. As each network sought to add affiliated stations to supplement its owned stations, the basic business arrangement was the same as in the radio affiliation agreement: The networks provided programming and paid station compensation in return for the right to sell program time periods to national sponsors.

The radio affiliation formula was transferred intact to television.[35] The networks sold time to national advertisers at rates based primarily on the total number of viewers in the network markets included in the order.[36] As with radio, television programming at first came from the advertiser and its agency. After a network deduction for overhead and other expenses and an agency's commission on advertising sales, television stations netted about one-third of their normal rate-card figures for carrying network programming.[37] These station-compensation payments were still paid on a monthly basis.

The stations found the affiliation arrangement even more advantageous in television than in radio, given the expensive and complex nature of television. Television programming is costly and difficult to produce.[38] Attempting to prejudge public acceptance of programming concepts is an inexact science; where errors of judgment occur and a program fails to win an audience, networks absorb production costs without offsetting advertising revenues.[39]

Also, television has a limitless demand for programming, necessitating constant development of new programs. Given these complexities, stations naturally were anxious to secure network affiliations and a steady supply of new programming. Finally, successful network programs produce increased numbers of viewers for stations, and these audiences in turn can be used to raise prices charged for the sale of local advertising time.

Over the years television has become still more complicated, with resulting changes in the basic affiliation arrangements. As the cost of television production continued to escalate in the late 1950s and early 1960s, advertisers and their agencies were no longer willing to take on the high costs and risks of program production. With a few exceptions, such as the daytime soap operas,[40] the networks took over responsibility for providing all programming for their schedules.[41] In the case of entertainment programs, the networks now generally purchase shows from outside suppliers;[42] for news and sports programs, networks do their own production.[43]

With advertisers no longer supplying programs, the networks began to sell individual minutes or other time segments in their programs to national advertisers, causing a key change in industry economics.[44] Network pricing formerly had been based on a composite rate, reflecting the prices of each program on each station in a network lineup. With the shift away from selling time periods to selling partial sponsorships and individual advertisements, the networks began to base prices more on what the market would pay. A popular program thus would be priced at as high a rate as advertisers would be willing to spend to reach the audience attracted by the program, and refinements in audience-survey techniques made these calculations increasingly precise.[45] Network sales processes also provided for volume discounts, seasonal discounts, and other special sales packages.[46] Finally, the network inventory of commercial spots expanded as the basic unit of sale shifted from discrete time periods to minute spots and later to thirty-second commercial announcements.[47]

As networks changed the manner in which they sold time to national advertisers, adjustments had to be made in the affiliation formula for station compensation. Stations no longer were paid on the basis of time periods cleared for network programming; rather, compensation was determined by an elaborate formula based on the amount of commercial advertising carried by the stations.[48]

The affiliation agreements of the three television networks are complex documents, but their basic computations follow similar formulas and arrive at similar bottom-line figures.[49] Stations report on a monthly basis the number of hours of network programming carried during the reporting period. Adjustments are made to account for periods cleared in various parts of the day. For example, for an hour program aired between 9 A.M. and 5 P.M., an NBC affiliate would receive less than half the value of an hour cleared during prime time.[50] Computations are then made to compensate the network for certain overhead expenses. For example, NBC requires its affiliates to carry twenty-four hours of programming without compensation each month as "a means of sharing the overhead cost to NBC of providing network service."[51] This adjusted number of hours then is multiplied by a *network rate*, which represents the estimated value of the station compared with all the other affiliate markets.[52] New York, the largest television market in the country, receives the highest rate, while other cities are allocated rates based on the size of their potential coverage. A final deduction is then made to compensate the networks for securing music licenses for programs presented during the reporting period.[53]

Station compensation is an important revenue source for all network affiliates. But the average payment to television stations now represents about 10 percent of their total station revenues.[54] By way of comparison, in 1964 network affiliates' compensation averaged about 20 percent of total station revenues.[55] The networks claim that the high costs of television-program production, interconnection, and related operating expenses, as well as the affiliates' increased revenues from sale of local advertising, explain and justify the difference in percentage revenue figures.[56]

Recent FCC Regulation

The dominant position of the television networks became the subject of far-ranging FCC inquiries in the late 1950s and the 1960s.[57] These proceedings produced little in the way of basic industry restructuring, however, since the networks continued to function as the primary programming source for some 600 out of 700 commercial television stations.

The regulatory proceedings did produce a number of changes in network operations. The Prime Time Access Rule was the FCC's key regulatory action to lessen the networks' commanding position in the industry.[58] This rule limits the amount of network programming broadcast by affiliates during prime-time hours. In effect, network stations are prevented from airing more than three hours of network programs between 7 P.M. and 11 P.M. (6 P.M. and 10 P.M. Central Time) Monday through Saturday.[59] There are several exceptions for specific types of favored programs—public-affairs, children's, and special-events programs—that permit the networks to expand their schedules to accommodate these programs.[60]

The goal of PTAR was to create a market for independently produced programs, which could be offered directly to stations free of competition from network product.[61] The results appear to have fallen short of the intended goals. Instead of producing a vast selection of new and imaginative programs, PTAR has brought to the market only the most inexpensive types of programs—game shows, nature shows, and various locally produced public-affairs programs. The reasons for this result rest in large part on the economics of program syndication. The distribution of programs on film or videotape directly to stations is a costly process compared with network distribution, and the films and tapes of programs in PTAR periods must be distributed directly to stations for broadcast in each market. In addition, the half hour cleared for independent product generally occurs during the first hour of prime time, usually 7:30 P.M. to 8:00 P.M. Thus the programs presented generally attempt to appeal to a wide cross-section of the audience, from children to senior citizens. Since programs such as game shows and nature programs meet this objective, stations have turned largely to these shows, rather than experimenting with more elaborate productions.

Another interesting result of PTAR has been its economic effect on the networks. Adopted to curb the power of the networks, the rule has actually increased their economic power. The rule went into effect at a time when the networks' three-and-one-half-hour prime-time schedules provided more advertising minutes than national advertisers wanted to buy. The Prime Time Access Rule eliminated one half hour (and three advertising minutes) from each network's schedule, thereby tightening supply and permitting prices to rise to meet demand. Also, the elimination of one half hour of program time resulted in less program-development expense.

The economic effects of the Prime Time Access Rule were most beneficial for ABC, which began to show a profit for the first time in a decade largely as a result of the artificial increase in advertiser demand for network time occasioned by the rule. With fewer minutes available, national sponsors paid increased prices for all available time. ABC, which was in the weakest financial position, thus benefited the most.[62]

This result reflected the simple fact that there is no substitute for the efficiency and reach of network television as a national-advertising medium. When the supply of commercial minutes is restricted by any factor, advertisers will usually be willing to pay higher prices in order to reach the audience.

Another aspect of PTAR affected ancillary dealings between the networks and their affiliates. Before the rule was adopted, separate program-syndication divisions at the networks sold reruns of program series for local broadcasts to all interested stations, both network affiliates and independent stations. However, the FCC determined that the power inherent in the network-affiliation arrangement necessitated a rule prohibiting the networks from engaging in program syndication in the United States.[63] The Commission reasoned that a network affiliate might feel compelled to purchase a program series from its network-syndication division in order to protect its existing network affiliation. Although no evidence of this existed, the FCC determined that the danger was sufficient to support remedial action.[64]

Network-Affiliate Relations

With minor economic changes, the network-affiliate relationship thus exists today in much the same manner as it did when NBC created its first chain of radio stations. The network remains at a fulcrum between the advertiser and program supplier on one side and the local station on the other. The stations are quite willing to delegate responsibility for selecting, creating, producing, and/or packaging programs to the networks. In addition, the networks act as primary national-sales agents to sponsors as a means of supporting the program-acquisition and -distribution process. A portion of the advertising revenue naturally goes to affiliates as station compensation.

The affiliates' high degree of support for the network process can be seen from the long-standing affiliate relationships. This is true despite the FCC's restriction of affiliation agreements to two-year terms.[65] Further, stations commonly have gone to great pains to win network affiliation—efforts that again reflect the importance of the network link to their overall operations.

In most markets, especially in smaller cities, the networks have a great deal of discretion in determining whether to grant an affiliation to a station. In these situations, the network has several standards for acceptance of stations.[66] The network's goal is to guarantee that a potential affiliate will add to its overall service on a national basis. As a result, a network reviews the operation of the station to determine its performance and standing in the market. Additional relevant factors include the existence of commonly owned stations that might be network affiliates and an applicant's future plans for expanding its service. A primary network concern is naturally its existing coverage in a market and the manner in which this will be affected by the addition of the new station.

The past few years have seen unusual turnover in station affiliations, as a result of ABC's serious attempt to improve its coverage. As previously noted, ABC historically has been the weakest network. Financing requirements as well as programming and counterprogramming strategies all depressed its overall performance. Its key problem, however, was the fact that in many markets it lacked coverage capabilities comparable with those of NBC and CBS.[67] Indeed, in some two-station markets ABC had no affiliates at all; in other markets it was affiliated with a UHF station while the other networks had VHF affiliates with greater coverage capabilities. Whatever the popularity and appeal of ABC programming, its affiliate lineup placed it at a competitive disadvantage and made it more difficult for ABC to challenge the other networks' commanding rating positions.

ABC's first-place rating position over the past few seasons[68] has given it new power to secure affiliates. The list of top-rated ABC shows has become very attractive to many local stations. Both NBC and CBS have thus faced affiliate defections, which have in turn brought increased reach and strength to ABC.[69]

In some situations, of course, the networks do not judge a station's service standards, but rather seek to persuade particular stations—especially those in leading markets—to change network affiliations. If a network is doing the importuning, a station's decision is not always simply a matter of dollars and cents. To be sure, networks always consider the possibility of paying a premium price to stations in certain key markets, especially where the shift of a highly visible station may influence other stations leaning toward a change. But stations generally consider many intangible factors, such as a long-standing relationship with a particular network, that might tip the balance against a change. For example, one network's vice-chairman and president made an eleventh-hour personal pilgrimage to a key station in an effort to emphasize the value of the station's fifty-year relationship with the company. The trip was unsuccessful, however, since the station ultimately decided to change its affiliation.[70]

The programming considerations relevant to affiliates also involve more than prime-time ratings. For example, news programming in the early evening hours is a key type of local service, and local news is a primary revenue source. A station thus will determine whether a particular network's news programming provides a strong support for a local-news block. This consideration reportedly has been operating against ABC in its quest for an increased station lineup; whatever the strength of its prime-time programs, "ABC Evening News" (recently renamed "ABC World News Tonight") has not been in a strong enough position—until recently[71]—to challenge CBS or NBC.[72] This is a key reason for ABC's interest in increasing the appeal and reach of its early-evening news program.

ABC's competitive challenge necessarily increased the other networks' interest and attention concerning affiliate relations. Yet while the affiliates are receiving increased time, attention, and in some cases compensation, there are changes at work that will have a profound and long-lasting effect on the affiliation process. These changes involve both government regulation and technological change; in each case the possible impact may be substantial.

FCC Actions

The FCC's new interest came about not on its own initiative, but in reaction to a petition filed by a licensee. In 1976 the Westinghouse Broadcasting Company (Group W) filed a petition with the Commission requesting investigation of and action on alleged network abuses.[73] The general thrust of the petition was that the FCC should reassess the workings of the television networks to determine whether new regulations were necessary to govern business relationships between stations and networks. Beyond this general goal, however, Group W's immediate attention in seeking Commission action focused on the networks' reported plans to expand their early-evening news programs to one hour. As noted in its filing, this action would have made local stations face undesirable choices, such as either shortening their own early-evening news programs or else eliminating a half hour of their evening programming. Group W found these alternatives unacceptable.[74]

While the filing of the petition probably had the short-range effect of forcing the networks to postpone any plans for expanding their evening news programs,[75] the Westinghouse charges went far beyond this program-scheduling matter. Group W's central thesis was centered on the dominance of network power. It is interesting to note that a similar regulatory initiative by Group W was the primary impetus behind the adoption of the Prime Time Access Rule.

In its pleading, Westinghouse charged that the networks' changing modes of operations over the last twenty years—the shift from the sale of station time periods to the sale of individual spot announcements—brought increased power to the networks over the form and content of programming, and that the networks in turn expanded into areas previously programmed by local stations.[76] For example, Westinghouse charged that in 1960 the three networks programmed 434 half hours on a weekly basis, while in 1976—even with PTAR in effect—the combined weekly figure had grown to 530 half hours, representing two-thirds of the available time on all affiliated stations.[77] Further, Group W complained that stations generally have less involvement in and responsibility for the programming carried over their facilities.[78]

Westinghouse also raised serious economic arguments. It noted that average annual combined income from network operations (including income from the fifteen stations owned by the network companies) recently accounted for 43 percent of all profits in the television industry.[79] Group W also pointed out that during the early years of television the time charges to sponsors represented the aggregation of networks' stations rates, but that today there is no correlation between the amounts networks receive from advertisers and the amounts paid to affiliates for carrying network programs.[80] In practice, station compensation payments actually represent an expense of network operation that is largely controlled by the network companies' bargaining power over the affiliates.[81]

Under the prevailing system, Westinghouse charged, "an affiliate's network rate is simply an arbitrary figure used in calculating the payment to be made for each network commercial carried by the affiliate."[82] If a spot within a particular program remains unsold, the station thus receives less compensation even though the overall program time taken by the network remains the same.[83]

Group W also questioned other commercial dealings of the networks. For example, Group W believes that the networks undersell their affiliates in the national-advertising market; it alleged that the networks' control over station compensation has enabled them to control the pricing of commercial announcements.[84] It can be argued that by holding down station-compensation rates and thereby limiting the revenues of stations from network sources, the networks are able to control their expenses and decrease the average prices charged to advertisers. The interaction of these factors is said to be reflected in the fact that network advertising sales in recent years have grown at a rate exceeding that of national and regional sales by local stations.[85]

Westinghouse also argued that in recent years the networks have retained a greater portion of revenues from network operations than they did before.[86] Business factors reflect the high degree of control exercised by the network companies over the terms and conditions of their affiliation agreements.

The Group W filing also focused specifically on several aspects of affiliation agreements. For example, it charged that the key economic factor in the agreements—the establishment of the "network rate"—is determined generally by the network companies, with the stations having no real power in the bargaining process.[87] Westinghouse estimated that the average hourly compensation rate for a CBS affiliate was 12.7 percent of the station's network rate as set out in its affiliation contract.[88] In the case of ABC and NBC affiliates, Group W estimated the comparable average figure to be 14.5 percent of the network rate.[89] Such figures, it can be argued, reflect the high degree of economic control exercised by the networks over the financial commitments to their affiliates.

Westinghouse also questioned the amount of the contributions required of network affiliates to support network operations. As previously discussed, NBC affiliates are required to waive compensation for twenty-four hours of programming each month as a means of sharing network expenses;[90] CBS and ABC deduct a dollar amount as a similar contribution.[91] Group W charged that this system reduced station compensation and compelled stations to schedule as much network programming as possible in order to minimize the impact of this charge.[92]

Another network practice questioned by Group W was the payment formula based on commercial load. As noted, affiliates' compensation depends on the number of commercial positions sold within network programs. Where commercial minutes go unsold or where a noncommercial message—such as a network promotion—is substituted for a commercial position, the affiliate's compensation is reduced proportionally.[93] In connection with this, Westinghouse also questioned the networks' use of so-called "cut-in" announcements. These are spot announcements sold by networks but not fed to all affiliated stations. Rather, they are inserted by selected affiliates to meet the requirements of regional advertisers. Westinghouse charged that the use of cut-ins represented a loss of a potential sale directly between the station and the advertiser.[94]

Finally, Group W sought a review of the restrictions imposed on the duration of affiliation contracts. While network contracts are limited by Commission rule to two-year terms,[95] Westinghouse alleged that they actually operated as contracts in perpetuity, with the terms and conditions continuing unless terminated by the networks.[96]

Largely as a result of the Westinghouse petition, the FCC launched its broad-ranging inquiry into the basic business dealings between networks and affiliated stations.[97] A special study staff began work on the project in mid-1978.[98] In its notice setting out the parameters of the proceeding, the FCC announced that it would devote its attention to the primary aspects of the network-affiliate relationship—mainly program clearances by affiliates, availability of previewing to affiliates, and station-compensation plans.[99]

With regard to affiliate carriage of network programming, the FCC is concerned with whether the increase of network-program offerings (as documented in the Westinghouse petition) has been accepted by the affiliates, or whether other economic considerations have coerced these programming judgments.[100] The Commission also is attempting to explore possible future expansion of network programming, as well as the prospects for increasing commercial time in all network programs.[101]

In the area of station previewing of network programs, the FCC is examining a specific criticism raised by Group W. In its petition, Westinghouse charged that the networks had failed to provide a workable system by which network affiliates could preview future network programs prior to broadcast.[102] The networks do, however, provide some prescreening for programs and series episodes that might be particularly objectionable to large numbers of viewers.[103] The FCC wishes to assess the workings of the present system as well as the practical requirements of both the networks and the stations.[104]

Finally, on the crucial subject of station-compensation arrangements, in a prior policy ruling the Commission had established guidelines for setting station rates by networks:

> Any graduated payment plan wherein the average hourly rate of compensation varies greatly with, or is heavily influenced by, the number of hours taken and which as a practical matter, requires an affiliate to take the majority of its programs from the same network without regard to the merits of the programming offered, is barred by [the FCC's] rules.[105]

The Commission is examining whether the basic affiliation-compensation plans are consistent with this basic principle.[106] Further, the FCC also is concerned with the extent to which certain contract payments or allowances by affiliates, such as compensation or free hours, are tied to the networks' actual costs.[107] The FCC will also seek to determine the extent to which station compensation varies in relation to total amounts of programming carried by the stations.[108] Finally, the Commission will attempt to discover the extent to which provisions in affiliation contracts limit local stations' freedom to purchase from non-network program-supply sources.[109]

In addition to these issues, the FCC also is considering various questions related to the dealings of networks with program suppliers.[110] This part of the inquiry parallels to some degree an ongoing antitrust case that the Department of Justice is pursuing against ABC and CBS,[111] the main thrust of which is to limit the ownership by the networks of entertainment programs broadcast during prime-time hours. NBC reached a settlement with the Justice Department that incorporates most of the limitations on network production activities sought by the department.[112]

These questions do not by any means exhaust the study staff's concerns, however. The Commission has issued a *Further Notice of Inquiry*[113] in a process that will not be completed before 1981. For example, the study staff has expressed a keen interest in the impact of satellite technology on traditional network-affiliate relationships.[114]

Impact of Satellites

Beyond both the long- and short-term effects of the Commission's proceedings, other factors will have a substantial impact on network operations in the future. The changes largely will result from technological developments that will alter the mode of instantaneous program transmission and confront the network companies with a new challenge—competition.

Since the launching of the first communications satellite, commentators have predicted an eventual shift from land-based wire and microwave transmission systems to satellite systems.[115] Satellite distribution systems are far less costly than terrestrial ones since they use just two earth stations and one satellite, thus doing away with any need for expensive landlines or microwave relays. As a result, satellites are *distance insensitive*: A satellite transmission of 100 miles costs as much as a transmission of 10,000 miles. It was naturally thought that with their vast resources the commercial networks would be the first to take advantage of the apparent cost savings and efficiencies of satellite transmission. In fact, however, for a number of reasons that will be outlined later in this chapter, it has not been the commercial networks—but rather cable television, public television, and radio networks—that have sought to improve their services by changing to satellite feeds.

Several satellite companies provide satellite-interconnection facilities for a variety of uses throughout the United States.[116] The cable industry has used satellite interconnection extensively to supply "pay" programming to individual cable systems. With an expenditure of between $10,000 and $25,000, a cable operator can construct a ground station for reception of satellite program transmissions.[117] These facilities permit a cable operator to choose from such diverse program offerings as multiple feeds of first-run movies (such as "Home Box Office" or "Showtime"); a twenty-four-hour audio-video news service; a twenty-four-hour news-sports-movie service from an Atlanta, Georgia television station; a sports service from Madison Square Garden; and several religious-programming services.[118] Transmission of these programs, and of many others still on the drawing boards, is made possible by the economics of satellite technology, which permits a program supplier to reach any number of local outlets throughout the country via a single satellite channel.

In addition, the Public Broadcasting Service (PBS) and National Public Radio (NPR) have shifted to satellite transmission.[119] Again, the substantial cost savings are cited as a key factor in the change to satellite transmission. A further advantage is increased flexibility in operation and scheduling, since both PBS and NPR can transmit multiple programs simultaneously. Local stations thus can choose among program feeds to meet their service requirements. Indeed, PBS can offer four simultaneous program feeds, with some programs for national audiences and others for distribution on a regional basis.[120] Such duplicate simultaneous transmissions are made possible only by satellite distribution facilities.

With all this activity, the question regularly arises as to what the commercial networks are planning in the area of satellite transmission. Indeed, this question is high on the agenda of every regional and national affiliate meeting. A primary concern of affiliates is potential cost savings through a change to satellite distribution. For the networks, however, the entire subject involves many complex considerations involving complicated service requirements all affecting total distribution costs. Thus the networks are moving slowly to implement satellite distribution systems.[121]

To date, program-distribution use of satellites has involved one-way transmission from program distributors to local stations. Satellite transmission in these cases simply replaces the syndication process of supplying individual film or tape copies of programs directly to a local station or cable system. The complex operations of the commercial networks, however, involve more than one-way distribution. Each weekend many subnetworks are established for distribution of professional football and baseball games, involving multiple program distribution to multiple stations. For example, a particular National Football League game slated for regional coverage might be fed to a half-dozen or a dozen cities. These scheduling requirements clearly involve far more intricate arrangements than does bouncing a single signal off a satellite. Also, news programming often requires multiple program feeds, and switching requirements are made possible through use of the AT&T long-lines network and supplemental land-based common carrier companies.

Beyond these complex service requirements, there is also the question of whether existing domestic satellites have sufficient channel capacity to meet the networks' expanded needs. Even if the networks totally shifted to satellite use, such a change might be feasible only when the next generation of domestic satellites is in orbit.

While the networks continue to make plans, other companies are actively investigating the possibilities of providing competitive program feeds via satellite. For example, while not directly competitive to network programming, new program sources are now available via satellite.

The Independent Television News Association (ITNA), is a cooperative venture among some television stations that provides a daily supply of film and tape news material for insertion in local-news programs. A number of ITNA member stations receive feeds via satellite, while others are linked by common carrier facilities to ground receiving stations. Again, the one-way satellite distribution system permits the news material to be supplied efficiently and economically on a national basis.[122] There also are other occasional networks, such as the Hughes Television Network (owned by Paramount), the TVS Television Network (owned by Corinthian Broadcasting), and Robert Wold Company; these provide programs—some via satellite feed—for use by both network affiliates and independent stations.[123]

In addition to these expanding alternate distribution mechanisms, there has been an increase in program-production activity by syndicators. An example of this activity is Operation Prime Time (OPT), a cooperative station undertaking that markets several "made-for-TV" movies directly to stations. These multipart movies have been of consistently high quality and were produced at network prices. Audiences' and critics' reactions have encouraged further expansion of this "fourth-network" project.[124] Program-production ventures such as OPT are distributed via the classic syndication route, but represent a new type of serious competition—especially in the two- and three-station markets.[125]

Conclusion

Looking into the not-too-distant future, it is apparent that stations will be installing earth stations for satellite reception. The time frame for satellite development is fairly short. Many television-station engineers believe that their stations will construct or establish a ground link to a satellite ground station within the next two years.[126] The link to satellite transmissions is regarded as necessary whether or not the networks shift to satellite transmission at a future date.[127] Satellite-reception capacity is viewed as opening access to new and useful alternate programming sources.

The networks therefore may face real competition from program suppliers and advertisers who seek to bypass the networks in order to supply programs directly to local television stations. With the construction of satellite ground stations by a majority of commercial stations, program suppliers can attempt to establish ad hoc networks for their productions. Further, group efforts like OPT will probably be created to gain access to the television marketplace via satellite distribution.

The availability of competing program sources will necessarily have a direct impact on program clearances by network affiliates. Indeed, the expanding syndication market already is having an effect on program clearances in late-afternoon time periods.[128] Syndicated programs such as "Mike Douglas," "Phil Donahue," "Merv Griffin," and "Dinah Shore" have somewhat limited the distribution of some daytime network programs. The availability of top-rated prime-time programs for direct distribution to stations is likely to alter the usual acceptance rate of network programs by affiliates.

Further, the arrival of new program sources will result in greater emphasis on network practices concerned with program clearances by stations. This changed competitive circumstance also will be of primary concern to the FCC.

In addition to facing pressures from new, competitive programming sources, the networks also must continue to deal with increased production costs for news and sports programming—operations that will not benefit from any changes in the overall distribution pattern by satellite for network programs. The networks therefore may experience increased competition—and reduced profits—in the area of entertainment programming, as well as increased costs in their news and sports operations. At some future time the networks may ask for goverment protection from competing program sources in order to subsidize news and public-affairs programming; this situation obviously would create the same cross-subsidy policy problems as exist in the regulation of telephone companies.[129]

Any defection by stations from networks to competing program sources will be neither wholesale nor immediate. Affiliates are clearly comfortable with a system under which major programming decisions are made by organizations with long-standing track records. Further, the networks will still have the necessary resources to underwrite multiple program-development projects with varying prospects of success. And the networks will probably continue to be the primary suppliers of national-news and public-affairs programming as well as of sports broadcasts.

In addition to these considerations, it also must be remembered that affiliates operate as cooperative associations with elected representatives. This organizational framework may take on increased importance for the networks as a means of providing coordinated services to their stations—an advantage not enjoyed by ad hoc network-program suppliers.

Beyond these considerations, however, lie the harsh realities of commercial television's primary focus on profits and performance. As noted earlier, station operators often attach a certain intangible value to network affiliations, similar to the value of membership in an exclusive club. This factor was most significant when stations were owned by individuals, many of whose histories in the broadcasting business parallelled the development of the networks. Ownership transfers, mergers, acquisitions, and other changes have altered the "old boy" nature of affiliation activities. Station negotiations thus increasingly involve strictly business considerations, with bottom-line financial performance as the primary criterion. In light of these changes, any first-rate programming proposal with a prospect of solid economic return will be seriously considered by affiliates as an alternative to network service.

The network companies thus will need to contend with serious impacts on their operations. The FCC's inquiry and the potential shift to satellite distribution will have short-term, basic effects on the network companies. Long-term factors include the overall competitive posture of cable television and pay television, the possible impact of videocassettes and videodiscs, and the possibility of a shift to direct satellite-to-home transmission[130]—a fundamental change which while affecting the networks, would have a far more serious and long-lasting impact on local television stations.[131]

As previously noted, the basic affiliate-network relationship has undergone only minor changes—largely related to distribution of revenues—since first conceived in the early days of radio. While the network companies officially continue to predict a future little changed from the present,[132] many observers agree that the future will indeed be different. It must remain for the marketplace, possible congressional legislation, and FCC policy to shape these future changes.

Notes

1. *See* FCC, TV Broadcast Financial Data—1978, Release No. 19540 (July 30, 1979), table 2.

2. *See* Petition for Inquiry, Rule Making and Immediate Temporary Relief (RM-2749), filed by Westinghouse Broadcasting Company, Inc. (Sept. 3, 1976), at 13-15 [hereinafter cited as Westinghouse Petition].

3. *See* E. Barnouw, A Tower in Babel 181-88 (1966); FCC, Report on Chain Broadcasting 7-8 (1941) [hereinafter cited as Report on Chain Broadcasting].

4. Report on Chain Broadcasting, *supra* note 3, at 8.

5. *See* E. Barnouw, The Sponsor: Notes on a Modern Potentate 21 (1978); Report on Chain Broadcasting, *supra* note 3, at 7-8.

6. *See* E. Barnouw, A Tower in Babel 148-50 (1966); Weeks, *The Radio Election of 1924*, J. Broadcasting, Summer 1964, at 233, 235.

7. Report on Chain Broadcasting, *supra* note 3, at 8.

8. E. Barnouw, A Tower in Babel 190 (1966).

9. *Id.* at 204.

10. *Id.* at 191.

11. *Id.* n.5.

12. Report on Chain Broadcasting, *supra* note 3, at 21.

13. *See* Broadcasting Yearbook 1979, at C-344.

14. E. Barnouw, The Golden Web 57 (1968).

15. *See id.* at 58; Report on Chain Broadcasting, *supra* note 3, at 41-42.

16. *See* Report on Chain Broadcasting, *supra* note 3, at 40-41.

17. *See id.* at 37.

18. *Id.* at 92 (Regulation 3.104).

19. *Cf.* House Comm. on Interstate and Foreign Commerce, Network Broadcasting, H.R. Rep. No. 1297, 85th Cong., 2d Sess. 454-56 (1958) [hereinafter cited as Barrow Report], describing the station-compensation arrangement as subsequently applied to television.

20. *See* Report on Chain Broadcasting, *supra* note 3, at 40-42. *Cf.* Barrow Report, *supra* note 19, at 449-66 (television).

21. Report on Chain Broadcasting, *supra* note 3, at 31.

22. *See id.*

23. *Id.* at 91-92.

24. *See id.* at 66.

25. *See id.* at 36-40, 57, 62-66.

26. *Id.* at 52.

27. *Id.* at 91 (Regulation 3.101).

28. *Id.* at 92 (Regulation 3.105).

29. *See id.* at 65-66.

30. *Id.* at 92 (Regulation 3.107).

31. *See* S. Quinlan, Inside ABC 19-20 (1979); E. Barnouw, The Golden Web 187-90 (1968).

32. *See* E. Barnouw, The Golden Web 168-69, 172-74 (1968).

33. NBC v. United States, 319 U.S. 190 (1943).

34. *See* E. Barnouw, The Golden Web 295 (1968); Broadcasting Yearbook 1979, at B-176, C-344.

35. *See* Barrow Report, *supra* note 19, at 449.

36. *See id.* at 408-20.

37. *See id.* at 454-56.

38. *See* A. Pearce, *supra* at 8-12; R. Jencks, *supra* at 43.

39. *See* A. Pearce, *supra* at 10.

40. *See* E. Barnouw, The Sponsor: Notes on a Modern Potentate 68 (1978).

41. *See id.* at 57-58; Report and Order, Docket No. 12782, 23 F.C.C.2d 382, 389-90 (1970) [hereinafter cited as PTAR I], *modified*, 25 F.C.C.2d 318, *aff'd sub nom.* Mt. Mansfield Television, Inc. v. FCC, 442 F.2d 470 (2d Cir. 1970).

42. *See* PTAR I, *supra* note 41, at 389-90; Notice of Inquiry, Docket No. 21049, 62 F.C.C.2d 548, 557 (1977).

43. *See* A. Pearce, *supra* at 8-9, 12; R. Jencks, *supra* at 49; W. Paley, As It Happened 274, 301 (1979).

44. *See* E. Barnouw, The Sponsor: Notes on a Modern Potentate 58, 68-70 (1978); PTAR I, *supra* note 41, at 390-91.

45. *See* E. Barnouw, The Sponsor: Notes on a Modern Potentate 68-71 (1978).

46. *See id.*

47. *See* Westinghouse Petition, *supra* note 2, at 33 & Attachment A, chart #4; PTAR I, *supra* note 41, at 390.

48. For a detailed discussion of how station compensation is computed, see Westinghouse Petition, *supra* note 2, at 40-46 & Attachment H.

49. *See id.*, Attachment H at 5-7.

50. *See id.*, Attachment H at 6.

51. *Id.* at 43.

52. *See id.* at 33, 40-42.

53. *See id.*, Attachment H at 5-7.

54. *See* FCC, TV Broadcast Financial Data—1978, Release No. 19540 (July 30, 1979), table 4.

55. Westinghouse Petition, *supra* note 2, Attachment A, chart #7.

56. *See, e.g.*, Comments of ABC, Docket No. 21049 (June 1, 1977), at 21-32.

57. *See, e.g.*, Barrow Report, *supra* note 19; FCC, Interim Report by the Office of Network Study, Responsibility for Broadcast Matter (1960), *reprinted in* House Comm. on Interstate and Foreign Commerce, Television Network Program Procurement, H.R. Rep. No. 281, 88th Cong., 1st Sess. 197 (1963); FCC, Second Interim Report (Part I) by the Office of Network Study, Television Network Program Procurement, *reprinted in* House Comm. on Interstate and Foreign Commerce, Television Network Program Procurement, H.R. Rep. No. 281, 88th Cong., 1st Sess. 13 (1963); FCC, Second Interim Report (Part II) by the Office of Network Study, Television Network Program Procurement (1965); PTAR I, *supra* note 41.

58. PTAR I, *supra* note 41. The rule, as amended, is codified in 47 C.F.R. §73.658(k) (1979).

59. 47 C.F.R. §73.658(k) (1979).

60. 47 C.F.R. §73.658(k)(1)-(6) (1979).

61. *See* PTAR I, *supra* note 41, at 384; Report and Order, Docket No. 19622, 44 F.C.C.2d 1081, 1087 (1974).

62. *See* S. Quinlan, Inside ABC 185 (1979); R. Jencks, *supra* at 53.

63. PTAR I, *supra* note 41, at 397-98.

64. *Id.* at 398.

65. 47 C.F.R. §73.658(c) (1979).

66. *See* Barrow Report, *supra* note 19, at 208-47.

67. In 1956, ABC had only 68 "primary" affiliates, while NBC had 162 and CBS 149. Barrow Report, *supra* note 19, at 215.

68. *See* S. Quinlan, Inside ABC 232-37 (1979); American Broadcasting Companies, Inc., Annual Report 1978, at 4.

69. *See* S. Quinlan, Inside ABC 233 n. 1 (1979); Broadcasting, Sept. 4, 1978, at 19; Brown, *ABC-TV Reaches Affiliate Parity With Its Rivals*, N.Y. Times, July 31, 1979, at C15, col. 3.

70. *See* Broadcasting, Sept. 4, 1978, at 19-20.

71. *See, e.g.*, Broadcasting, April 30, 1979, at 48; Broadcasting, July 16, 1979, at 54.

72. *See* S. Quinlan, Inside ABC 245-55 (1979).

73. Westinghouse Petition, *supra* note 2.

74. *Id.* at 15-21.

75. Soon after the Westinghouse Petition was filed, the networks dropped their plans to expand their evening newscasts, attributing their decisions to affiliate opposition. Broadcasting, Oct. 25, 1976, at 22; Broadcasting, Nov. 29, 1976, at 22.

76. Westinghouse Petition, *supra* note 2, at 4-5.

77. *Id.* at 11, 15.

78. *Id.* at 5, 23-27.

79. *Id.* at 30.

80. *Id.* at 31-32.

81. *Id.* at 32.

82. *Id.*

83. *Id.*

84. *Id.* at 33-34.

85. *Id.* at 34.

86. *Id.* at 36-37.

87. *Id.* at 40-41.

88. *Id.* at 42 & Attachment H at 7.

89. *Id.* at 42 & Attachment H at 5-6.

90. *See* p. 79 *supra.*

91. Westinghouse Petition, *supra* note 2, at 43.

92. *Id.*

93. *Id.* at 43-44.

94. *Id.* at 45.

95. 47 C.F.R. §73.658(c) (1979).

96. Westinghouse Petition, *supra* note 2, at 46.

97. *See* Broadcasting, Jan. 17, 1977, at 19-20.

98. *See* Broadcasting, June 19, 1978, at 34.

99. Notice of Inquiry, Docket No. 21049, 62 F.C.C.2d 548 (1977).

100. *Id.* at 553-54.

101. *Id.* at 554.

102. Westinghouse Petition, *supra* note 2, at 23-27.

103. Notice of Inquiry, Docket No. 21049, 62 F.C.C.2d 548, 554-55 n. 12 (1977).

104. *Id.* at 554-55.

105. CBS Network Compensation Plan, 24 R.R. 520a, *reconsideration denied*, 1 R.R. 2d 696 (1963).

106. Notice of Inquiry, Docket No. 21049, 62 F.C.C.2d 548, 555 (1977).

107. *Id.*

108. *Id.* at 555-56.

109. *Id.* at 555.

110. *Id.* at 556-59.

111. United States v. ABC, Civ. No. 74-3600-RJK (C.D. Cal., complaint filed Dec. 10, 1974); United States v. CBS Inc., Civ. No. 74-3599-RJK (C.D. Cal., complaint filed Dec. 10, 1974).

112. United States v. NBC, 449 F. Supp. 1127 (C.D. Cal. 1978).

113. Further Notice of Inquiry, Docket No. 21049, 69 F.C.C.2d 1524 (1978).

114. Id. at 1530.

115. *E.g.*, W. Schramm, *Some Possible Social Effects of Space Communications*, in United Nations Educational, Scientific and Cultural Organization, Communication in the Space Age: The Use of Satellites by the Mass Media 12-28 (1968).

116. *See* Broadcasting Yearbook 1979, at E-46.

117. *See, e.g.*, Broadcasting, May 28, 1979, at 76.

118. *See* Broadcasting Yearbook 1979, at E-47.

119. D. Smith, Teleservices Via Satellite 191-213 (1978).

120. *Id.* at 202, 206-07; Frost & Sullivan, Inc., The Commercial Satellite Communications Market in North America 7 (1979).

121. *See, e.g.*, Broadcasting, March 27, 1978, at 62; Broadcasting, May 21, 1979, at 56, 84-85; Broadcasting, Aug. 27, 1979, at 7.

122. For a more complete description of ITNA and its operations, see S. Robb, Television/Radio Age Communications Coursebook 2-42 to 2-43 (1978).

123. *See* Broadcasting Yearbook 1979, at D-43, E-47.

124. *See, e.g.*, Broadcasting, March 19, 1979, at 64; Broadcasting, Aug. 27, 1979, at 28.

125. In early 1979 Mobil Corporation presented the British-produced series "Edward the King" on a forty-nine-station ad hoc network, achieving ratings that in some major markets surpassed those of competitive network offerings. *See* Broadcasting, Nov. 20, 1978, at 68; Broadcasting, Jan. 29, 1979, at 53.

126. In March of 1979 RCA announced that it was testing the feasibility of a plan under which it would supply all commercial-television stations with a free earth station capable of receiving four signals. *See* Broadcasting, March 19, 1979, at 86-87.

127. Indeed, one program distributor (represented by the author) has asked the FCC to require every commercial-television station to have its own earth station. Petition for Rule Making (RM-3402), filed by National Producers' Corporation, July 10, 1979. Not surprisingly, broadcasters have expressed opposition to such a rule. *See* Broadcasting, Sept. 3, 1979, at 70.

128. For example, in 1976 nonclearances by NBC affiliates were greater for "Somerset" at 4 P.M. weekdays than for virtually any other program in that network's entertainment lineup. *See* Comments of NBC, Docket No. 21049 (June 1, 1977), at 47-53.

129. *See, e.g.*, AT&T, Long Lines Department, 61 F.C.C.2d 587, 607-09 (1976) *modified*, 64 F.C.C.2d 971 (1977), *appeal docketed*, No. 77-1333 (D.C. Cir. April 4, 1977).

130. *See* Broadcasting, Aug. 6, 1979, at 27-28.

131. *See* Broadcasting, Aug. 20, 1979, at 5.

132. *See, e.g.*, N.Y. Times, May 30, 1979, at C22, col. 1; N.Y. Times, July 26, 1979, at C19, col. 1; Broadcasting, Sept. 24, 1979, at 27.

10 Restructuring the Television-Program Distribution Process

George L. Back

Robb observes that the Prime Time Access Rule[1] may have been a failure in that it has not supplied us with diverse programming.[2] I would like to address that question directly and suggest that the FCC should consider PTAR a total success and that the Commission should expand—perhaps even double or triple—the amount of prime time set aside for local stations beyond the half-hour from 7:30 P.M. to 8:00 P.M., which is very limiting to a station's programming capabilities. PTAR has changed the potential structure of network prime-time television and has increased the number of program producers and suppliers. It has diversified programming and has increased local production. I therefore consider it a success and hope that the FCC will see fit to increase and expand its application.

Robb discusses the impact of new technologies on the development and distribution of television programming. While it is undoubtedly true that there will be widespread use of satellites and a proliferation of receiving earth stations,[3] this alone will not break the networks' hold on the distribution process. When the signal for a program is bounced off a satellite and comes down into the television market, it must still go through a process of getting to the local station. Except where the signal receiver is at the station itself, this process requires the use of circuits—known as *loops*—controlled by AT&T. In small markets there may not be enough loops to get satellite or other signals to the local television station. If a station only has one loop, and that loop is in continuous use receiving a network feed, a syndicator or other alternate source of real-time programming cannot be used. This would require either costly construction of additional loops or the use of delayed programming, thus incurring greater costs for the station. The point here is that the networks are at an advantage and that the onset of satellite communications is not in and of itself enough to change this.

Cable television, likewise, is unlikely to be a principal source of alternative new programming. At a recent cable convention, most cable operators, when asked what they would like to see the FCC do for their future, spoke in terms of the importation of more distant signals. The easiest and cheapest way to get programming is from distant cities' broadcast signals. In other words, if the Commission would allow it, cable operators would like to have perhaps twelve independent signals from all over the country.[4] That way they would not have to program anything.

This is not quite the same as what Anselmo discusses in chapter 11.[5] In any event, the cable-industry approach is not very promising from the point of view of developing new programming.

In speaking of alternative programming for the future, I would like to offer a personal warning: I expect future alternative programming to be frighteningly similar to what is now on the air. This is because the so-called "cost per thousand"—the basis on which the advertising agencies now buy time from CBS, NBC, and ABC—will apply equally to alternative programming. Consequently, mass-appeal programming will continue to enjoy an enormous advantage in the advertising marketplace. If anything, the amount of funds to be supplied for future alternative programming will not be as large as for current programming; so program quality is unlikely to improve substantially.

The following example illustrates some of the difficulties that beset those who seek to compete with the "big three" networks. In 1977 Paramount Pictures, the parent company of the Hughes Television Network, unsuccessfully attempted to start a Saturday-night network.[6] It lined up a number of stations (mostly independents, because they were the ones who had the time to give), and then took that list of stations to the advertisers on Madison Avenue. The advertisers would not pay what Paramount needed to produce the programming, because the stations' existing ratings were not as good as Paramount's projections. Surprisingly, about thirty network-affiliated stations were willing to join the Saturday-night network, and of these about half were affiliated with ABC, the leading network at the time. The reason for this was (as Robb points out[7]) that ABC, being the newest network, lacked strong "old boy" connections, and some of its affiliates' money makers thought that Paramount's deal was better than ABC's; further, the Paramount plan didn't take up too much of the stations' time. Nevertheless, the lineup of stations that Paramount assembled simply did not add up to a salable package, and its plans for the Saturday-night network had to be suspended.

In retrospect many reasons could be cited for the demise of the Paramount television service, including:

1. Ratings of cleared time periods didn't equal Paramount estimates, causing major agencies to worry about diverting budgets from ABC, CBS, and NBC.
2. The network was poorly designed. It should have been scheduled for 7-10 P.M., not 8-11 P.M., in order to secure higher ratings from one hour less of network competition.
3. There was a lack of commitment from the producer.

Finally, with respect to restructuring the television-program distribution process, it appears that no new "free broadcast" commercial network will ever arise out of the traditional television power axis of major Hollywood producers and Madison Avenue advertising agencies; they have too much invested in the status quo. The impetus will have to come from elsewhere.

Notes

1. 47 C.F.R. §73.658(k) (1979).

2. *See* S. Robb, *supra* at 80.

3. *See* S. Robb, *supra* at 86-88.

4. Indeed, the Commission now seems headed toward doing precisely that. Report, Docket No. 21284, 71 F.C.C.2d 632 (1979); Report, Docket No. 20988, 71 F.C.C.2d 951 (1979); Notice of Proposed Rule Making, Dockets Nos. 20988 & 21284, 71 F.C.C.2d 1004 (1979). *See* Broadcasting, April 30, 1979, at 21-23.

5. *See* R. Anselmo, *infra* at 101-103.

6. *See* Broadcasting, April 11, 1977, at 48-49; Broadcasting, June 20, 1977, at 45-46.

7. *See* S. Robb, *supra* at 82, 90.

11 Distribution of Specialized Programming to Minority Audiences

Rene Anselmo

In general, the networks do a good job through their programming and serve the public they set out to serve—the mass audience. But unfortunately they have kept everyone else out of the business of national program distribution. Whether this is the result of direct lobbying or behind-the-scenes lobbying, or of other factors, until recently no one else has been given an opportunity to try to serve the audiences the networks say they are not interested in. It is one thing for the networks to say a million or ten million people are not of much interest to them and that they will not program for them. But it is quite another thing to use technology effectively to block anyone else from attempting to serve those people—which is just what the networks and the FCC have done.

This seems likely to change now. Signals can be put up on satellites and made available to every city, town, and hamlet in the United States. What is needed is what I call "people's over-the-air free cable television." With such a system, we could do in essence what cable television does. For example, we at the Spanish International Network (SIN) could take our Los Angeles signal, put it on the satellite, and bring it down in Denver to a television station that would serve that city's Spanish community. At present, although about 20 percent of the population in Denver is Spanish-speaking,[1] they have only about two hours of television programming a week on one of the five stations in Denver.[2] That is all the Spanish-language service that exists for 20 percent of the population, and that is why the SIN proposal to provide free television service to Denver's Spanish-speaking community seemed like a fairly intelligent plan. It seemed to us that these people deserved some free television. And we would not even be "stealing" anyone else's signal (as cable operators do), because it would be our own signal. What possible objection could there be?

Nevertheless, the cable industry was unhappy about the plan, saying that such a scheme might spell the end of the cable industry.[3] And maybe it would. I think that the networks and the FCC are largely responsible for the cable industry anyway. In any event, the plan was pending at the FCC for years until finally, in June of 1979, SIN was granted a permit to implement it.[4]

This brings us to a consideration of the new Translator Inquiry.[5] (A *translator* is a repeater of a signal on another frequency in a different location.) The Commission's rules say that a VHF translator can be used only within a television station's primary service (Grade B) area.[6] But why not permit a translator in another market? Furthermore, by limiting (to between 1 watt and 1 kilowatt) the amount of power translators can have,[7] we protect the networks and the cable industry instead of serving the public. Why not a 10-kilowatt translator, or a 50-kilowatt translator, as long as it serves the public? Instead of "translators" I now call them LTDs, for "limited television delivery."

In other words, if no one is doing all sports, for example, in a particular market, one can do all sports—or all anything else, for that matter—and thus go into format television. The Commission's old-fashioned network-inclined rules[8] would prohibit this, of course; but the FCC should override those rules. It should let anyone go into any market and put on a station at any power to provide a service that is not presently being provided, as long as it does not interfere with other broadcasters' signals.

SIN is applying to go into every city in the United States that has a Spanish-speaking population of 40,000 or more, using the argument that no one is giving the Spanish-speaking people a signal and that we would like to provide it.[9] For instance, there are about 150,000-200,000 Spanish-speaking people in Washington, D.C., who have no Spanish-language radio or commercial television.[10] Assuming that an unused UHF frequency exists, we could put a 1-kilowatt translator on it that would work off a satellite or pick up our New York-area station via microwave. But why not provide them with a *decent* signal? Why not 10 kilowatts, as long as it does not interfere with other broadcasters? Why limit it? Who has the Commission been protecting all these years? The answer is simple: the networks.

The issue here is not ownership of these stations. SIN is interested in the outlet for its network programming. It would be willing to build these stations and turn them over to local groups.[11] Meanwhile, however, the capabilities exist, but no one is doing anything with them and the service is not being rendered.

This is the type of issue that is facing the Commission, and the FCC's decision on this question may well determine the future of this industry. It is the networks that should be asking the Commission to open up the spectrum to create more frequencies for over-the-air television; otherwise they will eventually be destroyed by the cable industry and pay television.

We have recently been working on bringing in quite a bit of programming from Europe and South America via satellite,[12] and we are now working on a morning show that would resemble the "Today" show on NBC except that it would be in Spanish. It would have live satellite feed from Mexico, Spain, and Argentina, so that there would be live communications throughout the Spanish-speaking world. Because the satellite rates are going down, this new programming is coming in; and all foreign-language pro-gramming is going to open up with the use of satellites.

Nevertheless, I would agree with Back that the prospects for better and more diverse programming are generally dim, given the present number of frequencies allotted to television.[13] But if additional frequencies are opened up, since there is a limit to how much mass product can be sold in a market, someone will eventually have to do something better or at least something unique in order to be successful, just as was the case with cable. But if the FCC continues to limit the frequencies, the "alternative" programming of-fered will be no different from what the networks currently provide.

Notes

1. This percentage is the author's estimate, based on 1970 U.S. census data.

2. *See* Broadcasting Yearbook 1979, at B-92.

3. *See* Broadcasting, May 1, 1978, at 64.

4. *See* Broadcasting, June 18, 1979, at 29. At the same time, SIN was granted permits for UHF translators in four other cities, *id.*, but only the Denver translator is to be fed by satellite. *See* Broadcasting, Aug. 27, 1979, at 37.

5. Notice of Inquiry, BC Docket No. 78-253, 68 F.C.C.2d 1525 (1978).

6. 47 C.F.R. §74.732(e)(1) (1979).

7. 47 C.F.R. §74.735 (1979).

8. *E.g.*, the requirement that every station devote time to the presenta-tion of programs devoted to the discussion of public issues. Fairness Report, 48 F.C.C.2d 1, 9-10 (1974), *reconsideration denied*, 58 F.C.C.2d 691 (1976), *aff'd in part and rev'd in part on other grounds sub nom.* Na-tional Citizens Committee for Broadcasting v. FCC, 567 F.2d 1095 (D.C. Cir. 1977), *cert. denied*, 436 U.S. 926 (1978).

9. *See* Broadcasting, Aug. 27, 1979, at 37.

10. *See* Broadcasting Yearbook 1979, at B-93 (five hours of television per week on the PBS outlet). *See id.* at C-40, D-89, D-104 (radio).

11. *See* Broadcasting, Aug. 27, 1979, at 37.

12. *See* Spanish International Network, 68 F.C.C.2d 1260, 1261 (1978).

13. G. Back, *supra*, at 98-99.

Part IV
The Government and the Networks

12 Federal Regulation of Network Practices

Richard E. Wiley

Introduction

In terms of economics, the television industry is simply another average-sized American industry. Indeed, economists have noted that the annual revenues of television stations and networks are similar to those of industries such as paperboard-box manufacture or fruit and vegetable canning.[1] In the communications field, the revenues of the television industry are small compared with those of AT&T and its subsidiaries.[2] Even in the field of advertising, where the television networks are commonly thought to be a dominant force, the networks account for only about 9 percent of annual U.S. advertising volume.[3]

Why then do congressmen, FCC commissioners, and other public officials devote so much time and energy to this single industry? Why does broadcasting, and especially television, provoke so much public attention and debate? The answers probably have little to do with balance sheets and annual revenues but instead are related to widespread concern regarding television's presumed power as a medium of entertainment and information, and to many people's belief that this power is unduly concentrated in the three networks.

The Political and Cultural Influence of Television

Discussions of television's supposed power involve both political and cultural issues. The role of television in political debate may be illustrated by reference to a recent D.C. Circuit Court decision regarding the coverage of national-defense issues by CBS, *American Security Council Education Foundation* v. *FCC*.[4] The American Security Council Education Foundation, a nonprofit educational institution interested in national-security issues, conducted an exhaustive survey of CBS news and public-affairs programming; it concluded that, over a long period of time, CBS's programming had been heavily weighted in favor of doing less to protect national security—a so-called "dovish" position. According to the foundation's characterization, in 1972 the "CBS Evening News" program presented viewpoints that, 62 percent of the time favored doing less about national security; 35 percent of the time favored continuing at about the same level;

and only 4 percent of the time favored doing more. The FCC's disposition of the complaint on procedural grounds[5] was ultimately upheld by the Court of Appeals sitting *en banc*,[6] after a three-judge panel of the court had insisted that the agency take a more detailed look at the facts.

In this case a detailed review of all CBS programming on defense-related issues over a period of years obviously would have been a massive and perhaps prohibitively expensive undertaking. In addition, categorizing each broadcast under one of the foundation's three rubrics would have involved many difficult and subjective decisions. The Commission's desire to avoid these types of decisions is thus quite natural. Despite these problems, perceptions about television's political power lead many to believe that such a massive and difficult undertaking would be well worth the cost and that without this kind of enforcement each network could distort national debate on important issues.

Other critics of television have focused on what they see as a use of the medium to corrupt our morals, our intelligence, and, indeed, the very culture of our society. As everyone remembers, former Chairman Newton Minow characterized television programming as a "vast wasteland."[7]

To some extent this criticism may reflect the fact that many Americans have unrealistically high expectations concerning the ability of technological advances to bring about a cultural renaissance. For example, Alexander Meiklejohn once stated that the introduction of commercial radio

> opened up before us the possibility that, as a people living a common life under a common agreement, we might communicate with one another freely with regard to the values, the opportunities, the difficulties, the joys and sorrows, the hopes and fears, the plans and purposes, of that common life. It seemed possible that, amid all our differences we might become a community of mutual understanding and of shared interests.[8]

When one's hopes and expectations are stated in such idealistic terms, some disappointment and bitterness naturally result after contact with the reality of what television is—and even what the average American wants it to be.

Although commercial television is not as good as it might be, it is much better than many of its critics would have us believe. It has brought into our living rooms presidential debates, the Vietnam War, third-world revolutions, racial conflict in many of our nation's cities, and the other great news stories of our time. Television has also given the American people a diverse stream of entertainment programming that has included high-quality offerings as well as shows whose redeeming character may be only their mass popularity. On this latter point, it should be recognized that most television programming is not produced for an elite audience and that the average American viewer's tastes do not necessarily mirror those of the average television critic or even those of the average FCC commissioner.

If television's critics sometimes belittle the medium's accomplishments, they also tend to exaggerate vastly its impact and power. Many people have commented on the pervasiveness of television, on the fact that more than 95 percent of American homes have television sets, and on surveys indicating that people spend many hours watching television programs. Indeed, in its somewhat ambiguous *Pacifica* decision,[9] the Supreme Court seemed to use a pervasive-impact theory to justify FCC regulation of "indecent" programming.[10] This type of reasoning overlooks the fact that a program's power and influence depend more on the courage and creativity of its author than on the nature of the medium. It is difficult to imagine that any television broadcast will ever have the impact of Luther's Ninety-Five Theses or of our own Declaration of Independence. Indeed, it is doubtful that any broadcast has rivaled the influence of Thomas Paine's "Common Sense" or William Lloyd Garrison's leaflets attacking the slave system.

This is not to suggest that television is powerless, only that the nature and scope of its influence may be considerably overstated. Even when television does play a role in expediting the dissemination of ideas and opinions, it may well be a follower rather than a leader. During the Watergate crisis, for example, the television news departments certainly were no more aggressive or influential than *The Washington Post* and *The New York Times*. Thus while television may be both powerful and pervasive, it has not totally eclipsed the spoken word or the "miracle" of movable type. In any event, television's great accomplishments will come more from the intelligence and resourcefulness of the people in the industry than from the technology of the medium itself.

Nevertheless, many people believe that television possesses almost supernatural powers and that the American people will be injured by these powers unless the government gets things under control.

Regulation of Program Content

The FCC's regulatory authority comes from a general statutory mandate to promote the "public interest, convenience and necessity."[11] In actual practice, however, the Communications Act gives the FCC little authority to supervise the content of programming. Section 326 forbids the agency from engaging in censorship or otherwise interfering with free speech through broadcasting.[12] Even aside from this express statutory prohibition, it is well established that broadcasting is a medium that is entitled to first amendment protection and that—except in narrowly defined areas such as obscenity and indecency[13]—censorship is impermissible.[14] This is why the FCC has never been in a position to regulate the quality of broadcast programming.

In many ways we are fortunate that the Congress did not authorize the Commission to act as a national arbiter of taste or quality. Such concepts are highly subjective in nature; what one person considers worthless may be a high artistic achievement to others. Indeed, it would be difficult or impossible to develop any practical or sensible means to define high-quality programming through rules and regulations.

Nevertheless, under its public-interest mandate the FCC does play a limited role in controlling the nature of a station's programming. It has stated that broadcasters have a responsibility to present a "reasonable" amount of news and public-affairs programming,[15] and under the fairness doctrine it requires stations to provide a "reasonable" opportunity for the presentation of contrasting views on controversial issues of public importance.[16] The Commission may impose only generalized programming requirements, however, and the private broadcaster has the primary responsibility for the selection and editing of program material. In the case of the fairness doctrine, for example, the broadcast licensee has wide discretion in determining what subjects or issues should be covered, the particular format of the programs to be devoted to each subject, the different shades of opinion to be presented, the spokespersons for each point of view, and the amount of time and scheduling of programming for each spokesperson or point of view.[17] The doctrine requires not equality of treatment, but only a reasonable opportunity for the presentation of differing views.[18] Furthermore, the broadcaster's judgment will not be second-guessed unless it is arbitrary or unreasonable.[19]

This policy of vesting wide discretion in the individual station licensee seems to be a sensible and practical approach to the problem of balancing first amendment concerns against public-interest considerations. As suggested in the discussion of CBS's coverage of national-security matters, a serious effort to enforce "fairness" in a vast amount of programming over a long period of time would be maddeningly complex. It is not surprising, therefore, that the FCC has established a policy of restraint in the enforcement of the fairness doctrine. In one two-year period (1973-1974) the Commission received 4,280 formal fairness complaints.[20] It resolved only 19 of these (0.4 percent) against the licensee.[21] In a sense the doctrine has come to be more of a goal or guideline to the licensee than an actual object of detailed enforcement, and this approach has been approved in the *American Security Council* case.[22]

Regulation of the Television Networks

When one considers the first amendment's protection of broadcasting, the generalized nature of licensee programming obligations, and the resulting difficulty of enforcement, it is not surprising that the FCC has used other approaches to deal with the perceived problem of network dominance. These efforts generally have focused on the structure of the television industry and on the financial relationships among the industry's component parts.

As former Commissioner Robinson has stated, however, the agency's continuing struggle with network dominance is an adventure worthy of Don Quixote. Robinson noted that "since the 1930's when the Commission first sallied forth in quest of a remedy for this evil . . . the Commission has doggedly pursued this aim of cutting down the networks' power. The intent has been noble, but the results have left the Commission, like its famous precursor, with a doleful countenance."[23]

The Chain Broadcasting Rules

Perhaps the earliest concern about network power arose well before the advent of commercial television, concerning standard-broadcast (AM) stations. In 1941 the FCC issued its Chain Broadcasting Rules, which were designed to lessen the networks' authority over their radio affiliates.[24] Among other things these rules limited the duration of affiliation agreements,[25] restricted the extent of station territorial exclusivity,[26] limited the use of so-called "option time" (requirements that affiliates give specified amounts of time to the networks on demand),[27] required stations to refuse network programming they deemed unsuitable,[28] and forbade network control over station rates for non-network time.[29] In 1977 I made a determined and ultimately successful effort to have the FCC eliminate all remaining vestiges of these rules; after thirty-six years they had outlived their usefulness, since network radio is simply not what it was in 1941.[30]

The Barrow Report

The FCC's struggle with the television networks did not begin in earnest until 1955. It is interesting that part of the impetus for its action then—as with the present inquiry[31]—came from a petition filed by Westinghouse Broadcasting Company (Group W). In July of 1955 the agency appointed a Network Study Committee of four commissioners to conduct a broad-ranging inquiry into network practices.[32] The committee's expert staff was headed by the late Dean Roscoe L. Barrow of the University of Cincinnati Law School. Under his leadership this staff pursued an intensive investigation through 1956 and early 1957. The Commission's study included searches of network files; interviews with representatives of various components of the industry; and extensive questionnaires sent to networks, stations, program suppliers, advertisers, agencies, and spot representatives. The effort culminated in October of 1957 when Dean Barrow sent the Commission a staff report that included some thirty-seven recommendations for further analysis or agency action.[33] As is often true of this type of study, many of its recommendations became likely candidates for further review or investigation.

The Prime Time Access Rule

In a proceeding that was a spinoff of the Barrow Report, Westinghouse Broadcasting Company proposed that network affiliates be limited to three hours of network programming during the four prime-time hours (7 P.M. to 11 P.M. Eastern Time).[34] This would free one hour of prime time for programs from non-network sources. After a long debate over the Westinghouse concept and other similar ideas, the Commission finally acted in 1970 by adopting the first version of the Prime Time Access Rule.[35] The agency also adopted two other rules that were designed to control network dominance, one prohibiting the networks from engaging in domestic syndication of reruns, and the other preventing them from holding a financial interest in programming not produced by the network.[36]

The practical effect of the latter two regulations on the network-dominance problem is difficult to determine. In the case of PTAR, however, there is reason to believe that it has not reduced network power or even, as we will show, contributed to diverse programming. While PTAR may have limited network operations by giving the networks fewer hours in which to present their programs, it also may have enhanced the networks' power over their affiliated stations. With only three hours of programming available, the networks perhaps can expect a greater percentage of stations to clear their programs. Moreover, the Commission's decision to restrict network operations under PTAR did not seem to concern some network executives. During the last in a long line of public proceedings concerning the rule, some networks actively favored—or at least failed to oppose strenuously—retention of PTAR.[37] Why did these corporations favor restrictions on their own activities—restrictions aimed at curbing their economic power? The answer apparently involves issues of economic benefit. In the early 1970s the nation was in the middle of a recession, and some networks may not have wished to create an additional time period in which they would be expected to compete with one another.

But the success or failure of the Prime Time Access Rule obviously does not depend on the happiness of network officials. The true measure of success or failure of the rule must be its effect on programming. And almost everyone would agree that in this area the record to date has been at best uneven and at worst miserable. A major premise of the rule was that it would promote diversity in prime-time programming. But as many had predicted, the access period has been dominated by game shows, animal shows, and revivals of programs that had been cancelled by the networks. There is nothing intrinsically wrong with this kind of programming, but there is no reason for the government to create a protected zone for it.

Another theory behind PTAR was that it would lead to a rennaissance of programming for specialized audiences.[38] However, the mere replacement of the networks with syndicators has not fulfilled this hope. The economic incentives behind the programming game remain unchanged and suppliers continue to seek the largest-possible audience shares. The only results of changes in programming strategies have been less high-quality programming because of relative inefficiencies of syndication operations, and more focus on low-budget types of programs.

The proponents of the rule also anticipated more innovative programs during the access period, but this was never a likely possibility. Program-pilot development is extremely expensive. A half-hour network pilot averages about $300,000, a one-hour pilot $550,000, and a two-hour pilot $1,000,000.[39] Syndicators could not be reasonably expected to incur such costs on any regular basis. And experience under the rule bears this out.

In 1975 the Commission voted to keep the rule in order to give it a full and fair test in actual operation.[40] At that time I expressed serious reservations about the wisdom of our decision,[41] and I remain skeptical. Once a rule like this has been in operation for a number of years and people have come to rely on it, however, it may be difficult to eliminate the rule in its entirety. Thus PTAR, in one form or another, is likely to be around for some time.

The Present Network Inquiry

Despite the unhappy history of FCC efforts to curb network dominance, the Commission followed my 1977 suggestion that it institute a new overall study of network-programming practices.[42] Almost two decades had elapsed since the release of the Barrow Report, and recent developments suggested that a new inquiry was warranted. As had been the case with PTAR, the inquiry was prompted in part by a petition filed by Westinghouse Broadcasting Company—which is generally recognized to be the largest group-station owner aside from the networks.[43]

This proceeding, however, does not propose the adoption of new rules or regulations; it is intended solely as "a fact gathering inquiry designed to provide the Commission with information necessary to a thorough understanding of television networking."[44] Moreover, the agency stressed that it had not "reached any conclusions, even of a tentative nature," regarding the issues raised.[45]

While the inquiry considers a number of matters related to the general allegation of network dominance, its primary focus is on the relationship between the networks and their affiliated stations.[46] This emphasis is in keeping with the agency's traditional policy of giving the individual licensee the right and responsibility to program his station. The Commission has "consistently maintained that responsibility for the selection and presentation of broadcast material ultimately devolves upon the individual station licensee, and that fulfillment of such responsibility requires the free exercise of his independent judgment."[47]

It is also well established that responsibility for independent programming judgment cannot be delegated to a network or to any other entity.[48] Accordingly, the inquiry will consider whether "particular network practices may improperly compromise or restrict the programming discretion of the broadcast station licensee."[49] In examining this issue, the Commission stated, it would devote some attention to the relationship between the networks and the program-production community.[50] The FCC noted that "station discretion can be meaningfully and effectively exercised only in circumstances where this market is in a healthy, competitive state and is in a position to offer alternative sources of programming."[51]

While all of us would concur with this expression of the need for competition in program supply, the FCC's experience with the Prime Time Access Rule demonstrates that the artificial promotion of alternative program sources may not be in the public interest. Rather than diversity and innovation, such an approach may result in a monotonous sameness among programs. For this reason, the Commission must use caution in tinkering with the market in pursuit of abstract objectives such as licensee discretion, program diversity, and competitive innovation. It is also hoped that at the conclusion of the inquiry, the commissioners will not feel compelled to adopt rules merely to justify the time and expense of the proceeding. If failures and deficiencies are demonstrated, regulatory action may well be desirable or required; but the system should not be tinkered with unnecessarily.

Several more specific issues were raised in the inquiry. As previously indicated, the two general areas of investigation are networks' relations with (1) their affiliated stations and (2) their program suppliers.

Network-Affiliate Relations. The first matter affecting network-affiliate relations involves clearance of network programs—acceptance for broadcasting by affiliates—and division of time between the networks and their affiliates. Westinghouse has alleged that since 1960 there has been a substantial expansion of network schedules.[52] The big three have responded that this increase is largely attributable to ABC's development into a fully competitive network, since expansions of program time by CBS and NBC have been only 9 and 5 percent respectively.[53] Moreover, the networks alleged that the existence of the Prime Time Access Rule blocks any growth during the hours of highest audience viewing.[54] Although Westinghouse's contention relates to a very important issue, available information does not suggest that any significant expansion of network schedules is likely in the near future.

The Commission also sought comment on whether the present level of affiliate clearance, which is very high, may result from either contractual provisions or economic relationships that are coercive in nature.[55] It is commonly alleged that clearances are something less than voluntary, but it is not always clear what these charges mean or whether violations of FCC policy are involved. The inquiry should resolve this issue one way or the other.

A second issue of concern to some affiliates relates to previewing or prescreening of network programs. Westinghouse has claimed that information about upcoming network programs is so sparse that affiliates lack enough warning to preempt programs deemed unsuitable for their audiences and to substitute other programming.[56] The networks have responded that they make programs available for previewing as soon as they have been reviewed, edited, and readied for broadcast.[57] My own view is that although production delays may have restricted some affiliates' opportunities to preview programs and to make their decisions, I am not convinced that production schedules should be subject to FCC regulation. If a problem exists in this area, it can and should be solved through responsible self-regulation by the industry.

Another Westinghouse complaint concerned what it believed to be the relatively low level of compensation paid by the networks to affiliates.[58] As Robb discusses in more detail in chapter 9, an affiliate's network compensation depends on its number of viewers, the size of its market, and other similar factors.[59] The Commission noted in the inquiry that stations' earnings per se were not a matter of government concern.[60] The FCC has raised questions about graduated-payment plans, however, in which the average hourly rate of compensation is heavily influenced by the number of hours cleared. The Commission's concern is that such plans may create an unreasonable obstacle to competition from independent syndicators.[61] On the other hand, one network has argued that the Commission-mandated higher compensation sought by Westinghouse might act as an even greater disadvantage to syndicators; ironically, it might make clearance of network programs more economically attractive by raising hourly rates.[62]

While the present graduated-payments plan is a legitimate subject of inquiry, similar plans were considered in the Barrow Report and found to be acceptable.[63] Moreover, many stations routinely preempt network programs and substitute syndicated material, which often consists of sports events or feature films. Stations presumably would do so on a regular basis only if they found this to be economically attractive.

Network-Program Supplier Relations. Turning to the second part of the Commission's inquiry, the discussion of network-program supplier relations is divided into six areas:

1. network interests in syndicated programs produced by independent suppliers;
2. network-produced entertainment programming;
3. contractual tying agreements relating to independent producers' use of production facilities and program options;
4. exclusive exhibition rights to new programs;
5. exhibition rights to reruns of network-produced programs;
6. relations between the networks' owned-and-operated stations and program suppliers.[64]

Many of these questions are being examined concurrently by the U.S. District Court for the Central District of California in connection with antitrust suits that the Justice Department has brought against the three networks.[65] The department and NBC have entered into a conditional-settlement agreement,[66] which is being opposed by the other networks.[67] In view of the status of this judicial proceeding, it would be inappropriate to comment on its merits in any detail here. It should be pointed out that existing rules forbid the networks from engaging in domestic syndication or holding a financial interest in non-network-produced programming[68] but that this prohibition may not have the effect the Commission intended. The FCC wanted to prevent networks from using their muscle on program suppliers who were attempting to sell their products in a very limited marketplace. Conversely, however, the rules may have prevented smaller independent programmers from sharing some of the risks of program failure with the networks, by giving the networks title to reruns. As former Commissioner Robinson noted, "the ultimate practical effect of this prohibition has not been to reduce network power or to strengthen independent producers—as was intended—but simply to increase the dominant position of the major Hollywood film producers, those large enough to possess the risk capital to invest in programming without network support."[69]

The Risks of Regulation

I cannot say whether the Commission's policy has been beneficial or not. Its experience suggests, however, that in adopting the task of curbing network dominance as an end in itself, the FCC may develop policies the real effects of which may prove to be contrary to the purpose intended and perhaps even inimical to the public interest. In a complex industry such as television broadcasting, economic relationships make it difficult to predict the effects of particular regulations. Sometimes the best-laid plans result in the worst-made rules.

Some observers claim that as business and industry become more complicated, the need for government regulation increases. More commonly, however, the reverse may be true. The very complexity of modern industry may make free competition the only way to achieve coordination and efficiency. One can hope that the Commission's experience with the Prime Time Access Rule and other quixotic adventures may give it a healthy skepticism toward proposals for government intervention in the marketplace. This is not to suggest that there is no place for regulation of the broadcast industry or of network practices. But this role should be limited to protection of well-established and well-defined public-interest values.

In this connection it should be noted that Congress envisioned free competition as the basic scheme in the broadcasting field. In the landmark *Sanders Brothers Radio* case,[70] the Supreme Court stated that, in contradistinction to the pervasive regulation of telephone and telegraph common carriers, "Congress intended to leave competition in the business of broadcasting where it found it, to permit a licensee who was not interfering electrically with other broadcasters to survive or succumb according to his ability to make his programs attractive to the public."[71]

The Further Notice of Inquiry

In October of 1978 the Commission unanimously voted to adopt a *Further Notice of Inquiry*.[72] This notice provided additional specificity and fine tuning to the original notice's general discussion. It also detailed a study of prospects for new advertiser-supported networks that would include six areas of investigation: interconnection rates, spectrum allocation and channel assignments, the so-called "UHF handicap," FCC ownership policies, viewer and advertiser demand for television, and the economics of occasional or part-time networks.[73] The Network Inquiry Special Staff will report on whether developments in any of these areas may alter the prospects for new networks.

Finally, the inquiry will explore prospects for new networks employing different means of program delivery or financing. The staff will analyze whether new methods for delivering programs may affect the extent of concentration in the television industry in the next decade. Research areas include: cable-television networks; satellite-to-home broadcasting; and videocassettes, videotape-recording systems, and videodiscs.[74]

The ultimate result of the Commission's far-reaching inquiry is difficult to predict at this point, but it seems clear that the present commissioners, like their predecessors, are prepared to press forward with a searching inquiry into the structure and performance of the television networks.

Conclusion

In conclusion, I would like to stress a point that should be kept firmly in mind by the Commission and the courts as they consider various matters concerning the regulation of the television networks: These entities are *not* in the business of manufacturing paperboard boxes or canning fruits and vegetables; they are in the business of communications and are therefore entitled to a high degree of first amendment protection. Whenever regulations are proposed that will affect the nature and quality of the programming to be presented to the American people, it is incumbent on all of us to recognize that we are dealing in an extremely sensitive area and that the exercise of both caution and responsibility is called for.

In this spirit I express the hope that the broadcast industry will employ a healthy dose of respect for its obligations to the listening and viewing public and that, in considering the future of network regulation, government officials will learn from the misadventures of the past and avoid mistakes that they will later come to regret.

Notes

1. R. Noll, M. Peck, & J. McGowan, Economic Aspects of Television Regulation 1 (1973).

2. *Compare* FCC, TV Broadcast Financial Data—1977, Release No. 3686 (Aug. 14, 1978), table 2, *with* FCC, Statistics of Communications Common Carriers—1977, at 30.

3. Network advertising volume was $3.455 billion in 1977, as compared with total U.S. advertising volume of $37.990 billion. Television Bureau of Advertising, Inc., TVB Basics 21.

4. 607 F.2d 438 (D.C. Cir. 1979) (*en banc*), *cert. denied*, ____ U.S. ____, 100 S. Ct. 662 (1980).

5. American Security Council Educ. Foundation, 63 F.C.C.2d 366 (1977).

6. American Security Council Educ. Foundation v. FCC, 607 F.2d 438 (D.C. Cir. 1979) (*en banc*), *cert. denied*, ____ U.S. ____, 100 S. Ct. 662 (1980).

7. E. Barnouw, The Image Empire 197 (1970).

8. A. Meiklejohn, Political Freedom 86-87 (1965).

9. FCC v. Pacifica Foundation, 438 U.S. 726 (1978).

10. *Id.* at 748.

11. Communications Act of 1934, §§307(a), 309(a), 47 U.S.C. §§307(a), 309(a) (1976).

12. Communications Act of 1934, §326, 47 U.S.C. §326 (1976).

13. *E.g.*, FCC v. Pacifica Foundation, 438 U.S. 726 (1978).

14. *See, e.g.*, Red Lion Broadcasting Co. v. FCC, 395 U.S. 367, 389-90 (1969).

15. Report on Editorializing by Broadcast Licensees, 13 F.C.C. 1246, 1249 (1949); Fairness Report, 48 F.C.C.2d 1, 9 (1974), *reconsideration denied*, 58 F.C.C.2d 691 (1976), *aff'd in part and rev'd in part on other grounds sub nom.* National Citizens Committee for Broadcasting v. FCC, 567 F.2d 1095 (D.C. Cir. 1977), *cert. denied*, 436 U.S. 926 (1978); Report and Order, Docket No. 19154, 66 F.C.C.2d 419, 428 (1977), *aff'd sub nom.* National Black Media Coalition v. FCC, 589 F.2d 578 (D.C. Cir. 1978).

16. Fairness Report, *supra* note 15, 48 F.C.C.2d at 10-17.

17. *Id.* at 10, 14-16.

18. *Id.* at 16-17.

19. *Id.* at 17.

20. Memorandum Opinion and Order on Reconsideration of the Fairness Report, Docket No. 19260, 58 F.C.C.2d 691, 709 (1976) (dissenting statement of Comm'r Robinson).

21. *Id.*

22. American Security Council Educ. Foundation, 63 F.C.C.2d 366 (1977), *aff'd*, 607 F.2d 438 (D.C. Cir. 1979) (*en banc*), *cert. denied*, _____U.S._____ , 100 S. Ct. 662 (1980).

23. Second Report and Order, Docket No. 19622, 50 F.C.C.2d 829, 889 (1975) (dissenting statement) [hereinafter cited as PTAR III], *aff'd sub nom.* National Ass'n of Independent Television Producers & Distribs. v. FCC, 516 F.2d 526 (2d Cir. 1975).

24. FCC, Report on Chain Broadcasting 91-92 (1941).

25. *Id.* (Regulation 3.103).

26. *Id.* at 91 (Regulation 3.102).

27. *Id.* at 92 (Regulation 3.104).

28. *Id.* (Regulation 3.105).

29. *Id.* (Regulation 3.108).

30. Report, Statement of Policy, and Order, Docket No. 20721, 63 F.C.C.2d 674 (1977).

31. *See* Notice of Inquiry, Docket No. 21049, 62 F.C.C.2d 548, 549 (1977) [hereinafter cited as Notice of Inquiry]; Further Notice of Inquiry, Docket No. 21049, 69 F.C.C.2d 1524, 1525 (1978) [hereinafter cited as Further Notice of Inquiry].

32. FCC Delegation Order No. 10 (July 22, 1955), *reprinted in* House Comm. on Interstate and Foreign Commerce, Network Broadcasting, H.R. Rep. No. 1297, 85th Cong., 2d Sess. 667 (1958) [hereinafter cited as Barrow Report].

33. Barrow Report, *supra* note 32.

34. *See* Report and Order, Docket No. 12782, 23 F.C.C.2d 382, 383 (1970) [hereinafter cited as PTAR I], *modified*, 25 F.C.C.2d 318, *aff'd sub nom.* Mt. Mansfield Television, Inc. v. FCC, 442 F.2d 470 (2d Cir. 1970).

35. PTAR I, *supra* note 34, at 384.

36. *Id.* at 397-99.

37. PTAR III, *supra* note 23, at 833-34.

38. *See id.* at 836. *But cf. id.* at 835 ("diversity of programming was a hope, rather than one of the primary objectives.")

39. S. Robb, Television/Radio Age Communications Coursebook 2-34 (1978).

40. *See* PTAR III, *supra* note 23, at 837, 847.

41. *Id.* at 888 (concurring statement).

42. Notice of Inquiry, *supra* note 31.

43. Petition for Inquiry, Rule Making and Immediate Temporary Relief (RM-2749), filed by Westinghouse Broadcasting Company, Inc. (Sept. 3, 1976) [hereinafter cited as Westinghouse Petition].

44. Notice of Inquiry, *supra* note 31, at 550.

45. *Id.*

46. *Id.* at 553-56.

47. En Banc Programming Policy Report, 44 F.C.C. 2303, 2312 (1960).

48. *See* Barrow Report, *supra* note 32, at 130-38; Notice of Inquiry, *supra* note 31, at 548.

49. Notice of Inquiry, *supra* note 31, at 549.

50. *Id.* at 549, 556-59.

51. *Id.* at 549.

52. Westinghouse Petition, *supra* note 43, at 11.

53. Notice of Inquiry, *supra* note 31, at 553-54 & n. 9.

54. *See, e.g.*, Comments of ABC, Docket No. 21049 (June 1, 1977), at 7-8.

55. Notice of Inquiry, *supra* note 31, at 554.

56. *Id.*; Westinghouse Petition, *supra* note 43, at 23-27.

57. *See* Notice of Inquiry, *supra* note 31, at 554-55 & n. 12.

58. *Id.* at 556; Westinghouse Petition, *supra* note 43, at 30-46.

59. S. Robb, *supra* at 79, 84-86.

60. Notice of Inquiry, *supra* note 31, at 555.

61. *Id.*

62. *See* Comments of CBS Inc., Docket No. 21049 (June 1, 1977), at 46-47.

63. *See* Barrow Report, *supra* note 32, at 466-67.

64. Notice of Inquiry, *supra* note 31, at 556.

65. United States v. ABC, Civ. No. 74-3600-RJK (C.D. Cal., complaint filed Dec. 10, 1974); United States v. CBS Inc., Civ. No. 74-3599-RJK (C.D. Cal., complaint filed Dec. 10, 1974); United States v. NBC, Civ. No. 74-3601-RJK (C.D. Cal., complaint filed Dec. 10, 1974).

66. United States v. NBC, 449 F.Supp. 1127 (C.D. Cal. 1978) (order approving consent judgment).

67. *Id.* at 1138-40.

68. 47 C.F.R. §73.658(j) (1979).

69. PTAR III, *supra* note 23, at 890 n. 3 (1975) (dissenting statement).

70. FCC v. Sanders Bros. Radio Station, 309 U.S. 470 (1940).

71. *Id.* at 475.

72. Further Notice of Inquiry, *supra* note 31.

73. *Id.* at 1535-36.

74. *Id.* at 1536.

13 A Civil Libertarian's View of the Television Networks

Alan Reitman

The American Civil Liberties Union (ACLU) is strongly opposed to government control of programming as a general proposition. But we also believe that the first amendment requires presentation of a full diversity of different points of view. There are thus certain appropriate goals for the FCC with respect to programming and even network practices. The problem, of course, is to walk that fine line between direct government interference in particular content or particular programming, on the one hand, and on the other a kind of general review of programming that emphasizes trying to create diversity with different types of programming.

Wiley's doubts about the power of television seem overstated.[1] Certainly we cannot compare "Roots" and "Holocaust" with Martin Luther's Ninety-Five Theses, but the great demand for television time and coverage by politicians at campaign time seems to indicate that the power of television is at least equal to that of the printed word.[2] Recent surveys indicate that more people these days watch television news programs than read newspapers for their news.[3] While much might be said about the form and quality of television news coverage, it is safe to conclude that television has tremendous power as a means of communication.

One of Wiley's main topics in Chapter 12 of this book is his discussion of the fairness doctrine, which many people regard as the most significant issue of the moment.[4] The ACLU feels that the FCC has a proper role to play in implementing the fairness doctrine, because if this is not done, the opportunity for diversity—not only in the presentation of controversial programs but also through responses to attacks on the air, which also involve an element of equity and fairness—will be lost.[5] Wiley's figures on the fairness doctrine are also interesting in their indication that out of several thousand complaints brought to the FCC by citizens and citizens' groups, only 0.4 percent were thought to have any validity.[6] The networks have been the leaders in the campaign to eliminate the doctrine to protect the first amendment freedom of broadcasters, but these statistics indicate that broadcasters have nothing to fear from the FCC since it almost never interferes with content.

On the question of the Prime Time Access Rule,[7] which the ACLU supported before the Commission,[8] Wiley is correct in pointing out that it has not proved to be miraculous. But although it has not tremendously changed the kind of programming on television, nevertheless—given the great control and power the networks have over programming—the rule has been an improvement. Because of PTAR, there have been many interesting programs on significant subjects such as, to cite one recent example, the problems of black ghetto youths. There have been other shows dealing with science and the occult, as well as the much-maligned animal shows, which can be intriguing and informative and are certainly different from game shows, in any case. Thus although I would not say that PTAR has been a panacea, I think that its presence acts as a prod and that in some cases it has been a prominent factor in giving the public some different kinds of programming. It is unlikely that the marketplace would have given us anything as innovative or unusual as those "access" programs have been.

The question of FCC censorship has recently arisen in the context of the "family-viewing-time" litigation.[9] That case did not involve direct FCC regulation of the content of individual programming, which clearly would be improper, but rather the power of the agency to regulate by "raised eyebrow." It is questionable whether the result is very different. The family-viewing-time concept represented something that the FCC felt the public wanted and that (as the trial court found) the Commission, through conferences and other communications, pressured the networks to adopt.[10] A serious question exists as to whether, apart from the issue of regulation by statute or ruling, the power of the agency itself informing networks of what it thinks the public should or should not have does not really result in the same kind of force, and thus amount to censorship.

The networks' reactions to so-called "pressure groups" are also interesting. These groups obviously have first amendment rights of expression and protest; but when networks give in to such pressures, the population at large may be denied certain kinds of programming. It is often desirable for the networks to stand up to such groups, as ABC did in the recent "Soap" controversy, and even to oppose their own affiliates who may be more willing to yield.[11] This is not to suggest that we have a regulation or ruling on the question of the rights of pressure groups to express their views; but it is important for the networks themselves to understand their responsibility in the first amendment area and to keep offering different kinds of programming to the general public.

Notes

1. R. Wiley, *supra* at 107-09.

2. Political candidates spent about $40 million for television time in 1972. *See* FCC, 39th Annual Report/Fiscal Year 1973, at 46-47. The amount has increased greatly since then.

3. The Roper Organization, Inc., Public Perceptions of Television and Other Mass Media: A Twenty-Year Review, 1959-1978 (1979).

4. R. Wiley, *supra* at 107-08, 110.

5. *See* Red Lion Broadcasting Co. v. FCC, 395 U.S. 367 (1969).

6. R. Wiley, *supra* at 110.

7. 47 C.F.R. §73.658(k) (1979).

8. *See* Second Report and Order, Docket No. 19622, 50 F.C.C.2d 829, 856, 858, *aff'd sub nom.* National Ass'n of Independent Television Producers & Distribs. v. FCC, 516 F.2d 526 (2d Cir. 1975).

9. Writers Guild of America, West, Inc. v. FCC, 423 F. Supp. 1064 (C.D. Cal. 1976), *rev'd on other grounds sub nom.* Writers Guild of America, West, Inc. v. ABC, 609 F.2d 355 (9th Cir. 1979), *petition for cert. filed*, 48 U.S.L.W. 3736 (U.S. April 29, 1980)(No. 79-1717).

10. *Id.*, 423 F. Supp. at 1092-1128.

11. *See* Broadcasting, Aug. 22, 1977, at 24.

14 Competition Policy and the Television Networks

Heather Kirkwood

Wiley has indicated that the time and effort devoted to television may be misplaced for three reasons: (1) television is not a particularly large industry;[1] (2) television does not have as much power as commonly thought;[2] and (3) television is probably not an appropriate medium to serve a culture composed entirely of media critics.[3] All these points are well taken. However, even assuming that television is a small industry, that it does not have any more power than, say, a manufacturer of dog biscuits, and that by its nature it can cater only to the masses, it is still indisputable that television is very important to us. We may love it or hate it, but very few of us can say that it plays no role in our lives. Since television is important to us and since it is a commercial product, just like dog biscuits, consumers have at a minimum the right to expect that the market will supply them with that product in a manner that reflects their demand.

At the Bureau of Competition our first interest lies in examining the extent to which the present system fulfills consumer demand, whatever that demand may be. To do this, one must thoroughly examine the present industry structure, conduct, and performance. Second, and more important, one must ask if there are clearly indicated changes in industry structure or behavior that would result in an array of products more fitted to consumer demand. This is the crux of the problem in media. Whereas in most industries there is only one identifiable consumer and one identifiable product, in television and most other media there are two: the viewer and viewer entertainment, on the one hand, and the advertiser and advertising time on the other. What pleases one consumer, the viewer, is not necessarily going to please the other consumer, the advertiser, and vice versa.[4]

This peculiarity explains the sharp disagreement at the Network Television Conference on the value and use of ratings. Some of the speakers have adamantly argued that the ratings work extremely well,[5] while others vehemently disagreed. Perhaps the answer is that although the ratings work very well for advertisers, they may not work as well for viewers. To the extent that simultaneously reaching optimum results for the viewer and the advertiser is impossible, tradeoffs must be made. One of the goals of competition policy may be to define the terms of that tradeoff.

At the end of his chapter, Wiley warns us that the government should think long and hard before tinkering with the present system, since past

127

tinkering has more often than not been unsuccessful in achieving its intended goals.[6] Wiley also emphasizes that given this situation, the government should for the most part prefer the marketplace solution.[7]

As a member of the Bureau of Competition staff, I am certainly in general agreement with that conclusion. It is important to note, however, that the marketplace solution in television may well be geared for only one set of consumers: the advertisers. The advertisers cannot completely disregard the needs of the viewers, of course, because the advertisers want the largest number of viewers per program delivered to them. However, they also want their viewers to be good potential purchasers of their products, and they want those viewers to be in a receptive state of mind to listen to their advertisements. The marketplace places very stringent demands on the networks to meet these criteria. But because television is free to viewers, the marketplace does not measure the intensity of viewer satisfaction with particular programming. It measures (through the ratings system) whether or not a viewer is watching the program, or whether certain viewers are watching the program; but it does not measure how strongly the viewer wants a particular program. Even if it did, television does not at the moment have any way of making the viewer pay for programs he especially wants.

This raises the question of whether anything can or should be done to improve viewer welfare. One suggestion made in this book is that we should wait for new technology, such as pay-cable television, to help supply alternatives.[8] One question now under consideration is whether that approach is satisfactory. Wiley is correct in saying that we must move carefully before tinkering with the present system; nevertheless, we presently have the tools available to make valid predictions of the outcome of any changes we might make. In many instances, in fact, we have had those tools for quite a while. Wiley noted that PTAR was adopted in hopes that it would provide diversity and specialized programming. But it was also predicted by many at that time that the rule would result at least initially in game shows, animal shows, and the like, given the economics of networking.[9] Thus it has also been said that the real goal of PTAR was not to increase diversity but rather to increase the sources of programming.[10] Robb observes that PTAR may have succeeded in that goal, even while failing to supply diversity or culture.[11] The point is that if accurate predictions can be made, and if we carefully and realistically define our goals and the tradeoffs we are willing to make to achieve those goals, then perhaps we can avoid being disappointed with the results.

In conclusion I note that the FTC's examination of "media concentration" is undertaken predominantly from an economic viewpoint. Much concern has been expressed, however, that there exists an excessive concentration of other forms of power—political power and power over ideas—in the hands of the networks.[12] These are very significant issues that we will certainly be considering in our study of media concentration.

Notes

1. R. Wiley, *supra* at 107.

2. *Id.* at 109.

3. *Id.* at 108.

4. *Cf.* Citizens Committee to Save WEFM v. FCC, 506 F.2d 246, 268 (D.C. Cir. 1974)(en banc).

5. *E.g.*, D. Blank, *supra* at 27-28; H. Eaton, *supra* at 60.

6. R. Wiley, *supra* at 118.

7. *Id.* at 117.

8. *E.g.*, H. Eaton, *supra* at 59.

9. R. Wiley, *supra* at 113.

10. *See* Second Report and Order, Docket No. 19622, 50 F.C.C.2d 829, 835, *aff'd sub nom.* National Ass'n of Independent Television Producers & Distribs. v. FCC, 516 F.2d 526 (2d Cir. 1975).

11. *See* S. Robb, *supra* at 78-81.

12. *See* A. Pearce, *supra* at 16-20.

15 Regulation as a Check on Network Power

Earle K. Moore

Wiley has given us some figures by which to measure the importance of television, figures as to gross revenues of networks and television stations.[1] Some other figures that are more significant are the figures as to net revenues or profits. It happens that television stations are just about the most profitable businesses in the American system. Network-owned television stations earn well over 300 percent per-annum return on net tangible investment.[2] That is not only an unusually high figure, but ordinarily such high profits would indicate a lack of free competition. All other television stations earn an average of a little more than 100 percent per annum on net tangible investments.[3] They also take down to net income a very high percentage of revenues.[4] If we were to value television stations as the stock market and investors value businesses, television would rank much higher than is indicated by the gross-revenue figures.

One thing that Wiley mentioned was the rule about licensee discretion.[5] It is well known that the station owner is a frontispiece and is responsible to the public. The Commission would have him be held responsible for everything that goes on the air over his station.[6] Yet in fact he is not permitted to preview the programming that he gets from the network, which is his principal program supplier and programs his most valuable time.[7] Wiley states that although this may be regrettable, it is no concern of the Commission.[8] It would seem that the Commission is being unfair to its licensees if on the one hand it holds them totally responsible and accountable, but on the other hand they cannot preview the programming they are getting from other licensees. If the rule on licensee discretion or responsibility is to mean anything, the licensees must have the right to preview the programming that they are broadcasting to their service areas.

I also take issue with Wiley's suggestion that perhaps graduated affiliation rates pose no problem.[9] It has long been Commission policy that one program cannot be tied into another, so to speak; the station must be free to take whatever programs it thinks will serve its audience and to reject any programs it thinks its audience will not want to see or will find objectionable.[10] Empirically, after all, the station is the final judge. Yet even though it has the right and indeed the obligation to look at all the programming and to pick out only the programming it wants, there is a suggestion that graduated rates are acceptable. Although graduated rates stop somewhat short of tie-ins, they do penalize a station financially if it does not take the whole schedule.[11] If there is any validity in the concept of licensee responsibility and licensee discretion, the networks ought not to be able to use absolute contractual or financial pressures on their licensees to take programming that the stations do not want to take.

Another important area is the Prime Time Access Rule.[12] Prime-time access, judging from some of the game shows, has certainly not been an unqualified success from the aesthetic point of view. But it has had some virtues. Before PTAR many licensees around the country really did not know how to program; they were not used to having the responsibility for a lot of time in which there was a big audience; they were not used to thinking about what the audience wanted. But with access time they had to do that; and they began to find out that they could program, that in some cases they could make judgments that were better, at least for the local market, than those the networks might make in trying to serve every market in the United States simultaneously.

A considerable amount of local and regional programming has been developed—programming that might be of interest in Arkansas but not in New York.[13] This development has been healthy. It is better to try to preserve some of the existing differences in this country than to try to make everyone always watch precisely the same thing. It is also a fact that the most recent projection by the Commission is that part of the time ought to be used for public-affairs programming, community service, and so on,[14] and a great many stations have developed and are presenting public-affairs programs in access time. This is also a very healthy development. We are used to seeing programming about some important national issues from the networks very occasionally; but we have not seen too much programming by local stations about local problems in valuable time periods. On Sunday mornings we may see a few people talking, but that has been the extent of it. PTAR has succeeded to some extent in getting local stations to accept the idea that they can present worthwhile, valuable, well-produced public-affairs programming.

One obstacle to the full realization of the goals underlying PTAR is the networks' ownership of five major-market VHF stations each, while other multiple owners are prohibited from growing to similar proportions.[15] Thus while the networks have strong captive buyers for the programs they produce, independent program producers must sell to one of the big three or face difficulties in financing their programs.

Perhaps this state of affairs is not in the public interest, and the networks should be made to sell their O&O stations and hunt for buyers like everyone else. This would kill two birds with one stone, since it would go a long way toward eliminating the perennial problem of network power that has been spoken of so much at the Network Television Conference.[16]

Notes

1. R. Wiley, *supra* at 107 & n.2.

2. *See* FCC, TV Broadcast Financial Data—1978, Release No. 19540 July 30, 1979, tables 3 & 12.

3. *See id.*

4. *See id.*, table 3.

5. R. Wiley, *supra* at 110, 114-15.

6. *E.g.*, Licensee Responsibility to Review Records Before Their Broadcast, 31 F.C.C.2d 79 (1971); En Banc Programming Policy Report, 44 F.C.C. 2303, 2313-14 (1960).

7. *See* Petition for Inquiry, Rule Making and Immediate Temporary Relief (RM-2749), filed by Westinghouse Broadcasting Company, Inc. (Sept. 3, 1976), at 23-27 [hereinafter cited as Westinghouse Petition].

8. R. Wiley, *supra* at 115.

9. *Id.*

10. *E.g.*, FCC, Report on Chain Broadcasting 62-66, 92 (1941)(Regulation 3.105). The current version of this rule is codified in 47 C.F.R. §73.658(e) (1979).

11. For explanations of how affiliates' compensation is computed, see S. Robb, *supra* at 79, 84-86; Westinghouse Petition, *supra* note 7, at 40-46 & Attachment H.

12. 47 C.F.R. §73.658(k) (1979).

13. *See* Second Report and Order, Docket No. 19622, 50 F.C.C.2d 829, 835-36, *aff'd sub nom.* National Ass'n of Independent Television Producers & Distribs. v. FCC, 516 F.2d 526 (2d Cir. 1975).

14. *Id.*, 50 F.C.C.2d at 840-44.

15. 47 C.F.R. §73.636(a)(2) (1979); Report and Order, Docket No. 16068, 22 F.C.C.2d 696, 700 (1968).

16. *See, e.g.*, A. Pearce, *supra* at 3, *passim.*

**Part V
First Amendment
Considerations**

16 Broadcast Regulation and the First Amendment

Oscar G. Chase

Introduction

In thinking about regulation of networks, one of the most basic questions is how far the free-speech guarantees of the first amendment allow Congress or a federal agency like the FCC to go. Acknowledging that no one could fully treat that question in a chapter of this length, let me attempt a reasonable compromise. I will first discuss some recent first amendment developments in the law of broadcasting that are of special interest and will then try to relate those legal "passages" to a single currently lively issue—the right of access to the broadcast media, that is, the right of members of the public to express themselves over the air (or through cable) free of control of content by the licensee.

It is axiomatic that broadcasting occupies a special place in first amendment theory. The Supreme Court and society generally have permitted a degree of government control over broadcast content that would be unthinkable if applied to other media. The government's role in broadcast regulation has historically been justified by reference to the scarcity of the electromagnetic spectrum, the attendant need to keep competing users from drowning each other out, and the desire to ensure that those users blessed with government licenses operate in the public interest.

A major goal of government regulation has been diversity of programming—the notion that the airwaves should not be the exclusive personal podiums of the licensees but should be used to bring a wide range of ideas and experiences from many sources to the American people. Recent decisions have endorsed growing government control, but this has come, ironically and regrettably, at the expense of diversity in broadcasting. Proponents of greater public access to the airwaves cannot be comforted by these shifts in the nature of and the justification for broadcasting regulation.

Recent Developments

A Starting Point: The NBC Case

In order to discern these trends it is necessary to adopt a baseline or starting point. *NBC* v. *United States* was the case in which the Supreme Court first addressed the constitutionality of FCC regulations over content.[1] At issue were the Chain Broadcasting Rules, designed to limit the degree of control the networks could exercise over their affiliated radio stations.[2] The rules did not deal directly with content but affected it indirectly insofar as they prevented the networks from totally dominating the broadcast content of local licensees' programming.

In quickly disposing of the first amendment arguments of the broadcasters and networks, the Court sounded a theme that became a leitmotif of constitutional doctrine. Because of the limited nature of the broadcast spectrum it cannot be used by all; some government control is necessary to prevent chaos. "That is why, unlike other modes of expression, it is subject to governmental regulation."[3] Thus denial of a license by the FCC would be valid as long as the denial was prompted by the Commission's concern for the "public interest, convenience, and necessity" which the Communications Act of 1934 established as guidelines for Commission action.[4] The Court noted that the case would be "wholly different" if Congress had authorized the Commission to choose among applicants on the basis of their "political, economic or social views."[5] Presumably the first amendment would not allow the government to base licensing decisions on ideological or other factors related to speech.

The Red Lion Case: The Fairness Doctrine Upheld

While the NBC decision endorsed FCC control over broadcast content only insofar as the *source* of content was concerned, the Supreme Court went further, endorsing control over *actual* content, in Red Lion Broadcasting Co. v. FCC.[6] Principally at issue was the power of the FCC, under the fairness doctrine, to require a broadcaster that had permitted its facilities to be used for a personal attack to grant the victim of the attack air time for a reply. In other words, the FCC was forcing the licensee to give air time to one whose views might be anathema to it.

After disposing of the broadcasters' statutory objections,[7] the Court turned to their constitutional argument. "Their contention," as the Court put it, "is that the First Amendment protects their desire to use their alloted frequencies continuously to broadcast whatever they choose, and to exclude whomever they choose from ever using that frequency. No man may be prevented from saying or publishing what he thinks, or from refusing in his speech or other utterances to give equal weight to the views of his opponents."[8]

Referring back to the NBC theme, the Court rejected the argument. It reiterated that the peculiar nature of broadcasting necessitates some government regulation. "It would be strange," said the Court, "if the First

Amendment, aimed at protecting and furthering communications, prevented the Government from making radio communication possible by requiring licenses to broadcast and by limiting the number of licenses. . ."[9] The Court went on to infer from this unassailable position that the government could require a broadcaster to share his frequency with others. And since Congress therefore could divide the airwaves up in any of a variety of ways, it certainly had the power, through the FCC, to make a licensee share time on his frequency with one whose views are different from his.[10] The Court further answered the broadcasters' constitutional objections by reference to the countervailing rights, not of the offended victim of the attack, but of the public. It—or better put, *we*—have a right to hear diverse viewpoints; this right, given the scarcity of broadcast licenses, overrode any first amendment claim that the broadcaster could muster.[11] In much-quoted language the Court stated that "it is the right of the viewers and listeners, not the right of the broadcasters, which is paramount."[12]

The validity of the diversity principle can be seen to depend on the scarcity principle. Together they underlie most constitutional decision making in the broadcasting area.

The Diversity and Scarcity Principles Applied

The principles of diversity and scarcity have been used by the federal courts of appeals to affirm the expansion of Commission control over content in a variety of contexts. In *Banzhaf* v. *FCC*,[13] a D.C. Circuit decision, the Commission was held to have the power to apply the fairness doctrine to commercials, thereby requiring, in effect, "antiadvertising." In *Yale Broadcasting Co.* v. *FCC*, the same court endorsed the Commission's issuance of an order requiring broadcasters to know the content of records that might be "drug oriented" and to make judgments regarding the suitability of playing them,[14] an order that was seen by many as a veiled command to delete such music altogether.[15]

A series of cases in the Second Circuit upheld further FCC intrusion into the program-selection process through the Prime Time Access Rules. Somewhat simplified, PTAR III (the latest of these rules) prohibited television stations in major markets from broadcasting more than three hours per evening of network-produced programs, but allowed an exception for what could be called "favored" programming (children's, documentary, news, and public-affairs programs).[16] It was upheld in *National Association of Independent Television Producers & Distributors* v. *FCC*.[17]

Not all the decisions have expanded the Commission's control over content, however. An admitted exception to the growing scope of FCC power was found in *New York State Lottery Commission* v. *United States*.[18]

There the Third Circuit held that the Commission acted unconstitutionally in attempting to bar the news broadcast of winning lottery numbers.

The Pacifica Case: The Culmination of FCC Power

The culmination so far of the trend toward enlarged FCC power is the Supreme Court's 1978 decision in *FCC* v. *Pacifica Foundation*.[19] That case is noteworthy not only for its impact on free speech in broadcasting, but also because of its radical departure from the all-important diversity principle which, as we have seen, has buttressed the FCC's power in the past.

The Pacifica Foundation is one of the most "diverse" broadcasters in the country. And it was at its most "diverse" on a Tuesday afternoon in October of 1973 when its New York station, WBAI, broadcast a recording by comedian George Carlin entitled "Filthy Words." Carlin's monologue was a treatment of, as he put it, the words you couldn't say on the airwaves. This particular broadcast was preceded by a warning that it included sensitive language that might be considered offensive by some. It happened that someone who tuned in in midprogram (and thus did not get the benefit of the warning) heard the broadcast while driving with his young son and subsequently complained to the FCC. The Commission chastised Pacifica and, in effect, put the station on a kind of probation.[20]

If, as the Supreme Court told us in *Red Lion*, the most important consideration in deciding broadcasting cases is the listeners' right to diverse programming, one would have naively expected the Court to reverse the FCC's action. Instead it endorsed the Commission's action in glowing terms. This result was traceable in part to the distaste which Mr. Justice Stevens, the Chief Justice, and Mr. Justice Rehnquist clearly felt for the monologue in question. Although not obscene, it was—they concluded—indecent and thus not entitled to the ordinarily rigorous protection that the first amendment offers to speech in general.[21] This aspect of the case is not only relevant to broadcasting but also holds implications for other areas.

Of greater interest here is the second part of Mr. Justice Stevens's opinion, which was joined in by Justices Powell, Blackmun, and Rehnquist, as well as by the Chief Justice, to constitute a bare 5-4 majority. Again there is a reference to the special nature of the broadcast media. The Court found two factors of special importance, but they were not the factors relied on in *Red Lion*. Rather, the Court stressed the pervasive impact of broadcasting in our lives and the unusual manner of its entry into our homes, where, since we frequently tune in in midprogram prior warnings may not have reached us.[22] A second distinguishing factor of importance, said the Court, is the ease of access children have to broadcasting without parental supervision.

This too was thought to justify banishing indecency from at least daytime broadcasting.[23]

Whatever one's view of the merits of the *Pacifica* case, one must admit that, far from promoting the much-espoused diversity of broadcasting, it limited the fare we are likely to receive. Moreover, the scarcity principle—so important as an early justification of content control—does not support the result in this case. In fact it would seem to require a contrary result, since Pacifica was providing an otherwise unavailable point of view.

Perhaps, then, the *Pacifica* case signals the demise of the scarcity and diversity principles, or at least limits their vitality to cases in which they are used to uphold Commission power as opposed to cases in which the FCC's actions would strike at them. On the other hand, *Pacifica* simply may be a maverick case, based only on the distaste with which the majority viewed Carlin's language. This view finds support in parts of Mr. Justice Stevens's opinion, particularly his comparison of the broadcast to an obscene phone call.[24] But only two other members of the Court joined in that aspect of the opinion; a majority congealed only around the part of the opinion that dealt with the special nature of broadcasting.

Moreover, to try to reduce *Pacifica* to its facts is to miss a broader point. Attempts to control speech content are ordinarily made only when that content is offensive to most people. If the listener's interest in receiving diverse broadcasting will not prevail when the material is offensive, it is an interest with little weight. *Pacifica* comes close to answering, in the negative, the question saved in the *NBC* case: whether the government can make broadcast licenses conditional on the social or political views of the applicant.[25]

Midwest Video: Access to Cable Denied

Just one year after deciding *Pacifica* the Court decided another case involving the diversity problem, albeit in a rather different guise, and again came down against the proponents of diversity. In *FCC* v. *Midwest Video Corp.*,[26] the plaintiff, which operated a cable-television system, challenged FCC regulations under which it was required to set aside at least one of its channels as an "access channel" to be used by members of the public over whom the operator would have no editorial control.[27] The Supreme Court did not reach the constitutional issues, although it observed that the first amendment question was "not frivolous."[28] Rather, the Court struck down the FCC regulations on the basis of section 3(h) of the Communications Act of 1934, which states that "a person engaged in . . . broadcasting shall not . . . be deemed a common carrier."[29] The Court said:

As we see it, §3(h), consistently with the policy of the Act to preserve editorial control of programming in the licensee, forecloses any discretion in the Commission to impose access requirements amounting to common carrier obligations on broadcast systems.[30]

Certainly the decision is sensitive to the rights of cable operators and broadcasters to control the content of "their" speech. Just as certainly it is insensitive to the need to diversify the broadcast product.

FCC v. NCCB: Cross-Ownership Ban Upheld

The Supreme Court did serve diversity interests in a third recent case, *FCC v. National Citizens Committee for Broadcasting*, decided in 1978.[31] There the Court upheld the FCC's power to bar common ownership of a broadcast station and a daily newspaper located in the same community. As the Court said:

> The regulations are a reasonable means of promoting the public interest in diversified mass communications; thus they do not violate the First Amendment rights of those who will be denied broadcast licenses pursuant to them. Being forced to "choose among applicants for the same facilities," the Commission has chosen on a "sensible basis," one designed to further, rather than contravene, "the system of freedom of expression."[32]

Thus again we see the diversity and scarcity doctrines being used to justify the FCC's power.

While there is no simple way to reconcile all of these recent Supreme Court cases, the broad trend has been toward an increase in government power over broadcast speech that can no longer be simplistically justified by reference to the need for diverse programming. The diversity goal thus may no longer be the determining factor in broadcasting cases to which it is relevant, but neither is it a dead issue. The promotion of diverse programming through diverse ownership, the Court has told us, is acceptable, but the imposition of common carrier obligations is not, at least under the present statute. And the Court is prepared to accept limitations on "extreme" expression, notwithstanding the variety it adds to the airwaves.

Let us turn now to a related aspect of the access problem: Do members of the public have a constitutional right to air time?

The Right of Access

A Constitutional Right of Access?

Proponents of access have argued that the public enjoys a right to obtain access to broadcast time and print space that is superior to the right of total control asserted by media owners. Access champions find support for their view in the central purposes of the first amendment: to encourage the full airing of all viewpoints in the marketplace of political and other ideas. The modern concentration of media power in the hands of broadcast licensees and owners of major journals will, they urge, frustrate that purpose unless outsiders have at least some access to those media.

Media owners have argued that, on the contrary, they enjoy a constitutional right to control the vehicle of speech at issue, be it newspaper or broadcast. The first amendment, they note, prohibits the government from interfering with anyone's speech but it does not guarantee to all an equal platform for their ideas.

From a constitutional point of view, it is fair to say that the debate is over, at least for the time being. That is, it can no longer be cogently argued that the Constitution, in and of itself, guarantees any person a right of access to a particular medium.

The CBS Case. The Supreme Court first reached the problem in the context of the broadcasting industry in *CBS Inc.* v. *Democratic National Committee*, which concerned denials of access by broadcast licensees to two groups that wished air time.[33] One, the Democratic National Committee (DNC), sought a declaratory ruling from the FCC that broadcasters could not, as a general policy, refuse to sell time to responsible entities (such as DNC itself) to solicit funds or to comment on public issues. DNC's experience in the past had led it to believe that it might have difficulty obtaining time for those purposes. The second plaintiff, Business Executives' Move for Peace (BEM), had been rebuffed when it had sought to purchase a series of spots in which to express its views on the Vietnam War. The Commission, in response to complaints brought by these parties, took the position that there was a statutory obligation on the part of broadcasters to allow political parties access for the purpose of soliciting funds.[34] It found that no right, however, inured to any party to purchase other time against the wishes of the broadcasters, even if the time would be used to comment on public issues.[35]

A divided Supreme Court upheld the Commission's position. A threshold issue that particularly troubled the Court was whether the government was sufficiently implicated in the broadcasters' refusal to sell time to bring the first amendment into play. (The amendment has, of course, no applicability to purely private acts.) The Chief Justice, joined by Justices Stewart and Rehnquist, concluded that government action was lacking; and Mr. Justice Douglas agreed in a concurring opinion. Justices White, Blackmun, and Powell refrained from deciding that question, while Justices Brennan and Marshall found that state action was present.

The Chief Justice, although finding a lack of state action, went on to consider the substantive first amendment claim, assuming for the purposes of this part of his opinion that state action was present. Because of the manner in which the other justices voted, the opinion of the Chief Justice became the opinion of the Court only insofar as it did assume the existence of state action. Thus, the views he expressed on the substance of the first amendment problem are not merely *dicta*.

The Chief Justice offered a virtual cannonade of arguments against the access position, with two major underlying themes. The first was that the imposition of an access right would necessarily lead to increased government control over the media because it would require FCC policing of disputes over access time. The second was that the case was decided against the background of existing Commission requirements, pursuant to the fairness doctrine, that coverage of public issues must be adequate and must reflect opposing viewpoints. It is noteworthy that the licensee defendant in the *BEM* case, WTOP, had argued before the Commission and before the Court that in fulfilling its obligation under the fairness doctrine to discuss and offer diverse viewpoints on important public issues, it had broadcast full and fair coverage of the Vietnam War.[36]

Impact of Pending Legislation. This second theme raises an interesting question about the potential impact of the passage of any of several bills, now pending in the Congress, which (as part of a broader deregulation of broadcasting) would limit or eliminate broadcasters' fairness-doctrine obligations.[37] Could broadcasters then still refuse to accept requests to purchase air time? The Chief Justice's opinion seems to say that if there were no statutory fairness obligation, the access proponents would have a far stronger case.

Resolution of the issue thus put would initially depend on the presence or absence of state action. If broadcasters are truly private, they would appear to be under no greater obligation to make time available than is a privately owned newspaper to afford space in its pages. And the latter, we may rest assured, has no such obligation. In *Miami Herald Publishing Co. v. Tornillo*, decided in 1974, the Supreme Court held unconstitutional a Florida statute that imposed on newspapers a requirement that they provide free space to a candidate for elective office whom the paper had previously attacked.[38]

Ironically, legislation of the sort under discussion, which by eliminating the fairness doctrine would apparently make the pro-access claim stronger on the merits, would also, by its deregulatory thrust, weaken the claim that state action is present. This is because a principal point of reliance by those who sought to show state action in *CBS* was the comprehensive regulation of licensees by the Commission and the specific FCC endorsement of the no-access policy at issue there. Even in the absence of the regulation argument, state-action proponents could still rely on such factors as the public "ownership" of the airwaves and the licensees' favored status under government imprimatur. Still, these arguments were insufficient in *CBS* and are likely to remain so in future cases. The Court is simply unlikely to clothe broadcasters in the trappings of state action, with all that would entail from a constitutional point of view, contrary to its clear general trend toward a restrictive view of the state-action concept.[39]

What would be the consequence, in this context, of a holding that state action is present? The "horrible" depicted by Mr. Justice Douglas in his concurring opinion in *CBS* is that the broadcaster would then become for legal purposes a public forum.[40] It would assume the same status as a park, municipal theater, or thoroughfare, which when made available at all for speech purposes must be made available without regard to content and subject only to reasonable regulations of time and manner. Obviously a commercial radio or television station run in that way would find it difficult, if not impossible, to obtain sponsors, and would probably cease to function. Since the purpose of the first amendment is not to interfere with but to encourage speech, any such result would be abhorrent.

Similar reasoning underlies the opinion in *Avins* v. *Rutgers University*, where the Third Circuit rejected the contention of a would-be contributor to the law review of a state school that first amendment doctrine prevented the review from refusing to print his work because of disagreement with its content.[41] We can concur in the result there and yet find a place for public-forum concepts as applied to media that must depend for their continued existence on some form of advertising. We need only distinguish between advertising material on the one hand and editorial material on the other. Pragmatic considerations would not appear to prevent a court from requiring a state-supported publication or broadcaster from offering paid space or time to advertisers on a first-come-first-served or other noncontent basis. Some lower courts have already taken this position with respect to print media.[42]

Assuming for the moment the unlikely event that the Court would find state action on the part of broadcasters if Congress were to eliminate the fairness doctrine, and assuming further that a practical solution to the advertising-access problem is available, would the Court then hold that access is a matter of right? Several of the Chief Justice's major arguments against access (which do not depend on existing fairness obligations) indicate that the answer would still be in the negative.

One such argument against access was the captive-audience theory, which recognizes that a listener or viewer cannot ignore broadcast advertising with quite as much freedom as can the reader of a journal. "It is no answer to say that because we tolerate pervasive commercial advertisement we can also live with its political counterparts," the Chief Justice wrote.[43] This position, which would militate against access even in the absence of the fairness doctrine, is noteworthy because it appears to stand on its head the traditional view of commercial speech as somehow *less* protected than politically oriented speech. True, this two-tier approach to speech has been narrowed, if not eliminated altogether, by the 1976 *Virginia State Board of Pharmacy* case, in which the Court found a first amendment right to advertise drug prices.[44] But to elevate business commercials *over* political announcements seems misguided. There is far more reason to impose the burden of pervasive political messages on a democratic society than that of pervasive inducements to buy soap.

Yet *CBS* is not the only case in which the Court has been willing to distinguish between political and commercial advertising to the detriment of the political. In *Lehman* v. *Shaker Heights*, it held that a municipal bus line (clearly involved in state action) did not offend the Constitution by refusing to sell placard space to candidates for public office while making the space available to commercial advertisers.[45] The pervasiveness or captive-audience hurdle thus remains a considerable one.

Another argument advanced by the Chief Justice is that of wealth domination—the fear that only the rich would gain access because they alone could afford to purchase any meaningful amount of broadcast time.[46] Indeed, a judicially imposed access right after congressional elimination of the fairness doctrine would make this problem even more significant because there would be nothing to prevent domination by a particular viewpoint. Nothing, that is, unless coupled with the right of access would be some sort of constitutionally imposed fairness obligation.[47] And if there were, who would enforce it? Whether one's answer is the Commission or the courts, the result could well be, as Chief Justice Burger feared, the further involvement of government in programming. Nevertheless, it is particularly ironic for the fear of wealth domination to be raised as an objection to access when wealth already so completely dominates the allocation of television time and space in the print media.

In sum, even if the Court got past the state-action issue, it would likely not conclude that the elimination of the fairness doctrine leads to an access requirement.

The FCC as a Source of Access Rules

Although defeating the notion that the first amendment compels broadcasters to open their airwaves to others—even those who wish only to purchase time—the Court in *CBS* expressly left open the possibility that the Commission could by rule (or Congress by statute) impose an access requirement on the broadcasters.[48] Let us proceed on the assumption, therefore, that at least some narrowly drawn access scheme would be permissible under the Constitution, while admittedly not compelled by it.

The Supreme Court's decision in the already discussed *Midwest Video* case,[49] however, barring the imposition by the FCC of an access requirement on cablecasters, casts a cloud over the Commission's statutory authority to impose a system of access. The Court did note that it was not deciding that the Commission had no authority to impose access obligations on licensees,[50] but the language of the opinion is otherwise very broad; and the authority on which it rests—the "no common carrier" provision of the Communications Act[51]—applies to broadcasters as well as cable operators. Thus for any access requirement imposed by the Commission to be approved it would have to be minimal indeed. Even a requirement that as little as one hour per week of air time be turned over to members of the public would not be indisputably valid.

It is in any event unclear that the FCC is ready to impose anything of the sort.

In its recent review of the fairness doctrine in its 1974 *Fairness Report*, the Commission stated that it had not at that time found a plan that would allow access that it considered "both practicable and desirable."[52] It noted these objections: (1) a system of paid access would favor wealthy spokesmen; (2) a first-come-first-served system would not ensure that the most important issues would be discussed on a timely basis; and (3) any alternative system would require the FCC to determine who should be allowed on the air.[53]

The Commission returned to the problem in its *Opinion and Order on Reconsideration of the Fairness Report*, issued in 1976.[54] In the reconsideration opinion, it rejected a proposed access system under which one hour per week would have been set aside for broadcasting by citizen groups and the like. The Commission noted that in addition to the problems it had earlier elucidated there were certain "essential" requirements for an access system: (1) licensee discretion must be preserved; (2) no right of access must accrue to particular persons or groups; (3) the access system must not allow important issues to escape timely public discussion; and (4) the system should not draw the government, and particularly the Commission, into the role of deciding who should be allowed on the air and when.[55] These requirements appear to echo the concerns of the Supreme Court in the *CBS* case.[56]

In litigation challenging the FCC's *Order on Reconsideration* which I have just briefly summarized—*National Citizens Committee for Broadcasting* v. *FCC*—Judge McGowan, writing for a panel of the D.C. Circuit, expressed reservations about the FCC's conclusion.[57] The court remanded the access issue for further Commission inquiry; to date, we still await a response from the FCC.

A major difficulty with the four "essential" requirements the Commission has imposed (as Judge McGowan has also noted[58]) is the unavoidable tension between the requirement that licensee discretion be preserved and the requirement that the system must not draw the government into the role of deciding who should be allowed on the air and when. Taken to its logical conclusion, this tension appears to be an insuperable barrier to any access scheme. So long as the licensees enjoy discretion, their decisions will be subject to challenge before the Commission by disappointed applicants, and the government will be drawn into just such a role.

The solution to this dilemma lies in recognizing that no access system worth the name *would* allow licensee discretion, at least as to content. Under an access system that would reduce the licensee to the role of a traffic cop, it is unlikely that complaints to the Commission would materialize. Moreover, any complaints that might arise would be unlikely to involve the Commission in content-based decision making.

The Commission's problem is certainly not an easy one. There is a danger that an access system would result in overcoverage of some issues and undercoverage of others. But could this not be cured by retaining the fairness doctrine, insofar as it requires a licensee's overall programming to be balanced, while imposing a limited access system?

More difficult still is devising a traffic-control system for the licensees that would avoid the evil of content-oriented decision making on their part. The simplest system, first-come-first-served, might degenerate into a series of self-serving statements by "media hogs." On the other hand, to insist on "responsible spokespersons" is to enmesh the licensee in a quagmire. Establishment groups, almost by definition the most "responsible," are not likely to need this kind of access. Marginal groups may not meet the definition of responsibility, although it is they who are most in need of the access.

Perhaps as good a proposal as is likely to be made is that of the Committee for Open Media, which was discussed in the *NCCB (Fairness)* case by Judge McGowan.[59] Simplified somewhat, it would impose one hour of access time per week on each broadcaster, half of which would be made available on a first-come-first-served basis, while the other half would be reserved for "representative spokespersons." A highly attractive feature of this plan is that persons who are rejected because they are not "representative" can still be assured of eventual access on the first-come-first-served basis. Under such a system the Commission could demur reviewing decisions about representativeness or responsibility except where egregious patterns emerge. The Commission would thus have no greater role than it already has under the fairness doctrine.

Perhaps Jencks is correct in asserting that we ought not to have messages on the pros or cons of abortions during "The Waltons."[60] But this does not mean that broadcasters should not be required to set aside a separate time period during which the audience knows that such subjects will be discussed. One weekly hour of access time is, moreover, so minimal, and so far removed from the imposition of common carrier status, that it ought to be allowable under the Communications Act, even as construed in *Midwest Video*.

Nor must the *CBS* case be regarded as imposing a constitutional barrier to the adoption of such an access system. The *CBS* reservations about access should be kept in perspective as merely objections to the argument then before the Court that the Constitution *required* access in the teeth of the FCC's refusal to impose it. Those objections will not necessarily render unconstitutional an access system prescribed by the Commission. As the Supreme Court has reminded us in the cross-ownership case,[61] as long as the Commission's policy making reasonably furthers a legitimate interest within its statutory powers its judgment will be respected;[62] and the promotion of broadcast diversity has been repeatedly recognized by the courts as such an interest.[63]

Enhancing Structural Diversity

Without gainsaying the importance of the arguments in favor of public access to regular commercial channels, it is vital that we not overlook the potential role of structural diversification in opening broadcasting up to multiple voices. By this I mean devices that encourage diversity by affecting the structure of the broadcasting industry without making a broadcaster a common carrier. Structural solutions are particularly desirable because they tend to have a minimal impact on the free-speech rights of individual broadcasters.

Such structural devices include the rules barring multimedia ownership approved by the Supreme Court in *FCC* v. *NCCB*.[64] The Prime Time Access Rule, although narrowing somewhat a licensee's program choices by limiting the use of network programming at certain hours, may strengthen the part played in broadcasting by local voices and thus is also a judicially approved source of structural diversity.[65]

There are other potential structural mechanisms for increasing diversity that should not be forgotten. One important means of diversifying the voices heard on the air is to strengthen and increase the number of minority broadcasters. The Commission has adopted that policy[66] and taken steps, albeit limited ones, toward its implementation,[67] the results of which have begun to materialize.[68] However, the full realization of this goal will require more drastic means such as loan programs, license allocations, and other steps that may require government action beyond the Commission's present power.

Another salutary mechanism for increasing diversity would be increased financial support of public broadcasting. Great care must be taken, however, to guard its independence from government more effectively than has been done in the past.[69]

As the technology of broadcasting changes, new possibilities for creating diversity without silencing existing voices are likely to emerge. Let us hope that the Commission, or Congress where appropriate, is quick to seize them.

Conclusion

Given the network domination described in previous chapters,[70] the homogeneity of so much of broadcasting, and the powerful impact of television on American life, it is imperative that decision makers become more sensitive to the goal that broadcasting speak with many voices. When genuine diversity of speech does emerge we should be slow to stifle it. The FCC should thus see itself as first and foremost a guardian of free expression, not a policeman of broadcast content. It should not be too much to hope that structural diversity will be promoted. It cannot be too much to insist that the diversity that does emerge will be protected.

Notes

1. 319 U.S. 190 (1943).
2. FCC, Report on Chain Broadcasting 91-92 (1941).
3. 319 U.S. at 226.
4. Communications Act of 1934, §§307(a), 309(a), 47 U.S.C. §§307(a), 309(a) (1976).
5. 319 U.S. at 226.
6. 395 U.S. 367 (1969).
7. *Id*. at 379-86.
8. *Id*. at 386.
9. *Id*. at 389.
10. *Id*. at 390-91.
11. *Id*. at 390.
12. *Id*.
13. 405 F.2d 1082 (D.C. Cir. 1968), *cert. denied*, 396 U.S. 842 (1969).
14. 478 F.2d 594 (D.C. Cir.), *cert. denied*, 414 U.S. 914 (1973).
15. *See id.*, 478 F.2d at 603-06 (separate statement of Bazelon, C.J., on motion for rehearing *en banc*); Yale Broadcasting Co. v. FCC, 414 U.S. 914 (1973) (Douglas, J., dissenting from denial of certiorari); N.Y. Times, March 7, 1971, at 28, col. 3.
16. 47 C.F.R. §73.658(k) (1979).
17. 516 F.2d 526 (2d Cir. 1975).
18. 491 F.2d 219 (3d Cir.), *vacated as moot*, 420 U.S. 371 (1974).

19. 438 U.S. 726 (1978).

20. Pacifica Foundation, 56 F.C.C.2d 94 (1975).

21. FCC v. Pacifica Foundation, 438 U.S. 726, 741, 746-47 (1978).

22. *Id.* at 748.

23. *Id.* at 749-50.

24. *Id.* at 749.

25. NBC v. United States, 319 U.S. 190, 226 (1945). *See* p. 138 *supra*.

26. 440 U.S. 689 (1979).

27. *Id.* at 691-96. The access regulations were adopted in Report and Order, Docket No. 20528, 59 F.C.C.2d 294 (1976), and codified in 47 C.F.R. §§76.254, 76.256 (1976).

28. 440 U.S. at 709 n. 19.

29. Communications Act of 1934, §3(h), 47 U.S.C. §153(h) (1976).

30. 440 U.S. at 705.

31. 436 U.S. 775 (1978).

32. *Id.* at 802.

33. 412 U.S. 94 (1973) [hereinafter cited as CBS].

34. Democratic National Committee, 25 F.C.C.2d 216, 229-30 (1970).

35. *Id.* at 226; Business Executives' Move for Vietnam Peace, 25 F.C.C.2d 242, 247 (1970). The D.C. Circuit reversed both cases on this issue. Business Executives Move for Vietnam Peace v. FCC, 450 F.2d 642 (D.C. Cir. 1971).

36. 412 U.S. at 98.

37. H.R. 3333, 96th Cong., 1st Sess., §462(b) (1979); S. 622, 96th Cong., 1st Sess., §301 (1979). A third bill, S. 611, 96th Cong., 1st Sess. (1979), would leave the fairness doctrine intact.

38. 418 U.S. 241 (1974).

39. *See, e.g.*, Jackson v. Metropolitan Edison Co., 419 U.S. 345 (1974); Moose Lodge No. 107 v. Irvis, 407 U.S. 163 (1972).

40. CBS, *supra* note 33, at 161-62 (Douglas, J., concurring).

41. 385 F.2d 151 (3d Cir. 1967), *cert. denied*, 390 U.S. 920 (1968).

42. *See, e.g.*, Zucker v. Panitz, 299 F. Supp. 102 (S.D.N.Y. 1969).

43. CBS, *supra* note 33, at 128.

44. Virginia State Board of Pharmacy v. Virginia Citizens Consumer Council, Inc., 425 U.S. 748 (1976).

45. 418 U.S. 298 (1974).

46. CBS, *supra* note 33, at 123.

47. Cf. Red Lion Broadcasting Co. v. FCC, 395 U.S. 367, 390 (1969).

48. CBS, *supra* note 33, at 131.

49. FCC v. Midwest Video Corp., 440 U.S. 689 (1979).

50. *Id.* at 705 n. 14.

51. Communications Act of 1934, §3(h), 47 U.S.C. §153(h) (1976).

52. 48 F.C.C.2d 1, 28 (1974).

53. *Id.* at 29.

54. 58 F.C.C.2d 691 (1976).

55. *Id.* at 699.

56. CBS, *supra* note 33.

57. 567 F.2d 1095 (D.C. Cir. 1977), *cert. denied*, 436 U.S. 926 (1978).

58. *Id.,.* 567 F.2d at 1114.

59. *Id.* at 1112-15.

60. R. Jencks, *supra* at 51.

61. FCC v. National Citizens Committee for Broadcasting, 436 U.S. 775 (1978).

62. *Id.* at 796.

63. *E.g.*, *id.* at 796, 801-02; Red Lion Broadcasting Co. v. FCC, 395 U.S. 367, 389-90 (1969); Mt. Mansfield Television, Inc. v. FCC, 442 F.2d 470, 477-79 (2d Cir. 1970).

64. FCC v. National Citizens Committee for Broadcasting, 436 U.S. 775 (1978).

65. National Ass'n of Independent Television Producers & Distribs. v. FCC, 516 F.2d 526 (2d Cir. 1975); Mt. Mansfield Television, Inc. v. FCC, 442 F.2d 470 (2d Cir. 1970).

66. Statement of Policy on Minority Ownership of Broadcasting Facilities, 68 F.C.C.2d 979 (1978).

67. *Id.* at 982-84.

68. *See* Broadcasting, Aug. 28, 1978, at 30-31; Broadcasting, Sept. 25, 1978, at 27-28, 50-51; Broadcasting, June 11, 1979, at 19-20.

69. Carnegie Commission on the Future of Public Broadcasting, A Public Trust 41-51 (Bantam ed. 1979).

70. A. Pearce, *supra* at 3; S. Robb, *supra* at 73.

17 What Is First Amendment Theory?

James C.N. Paul

Many contemporary critics of first amendment decisions—particularly those of the Supreme Court—assert, almost as a recurring theme, that the courts are not paying enough attention to basic theory.[1] It is clear that there is no common consensus on what "first amendment theory" is; like economics, it is a dismal science and a very ephermeral one.

The first amendment in its essence is a standard by which things that affect communications are to be judged. As a standard, it calls for evaluative criteria, and therefore one must think of the values that are embodied in those criteria. There are four general themes or values that find their way at various times into opinions of the Court and into the writings of commentators on first amendment problems.

The first theme is that the first amendment really is a basic guarantee of individual autonomy—that individuals cannot be autonomous unless they have a right to self-expression.[2] This bears very heavily on problems of obscenity and of so-called "dirty words" in contexts other than broadcasting.[3]

The second theme is the famous justification of John Stuart Mill,[4] differently elaborated but more or less echoed by Holmes in his *Abrams* dissent: that we have free speech because truth can only find its way in the free marketplace of ideas, in the clash of debate and of ideologies.[5] That is the value the first amendment is trying to promote.

A third approach that has certainly found its way in and out of various opinions at different times is the philosophy articulated by Meiklejohn that the first amendment exists as a basic part of self-government, that self-government is impossible without it, and that the fundamental value of the first amendment is to permit interest groups to speak in the political process and to promote its functioning.[6]

A fourth and final justification is that, based on what little history is known about the first amendment and on eighteenth-century American writings, the amendment really does have to do with the press as a distinct beneficiary of rights.[7] The Founding Fathers believed that the press is a part of the state—that it is kind of a watchdog over official power (or abuse of power), over how the commonwealth is being run, and over those to whom we entrust its running.[8]

First amendment theory is very different from economic theory, and the interface of the two is difficult to work out. Clearly, first amendment theory is not coextensive with the ideas of Adam Smith, and it may very well justify tinkering with economic structures in the marketplace that do not work to serve first amendment goals. First amendment theory also may mean—and does mean in my view—that we treat different media differently under the law because they *are* different for many purposes.[9] Therefore, whether we are discussing scarcity or some other issue, it seems that what we should be looking at, particularly in television, is how that medium is being used under the present legal regime that controls it, in terms of furthering first amendment values.

These things may seem obvious, but they sometimes get lost in debates about application of the first amendment to this or that problem. If we return to and think about the values previously mentioned, or whatever other values have that kind of preeminent place in analysis of first amendment problems, it might lead to a more informed discussion of the access problem.

We must concern ourselves with the development of a regime of regulation of television that will best serve our first amendment values; and we must worry much more about the access problem than the Commission does. This is not to say that the FCC has not worried about it, but simply that this problem is not going to go away, that it is on the agenda, and that it is crucial to find ways of enlarging access to the use of this medium.

Access does not necessarily mean that everyone has the opportunity to air a message. But access could mean that we expand the obligation of the broadcaster to provide more opportunities for groups that it considers significant spokespersons for significant issues to develop programs and get on the air. It is obviously important to take into account the various practical problems that Chase has discussed;[10] and although it will not be easy, at least some of them can be solved.

The CBS policy outlined by Jencks poses a real issue.[11] CBS (like the other networks) said in effect that it was going to do all the public-affairs broadcasting and that no one else could use the airwaves controlled by CBS for that purpose.[12] This may be the best way of furthering first amendment values. But we should not simply take the broadcasters' word that that is so. There are very strong feelings among minority groups, for example, that minority concerns are not being adequately articulated over the national airwaves and in the national media.

I agree with those who say that detailed regulation by the FCC is not the solution to the problem of access. I also agree that not every aspect of the access problem is a constitutional issue. Nevertheless, we must insist that the broadcasting industry pay more attention to first amendment values than it generally has in the past.

Notes

1. *E.g.*, Blasi, *The Checking Value in First Amendment Theory*, 1977 Am. Bar Foundation Research J. 521, 525-26.

2. *See id.* at 544-48; T. Emerson, The System of Freedom of Expression 6 (1970).

3. *E.g.*, Cohen v. California, 403 U.S. 15 (1971).

4. J.S. Mill, On Liberty 32 (R. McCallum ed. 1947).

5. Abrams v. United States, 250 U.S. 616, 630 (1919) (Holmes, J., dissenting).

6. A. Meiklejohn, Free Speech and Its Relation to Self-Government 63 (1948).

7. *See* Blasi, *The Checking Value in First Amendment Theory*, 1977 Am. Bar Foundation Research J. 521, 532-38. The significance of such historical facts has, however, been deprecated in Lasswell, Book Review, 22 Geo. Wash. L. Rev. 383 (1953).

8. *See* Blasi, *The Checking Value in First Amendment Theory*, 1977 Am. Bar Foundation Research J. 521; New York Times Co. v. United States, 403 U.S. 713, 717 (1971) (Black, J.).

9. *See* Joseph Burstyn Inc. v. Wilson, 343 U.S. 495, 502-503 (1952); Kovacs v. Cooper, 336 U.S. 77 (1949).

10. O. Chase, *supra* at 147-49.

11. R. Jencks, *supra* at 48-52.

12. *See generally* Neubauer, *The Networks' Policy Against Freelance Documentaries: A Proposal for Commission Action*, 30 Fed. Com. L.J. 117 (1978).

18 Some Unanswered Questions about the First Amendment

Eugene Aleinikoff

There are several important questions about the first amendment and mass communications that have plagued us for many years. And, as Chase pointed out in chapter 16 of this book, these problems still have not been solved.

The first question that comes to mind is whether the first amendment has positive, as well as negative, ramifications. Is it, as we thought for so long, simply an injunction against government censorship or proscription of speech? Or does it go further and impose an affirmative obligation on the government to see that broadcasters and publishers provide channels of speech for various segments of our population?

This issue first became prominent in the *Red Lion* case.[1] There, against the wishes of the commercial networks, the fairness doctrine regulations of the FCC were upheld. They imposed a positive requirement that broadcasters not only air all sides and points of view on those controversial issues they cover, but also that they provide reply time to people for answering charges against their personal integrity. This led to a new movement among those concerned with free speech—largely through those people who were involved in media-reform movements—to think in terms of the positive aspects of the first amendment.[2] But the question of what positive action the government must take in order to comply with the first amendment has not been fully answered.

Since *Red Lion* was based on the scarcity of channels and the need for regulation to prevent interference between channels, its holding has not been extended to other media, although some commentators have argued that even the print media should be subject to some kind of fairness doctrine.[3] In the *Tornillo* case, however, the Supreme Court held decisively that in terms of access the fairness doctrine concept does not apply to any media other than those that had been subjected to such regulation under the Communications Act.[4]

This leads us to a second unanswered question: Why is there a difference between television and newspapers—between electronic and print media? Scarcity of frequencies has been cited again and again and has always been disproved. There are more television channels in most cities than there are newspapers, and there are certainly more radio frequencies almost everywhere. It is no more expensive to start a radio station than it is to start a newspaper in this country. It is not that there is no scarcity—there is a scarcity, and that will still be true even with twenty or more channels on the cable or from satellites. But there is an even greater scarcity of newspapers, so that this factor should not account for differential treatment of broadcasting and newspapers in first amendment terms. If anything, it seems that there should be less regulation of broadcasting rather than more.

There is, however, some reason for that difference, and not just that it started that way, with regulation of broadcasting and not of newspapers—not just because Thomas Paine lived in the 1700s and television began in the 1900s. There must be some other reason.

That is why I disagree to some extent with many commentators' views of the *Pacifica* case.[5] That case is, at least, an attempt to supply a reason (other than scarcity) for applying different rules to television and radio than to print media. Whether one calls it pervasiveness of television in our living rooms, or its availability to children, or something else, the difference exists and everyone recognizes it. As an illustration, political candidates still flood the last few weeks of their campaigns with millions of dollars worth of television commercials, much more than they spend on billboard and newspaper advertising. Obviously, candidates find that television has a greater impact than other media on potential voters.

We may need more first amendment training, since the first amendment we are dealing with today is different from the first amendment as perceived only in terms of print media. The *Pacifica* case was the first case to talk about this changed perception, apart from the old scarcity argument. *Pacifica* therefore may introduce some flexibility in dealing with these two different types of media, without one's having to be apologetic about making unreal distinctions.

A third important but unanswered question is: Whose first amendment is this anyhow? Is it the broadcasters' (as it is the publishers')? Is it other groups'—groups that would like to carry their messages to the people? Or does it belong to the people, who are entitled to full information from all sides so that they can know what is going on? The Supreme Court has said that the first amendment protects different kinds of people at different times, depending on the issues; and this is understandable. These cases are unusual in that they deal with conflicts, not between different basic constitutional principles, but between different people's rights under the same constitutional principle. No one has really solved this question.

There is a corollary to the question. Even if we were to conclude that the first amendment primarily protects the broadcaster, we still do not really know who "the broadcaster" is. Is it the local station that broadcasts as the outlet of the network? Is it the network as a program source? Is it the producer who produces programs for the network? Or is it the writer who creates those programs for the producer?

These are not idle questions, because arguments about these issues go on constantly. Indeed, a producer recently sued WGBH, Boston's public-television station, for having changed one of his programs about the situation of blacks in Britain, saying that it violated his freedom of speech to have the station change his program and then distribute it for broadcast by any number of local PBS stations. Although the producer was denied an injunction,[6] WGBH decided to show the unedited producer's version of the program as well as the edited version that the lawsuit attacked.

Perhaps the ultimate unanswered question is whether any of these issues are capable of being solved in our constitutional process—whether the Supreme Court really should be deciding on "seven dirty words" or should, for that matter, be taking on any of these things piecemeal. Perhaps, as Chase has implied, the FCC or the Congress, as representatives of the people, might really be the best ones to reach conclusions about how to make the communications apparatus that is developing so madly these days available for use by the American people.[7]

This does not mean that the FCC must accept the concept of three networks in television any more than it must go along with all the other broadcasting patterns that now exist. Maybe the networks will disappear of their own accord when more channels come into being—just as they disappeared, more or less, in radio. Everybody assumes that there are going to be technological innovations that will create multiple channels across the country in one way or another, whether by cable, by dividing or fractionalizing channels, or by drop-ins or some other means. Eventually everyone with a home receiver will get innumerable channels from direct satellite broadcasts.[8]

The question is whether we really want to have these issues solved in first amendment terms by the Supreme Court, beyond the Court's making sure that what the government does is not unreasonable and does not amount to censorship.

Thus as long as the Commission avoids censoring actual program content, there seems to be no constitutional problem with the FCC telling licensees that they must have ten hours of news programming a week or may not have more than twenty-five hours a week of entertainment programming. In fact, this is similar to what the Commission did in New Jersey when it encouraged WNET to increase the amount of its New Jersey-oriented programming.[9] Nor do there seem to be any problems connected with mandating that each station must broadcast a given number of hours on the political campaigns in its area; I would not consider that a violation of broadcasters' first amendment rights.

On the other hand, we must be particularly careful to avoid government censorship where public broadcasting is involved. Because it is a government-financed system, it involves state action to a far greater extent than does private broadcasting. If Congress were to attach conditions to appropriations for the Corporation for Public Broadcasting (CPB), earmarking them for specific programming (such as ballet), or barring their use for other types (such as news or public-affairs programming), this might violate the first amendment rights of CPB or of individual public stations. There are strong arguments on both sides of this question.

Yet even in cases involving public broadcasting there is an overemphasis on the first amendment. For example, in a recent decision, *Community-Service Broadcasting of Mid-America* v. *FCC*,[10] where the issue was what records public-broadcasting stations must keep of their public-affairs programs, the D.C. Circuit held that the requirement that public-broadcasting stations maintain audio recordings of "any program in which any issue of public importance is discussed"[11] was unconstitutional, as being in violation of the first amendment and as creating inequality of treatment, since commercial broadcasters were not subject to the same depth of regulation. The decision seems to imply that if the same kind of regulation were imposed on commercial broadcasters as on public broadcasters it might not then be unconstitutional. Why, we may fairly ask, should decisions of this sort be made on a constitutional basis?

A lawyer knows that if the law is not on your side, you argue the facts. A similar process seems to be at work here: If the statute is not on your side, you argue the Constitution. Perhaps we have become "overconstitutionalized," and it now may be time to retreat from this overemphasis on the first amendment and to focus instead on the Congress and the Commission as perhaps being more suitable agencies than the Supreme Court to deal with the extremely complex and ever dynamic problems in American broadcasting.

Notes

1. Red Lion Broadcasting Co. v. FCC, 395 U.S. 367 (1969).

2. *See, e.g.*, the proposal of the Committee for Open Media, referred to in O. Chase, *supra* at 148, and discussed by the FCC in its Opinion and Order on Reconsideration of the Fairness Report, 58 F.C.C.2d 691, 699 (1976), and by Judge McGowan in National Citizens Committee for Broadcasting v. FCC, 567 F.2d 1095, 1112-14 (D.C. Cir. 1977), *cert. denied*, 436 U.S. 926 (1978).

3. *E.g.*, Barron, *Access to the Press—A New First Amendment Right*, 80 Harv. L. Rev. 1641 (1967).

4. Miami Herald Publishing Co. v. Tornillo, 418 U.S. 241 (1974).

5. FCC v. Pacifica Foundation, 438 U.S 726 (1978).

6. Koff v. WGBH Educational Foundation, Inc., Civ. No. 78-1951-C-W (D. Mass. Aug. 9, 1978).

7. *See* O. Chase, *supra* at 146-150.

8. *See* Broadcasting, Aug. 6, 1979, at 27-28.

9. *See, e.g.*, Educational Broadcasting Corp., 61 F.C.C.2d 907, 908 (1976).

10. 593 F.2d 1102 (D.C. Cir. 1978) (*en banc*).

11. 47 U.S.C. §399(b) (Supp. V 1975). Regulations promulgated there-under, Report and Order, Docket No. 19861, 57 F.C.C.2d 19 (1975), were also held invalid.

19 The First Amendment and the Network Inquiry

Paul B. Jones

My duties as assistant general counsel of the FCC are focused on "special projects." This includes such diverse matters as the Network Inquiry,[1] the Children's Inquiry,[2] and the Commission's investigation of the potential of low-powered transmitters.[3]

Each of these areas contains profound first amendment implications. All of us at the Commission have a great responsibility since our decisions obviously play an important part in the development of first amendment doctrine. In discharging that responsibility we should be concerned with the development of a coherent first amendment theory.

There is an inherent dilemma in first amendment doctrine as it applies to the broadcast media. The first amendment supports regulation based on the theory of scarcity. This theory states that there are many who wish to broadcast and only a few who can actually do so. Given the scarcity premise, the theory is that the first amendment interests protected are those of the general public, the nominal "owners" of the broadcast spectrum.[4] However, those who have been granted a license to broadcast also have first amendment liberties, which reserve to them the right to select, edit, and broadcast material.[5] The Communications Act also affords broadcasters protection against censorship.[6] Although this is an oversimplification, therein lies the dilemma.

The speeches and discussions at the Network Television Conference reflect a concern about what many consider the failure of network-program content to satisfy the desires for greater variety in programming and for audience-specific programming. Apparently some people feel that they have not had an opportunity to participate effectively in the development of broadcast programming. Still others complain that they have been denied an opportunity to speak out and have their views presented via the broadcast media, and hence urge the adoption of access requirements.

The FCC's Network Inquiry staff is mindful of the first amendment dilemma inherent in our system of broadcasting—a system that permits regulation in the "public interest" while preventing the Commission from telling broadcasters what they must program in order to serve specific interest groups. It is always difficult to predict answers to first amendment problems, particularly with respect to the broadcast media. But the questions being addressed in the Network Inquiry are designed to analyze the

163

economic structure of our broadcasting system, with the ultimate goal being to increase viewer choice while minimizing the burden of regulation.[7] Perhaps, as Chase suggests, these goals can best be achieved through structural diversity.[8] But whatever the outcome of the inquiry, it will reflect the staff's continuing concern for the first amendment values that are so important a part of our constitutional heritage.

Notes

1. Notice of Inquiry, Docket No. 21049, 62 F.C.C.2d 548 (1977); Further Notice of Inquiry, Docket No. 21049, 69 F.C.C.2d 1524 (1978).

2. Second Notice of Inquiry, Docket No. 19142, 68 F.C.C.2d 1344 (1978).

3. Notice of Inquiry, BC Docket No. 78-253, 68 F.C.C.2d 1525 (1978).

4. *E.g.*, Red Lion Broadcasting Co. v. FCC, 395 U.S. 367, 390 (1969).

5. CBS Inc. v. FCC, 412 U.S. 94, 110-11, 124-25 (1973).

6. Communications Act of 1934, §326, 47 U.S.C. §326 (1976).

7. *See* Further Notice of Inquiry, Docket No. 21049, 69 F.C.C.2d 1524 (1978).

8. O. Chase, *supra* at 149-50.

Part VI
Reports from the Future

20 Cable and Pay Television

Peter A. Gross

I believe it was Lord Rothschild who advised a young colleague trying to learn about international monetary exchange that the subject was so complicated there were only two people in the world who understood it: a director of the Bank of England and an obscure clerk in the Bank of France—and that they thoroughly disagreed with each other.

"Reporting from the Future" is rife with uncertainties and disagreements. Conjectures about the impact of cable and pay television are particularly so because they are woven from guesses about technology, business, programming, politics, and law. But part of the excitement of our business is the very intensity of this mixture, the need to make these guesses and the way we consequently all pretend to be somewhat expert in areas beyond our training.

In boldness, then, perhaps typical of our new industry, I will begin conjuring up an image of the future in this uncertain area by stating that many of us in pay television think that most of what has been discussed in this volume is about to become ancient history and most of the major problems and issues in fact may not be such vibrant concerns in the future.

The Power of the Commercial Networks

In addressing the effect cable and pay television are likely to have on the commercial broadcast networks, it is helpful to begin with an understanding of where the broadcast networks get their power and influence. If I can offer a quick and somewhat simplistic overview, I think the major strengths and weaknesses of the commercial broadcast networks ultimately derive from their local delivery mode: use of the limited broadcast spectrum to reach homes. Use of the airwaves has led to a business with two significant and interacting attributes: financing by the intrusion of commercials, which translates viewership levels into revenue (and programming and promotion dollars); and the technical limitations of spectrum utilization, which translate the scarcity of the facilities available to reach the audience into programming decisions and power.

This chapter contains Mr. Gross's individual views. Although he wishes to acknowledge the helpful insights of many of his colleagues, he is not writing as a representative of Home Box Office.

The system of financing network broadcasting through commercial sponsorship is a historical consequence of limited-spectrum technology. Imagine yourself in the position of a broadcaster in the early days of radio and then of television, when you had the technical means of delivering an audio or video signal to a great number of homes, but had yet to figure out how this wonderful technology could be turned into a profitable business. Of course, you could try to make your profits from the sale of home receiving sets, but you did not have to be a broadcaster to manufacture or sell receiving sets. Eventually, you would have no business unless you could get somebody to pay you for broadcasting. You could not get the viewers to pay because of the nature of the reception devices used in their homes. You needed to find another way and the obvious one was to take the model from the print media—magazines and newspapers—and use a sponsorship or advertising-supported system. But unlike the print model, you could not have any subscription revenues; it all had to be from sponsorship. And the advertisements, to achieve their fullest value, had to intrude on the viewer's time and on the flow of the programming itself; the audience in the middle of a story could not choose to flip the page.

There simply was no feasible way to effect the usual economic system: direct payment by consumers for what they want. Instead, commercial sponsorship, an indirect and inefficient system, evolved as the sole means of financing broadcasting and the system itself both dictated the nature of programming and put an even higher premium on the available broadcast frequencies.

A commercial television network must cover its costs, including the cost of programming, and make a profit. It talks to a toothpaste manufacturer who says, in effect, "We'll put an advertisement for toothpaste in the middle of your program, on the assumption that it will have some effect on some of the people watching, so that the next time they go to buy toothpaste they'll be more likely to buy our brand." Although this system produces profits, it denies viewers the kind of leverage they could enjoy from paying directly for their programming preferences, it does not give broadcasters the revenues they could enjoy from a direct economic relationship with viewers, its efficacy depends on interrupting programs, and it makes raw audience size the goal of programming.

Because value to sponsors is almost exclusively a matter of the size of the audience, the advertising base achieved by the aggregate number of viewers reached by commerical networks translates directly into the revenues available for programming, promotion, transmission, and other expenditures. This tends to reduce programming decisions to attempts to maximize audience size at every moment. It also means that any would-be commercial broadcast-network competitor might find it prohibitively difficult to obtain the advertising base represented by the five VHF outlets owned and operated by each existing commercial network and the still-wider base represented by its affiliates. Without a competitive advertising base a network can not compete in the commercial-network business and access to that advertising base is foreclosed by spectrum limitations.

This has led to the intensified economics discussed at the Network Television Conference and in this volume,[1] where the more a network has, the less possible it becomes for a new network to compete. And the situation also itensifies the first amendment problems discussed in this volume: since no one else can reach the audience the networks can, we are faced with the odious choice of limiting their speech or, as a practical matter, limiting the ability of others to speak with equal reach and effectiveness.[2]

The commercial networks' power, then, has been the economic and historical consequence of broadcasting in the limited spectrum—a power vulnerable, for reasons outlined in the following section, to the new technologies, which remove the premium of spectrum allocation and allow direct-payment economics.

The Nature of Cable and Pay Television

Within the term "cable" in this discussion, I include not only coaxial cable, but all "hardwired" systems, such as fibreoptics. I do not want to focus on the use of cable systems to retransmit broadcast signals, although that undeniably is a very important part of what cable has been. Such retransmission provides a significant service to the public, but I expect it will become less significant in the future as more services originate specifically for cable subscribers.

It may be instructive to identify the functions or attributes of cable which are relevant to the commercial-network problems already discussed. First, cable does not rely on the limited spectrum to reach homes; it delivers a signal over a wire. Once the system is in place the actual costs of delivering programming are relatively low, particularly compared to television broadcasting,[3] and there are relatively easy ways to control the reach of the signal and thus provide for direct payment by consumers.[4]

Second, and more important, is cable's multiple-channel capacity. There may be nine channels of programming on broadcast television in the largest cities in the United States, but only one, two, or three, in most parts of the country.[5] In contrast, there are potentially as many as thirty-six channels on a cable system today in some of those cities—and with the right economics and technology, there could easily be more than 150. The multitude of channels dissipates the intensity of competition over gaining access to viewers. And no single source of programming could dominate the programming requirements of a cable system—even one affiliated with that source. Cable systems have both the capacity and the financial motivation to offer a wide and diverse range of programming and other services from a variety of sources. In fact, the practice of "tiering" a number of separate services is already becoming standard practice in the cable industry.

To understand the impact of multiple-channel capacity on cable programming and on public policy, it is important to recognize that cable television is not a variation of broadcast television. The issues in cable, from a public-interest or any other perspective, are wholly different from the issues presented by traditional broadcasting. I have suggested that the nature of broadcast programming results from spectrum scarcity and the advertising basis of television economics. A broadcast network has a single channel and wants to maximize its audience at all times. With relatively few broadcast stations in each market, programming designed to attract a large share of the widest possible group will be likely to realize higher viewership levels than will more diverse or specialized programming designed to appeal to a narrow audience segment. By gathering the largest possible audience at all times, potential advertising revenues, and hence profits, will be maximized.

On the other hand, a cable system with thirty-six or more channels to program sees financial benefits in programming for specific audiences in addition to addressing general audiences because its goal is not necessarily to maximize the audience at every moment on any one channel, but to maximize the combined revenues for all its channels.[6] Using some of its channel capacity to provide significant diversity and to appeal to specialized audiences adds subscribers and revenues. Thus, for example, programs for ethnic groups, instructional programs, programs for senior citizens, and medical, cultural, or financial channels can become economically feasible, as each of them adds or helps to keep subscribers and many of them garner previously untapped subscriber or advertiser revenues. There has been a stunning variety of programs and services proposed and, because the economics of cable (as well as the franchising process) encourage them, we are beginning to see some of them offered by cable systems.

A perhaps mundane example is local high school or college sports which rarely make much of a business for a commercial broadcaster, but many cable systems carry local sports with great success. There is no need to sacrifice children's programs to soap operas, or town-council meetings to game shows; cable systems find it profitable to offer all of them simultaneously. Urban cable systems serving the cultural mix of New York City began a number of years ago providing Chinese, German, French, black, Spanish, and a multitude of other specialized programming reflecting the cultural diversity of New York.

It is not that the individuals who operate cable systems are naturally more concerned about their community than are broadcasters; the point is that each broadcaster must maximize the audiences on his single channel at every moment of the day, while a cable operator benefits from direct payment by subscribers and the capacity to provide many channels of programming. The economics and technology of cable foster a natural democracy in programming which replaces the plurality programming of broadcasting.

The program diversity likely to be realized will take many forms, including general entertainment channels, movie channels, all-sports channels, and all-news channels. Variations of subscriber-supported and commercially supported services would seem a likely diversification in the future, as the present commercial networks and others wishing to enter that business will offer their commercially supported programming within a new kind of spectrum.

This is not a glimpse of "blue sky." It is presently occurring, and it is based on real numbers. Assume, for example, that a community has three broadcast television stations. Each broadcaster, in trying to maximize his revenues, will carry programming designed to attract the maximum audience at all moments. Simple math reveals that as a general rule he makes an unwise financial decision if he chooses to direct any programming to a specific audience that is smaller than one-third of the potential general audience available at that hour. With four stations, it is 25 percent; with five, it is 20 percent; and so on. Through this analysis, a broadcaster would have to be in a community with ten broadcast stations before it would make sense for him to direct programming at a special-interest group consisting of 10 percent of his potential audience (or 15 percent if he assumes that a third of that group will be part of the general audience watching his competitors). In contrast, a cable-system operator, with his multiple-channel capacity (and his ability, as discussed below, to derive revenues from the variety of programming carried during the course of a month) can profit from carrying both general- and specific-audience programming.

Part of the diversity of cable may inure to the benefit of advertisers by providing a new range of opportunities for advertisers of specialized products, since only advertisers aiming at the mass audience find it worthwhile to pay commercial network rates. An illustration might be the photographic-equipment industry. Photographic-equipment advertising on television is usually for Instamatic cameras, Polaroids, snapshot film, or other items that the average American family, but not necessarily the camera buff, would purchase. It may not be economically efficient to advertise very expensive cameras and equipment on commercial television, where the advertiser wishing to reach a specific audience must also pay for the large part of the audience he is not trying to reach. But with a multitude of channels available, a company like Nikon, Hassleblad, or Omega may find it attractive to sponsor an informative series on photography aimed at an audience which is much smaller but consists predominantly of its potential customers.

Perhaps the most significant consequence of delivering programming by cable is that it affords, as part of its diversity, the opportunity of direct and more efficient economics: payment by the consumer for what he wants. By using scramblers, converters, or frequency traps, a cable system can allow an individual viewer to pay for the programming he wants to see and neither the cable system nor the viewer is trapped in the syndrome of indirect economics and mass-appeal programming dictated by commercially supported broadcast television.

This affects the content of the service itself. The absence of commercial intrusions permits presentation of motion pictures, for example, in the same form as they were exhibited in theaters. Programming need not be broken into ten- or twelve-minute segments (each with its mini-plot designed to sustain viewer interest), but allows for sequences of greater duration. Pay television has a flexibility in rhythm and pace impossible in commercial television. Furthermore, the tastes and public images of advertisers are of no concern to the programmers and the viewing audience is limited to those desiring the programming. As a result, pay television offers a refreshing freedom from many of the content restrictions artificially imposed on traditional broadcasters. Viewers decide directly through their subscription dollars what they want to see.[7]

Although intelligently comparing the per-viewer revenues derived from pay-television exhibition and those derived from commercial exhibition is a slippery and not necessarily revealing task, it is difficult to understand how, except in extraordinary circumstances, an advertiser would be willing to pay more for a viewer to see his message than the viewer himself would be willing to pay to see the program without the message. A careful analysis of this issue must take into account the uniqueness of the particular pay-televison program and the intrusiveness of commercials. Some of the uniqueness may result merely from the lack of commercial interruptions—a phenomenon more significant in the presentation of a motion picture, for example, than in the carriage of a baseball game. Another possible source of uniqueness, and consequently consumer willingness to pay, is whether the programming is generally available to the consumer on commercial television. These factors suggest that a sorting out of program formats and contents between commercial and pay television (though both will be delivered by cable) will eventually occur through the consumer responses to the functional attributes of each, much as commercial television and radio eventually developed programming modes appropriate to each of them.

Feature films, for all the reasons discussed, appear to make functional sense in a pay-television schedule and the marketplace has indicated that it makes sense for us at Home Box Office (HBO) in licensing the motion-picture exhibition rights to pay significantly more per viewer than what a commercial network has traditionally paid. The license fees paid by HBO are already approaching the license fees paid by the three commercial networks, and that is occurring while we still serve a small percentage of the audience available to them. Our viewers have demonstrated an eagerness to pay for the programming they want.

Of course, while comparing pay-television license fees with those of the networks, I do not mean to imply that films or other programs are licensed to pay television instead of the networks. It is often a matter of uniqueness through sequence. Even when we become able to offer the movie companies as much as the networks as an industry—and I think that will be within a few years—we will not take movies away from commercial-television exhibition. There is no reason to think that a movie company would ever want to do business that way or that our subscribers would become unwilling to pay for an uninterrupted exhibition of a film because it will subsequently become available with commercials on broadcast television. What is beginning to happen is that during the period of perhaps six months to a year and a half after theatrical release a movie will be on pay television, then it will be on the commercial networks; and after that it will appear on syndicated television.

We are presently in a position to reap the benefits of the direct economic system. As that system extends, it can be expected to change programming and increase diversity. For example, people who really like opera—maybe a very small audience—may be willing to pay $100 each year for an opera a month out of Lincoln Center. No commercial broadcaster trying to run a profitable business could air a program aimed at so small an audience. The opera example is not as fanciful as it may seem. As more of the nation becomes wired and satellites are increasingly utilized, an impressive subscriber base can be obtained by a pay service which attracts a relatively small percentage of cable subscribers. The payment of $100 a year by 2 percent of U.S. television homes could easily produce $17 million in revenues.

Another aspect of the likely impact on programming results from the fact that pay- and cable-television services can be, and to date generally have been, made available to subscribers on a monthly subscription basis. In contrast, commercial broadcast television can be offered to advertisers on a moment-by-moment basis. This has suggested a newspaper or magazine approach to cable and pay programming, which again contrasts sharply with the broadcasters' approach. Since the revenues of a pay-television service and a cable system depend on retaining subscribers from month to month rather than maximizing audience at every moment, more variations, diversity, and even specific-audience programming can be provided on each service, on the same theory that includes crossword puzzles in newspapers despite the fact that the majority of readers may not attempt to solve them.

Cable and pay television, then, would seem to be logical and natural providers of television services in the future, with cable systems offering both commercially supported and subscriber-supported programming. But what other new technologies are likely to develop and what will their impacts be?

Other Developments

Communications technology is developing at an explosive rate. Perhaps in a few years the role of cable will be eclipsed and will not be part of any discussion about the future. Technology seems to be moving in a fairly consistent direction: toward expansion of the number of channels, the number of sources of available programming, and the ability to deliver discrete portions of cable offerings to individual subscriber homes; yet other technologies are also on the horizon.

Let us first examine some developments directly related to cable. The first is fibreoptics, the transmission of video signals by means of laser light waves through thin glass fibers.[8] Because the optical fiber provides such "clean" signals, a bandwidth capable of delivering a significantly greater number of video channels can be delivered over greater distances, and when fibers are bunched in a single wire the capacity (for video channels and other services, even with digital transmission) becomes prodigious.[9] This development can only dramatically enhance the capabilities of cable systems.

Perhaps the greatest impact of fibreoptics on television will come from a different direction. The fiber is also an efficient way for other signal carriers, such as telephone companies, to provide their services. Currently, there are technological as well as legal restrictions separating the roles of telephone companies and cable companies. The twisted pairs of wires used by telephone systems are not designed to deliver video signals and the point-to-multipoint downstream capacity of cable systems does not have the switching capacity necessary to the switched point-to-point accessibility of telephone service. With the telephone system's capability enhanced by fibreoptics and with the cable industry's development of addressable technology, technological capacities will no longer determine the different roles of the telephone companies, cable systems, and other carriers, so that these extremely portentious issues increasingly will have to be sorted out on a public-policy and legal basis.

Another experiment of interest is Warner's "QUBE" cable system in Columbus, Ohio.[10] That system permits cable subscribers to transmit messages "upstream" on the cable by pressing a button (while a computer rapidly scans all the subscribers to gather the data) and also permits the system to bill subscribers for certain programs on a per-view (rather than monthly) basis. Instant polls can be taken of viewers' reactions to questions raised on programs and the system could also be applied to the direct ordering of advertised merchandise, all processed and billed through the cable system. The experiment, which has received a great deal of attention and will so⊂n be tried in other cities,[11] is significant at least as an attempt to develop a capacity to test the variations in programming and consumer services which may be offered through cable.

Another technology which has affected, and will continue to affect cable television directly is the satellite delivery of television signals. Satellites are very much a part of our operations today. HBO began using satellites in 1975 for simultaneous distribution to cable systems, and there now are cable systems receiving our service, as well as the services of other program suppliers, in all fifty states. The use of satellites offers several obvious benefits. Satellite transmission is far less costly for a national program-service distributor than other available means. It eliminates the need for separate and costly interconnecting terrestrial network links to each cable system, resulting in ready access to a multitude of cable-system earth stations by satellite service. Major issues regarding the assignment of orbital slots, the assignment of frequencies, and signal strength remain as both technological and political questions.

Probably the most exciting and, in the long run, most important of the developments in the foreseeable future for cable is the delivery of "viewdata" or "teletext" services. They have been pioneered in Britain and France and now are being tested in both the United States and Canada.[12] These services, by using a combination of two-way technology, satellite delivery, videodisc storage, and computer technology can bring to the consumer's computer-printer-television of the future an incredible range of information and services. Some of the more primitive examples might be access to, and rapid facsimile reproduction of newspaper and magazine articles, airline schedules, stock-market information, recipes, comparative pricing data, learning programs, and emergency health procedures.

There are a number of current developments that are not related so directly to cable, but should be mentioned in any consideration of the future of television. One of these is the use of the satellite for direct broadcast to homes (DBS), which is discussed by Horowitz in more detail in this volume.[13] In response to his discussion, I offer the observation that as an increasing proportion of the country is wired for cable television, the prospects for community reception of satellite signals become more attractive than those for individual reception. If there were a wire going into every home and centralized antenna and storage capacity at a community level, it would seem redundant, wasteful, and uneconomic to provide satellite broadcasting to earth stations at every home. The cable system's "community antenna'' would seem to be a more practical and reliable way of relaying satellite-originated signals to homes.

Another such development is over-the-air-broadcast pay television, commonly called subscription television (STV). STV stations broadcast pay-television programming with a scrambled transmission and install unscramblers in subscribers' homes. As UHF stations, STV operators have the ability to reach homes in their broadcast areas without waiting for the costly construction of cable systems.

Multipoint distribution service (MDS) is an omnidirectional transmission, which is often used to deliver pay-television programming to apartment-building master-antenna systems and private homes. Like STV, it relies on the transmission of a signal not intelligible by the usual home antenna rather than the extension of cable-television lines. Unlike STV, however, actual line of sight between each reception point and the transmitter is required.

Videodiscs, cassettes, and recording devices are also part of a rapidly developing technology, and their significance in the future is the subject of sharp differences of opinion. The use of a videodisc for information storage (and, perhaps, as the original production medium for periodicals of the future) suggests a potential for them in educational and library contexts, and the use of recording devices for consumer time shifting has obvious benefits. Their success as an original home-entertainment medium seems less promising because of their likely cost and inherent inconvenience, especially compared to the delivery of programming by pay cable. If future cable systems offer subscribers large libraries of films and other entertainment which could be selectively ordered by the consumer for delivery on his television set when requested, only the rare program which is both unavailable and sufficiently valuable to justify the cost and inconvenience would be distributed by disc or cassette.

Conclusion

The major question that emerges is whether the kind of cable services envisioned in this chapter will materialize. I do not know whether it is likely and I certainly do not think it is inevitable.

Among the many problems facing the cable industry are political considerations. Political pressure in the past has come from many different directions, most notably from the commercial networks. The FCC was convinced a number of years ago to adopt regulations severely limiting the programming allowed on pay television. Basically, the Commission prohibited virtually all movies more than three years old, most sports events, and all advertising, and required that at least 10 percent of the programming mix consist of programs other than movies and sports.[14] HBO, along with other cable- and pay-television companies, asked the U.S. Court of Appeals for the District of Columbia Circuit to declare the rules invalid. The commercial networks intervened saying that the rules were much too lax. The court upheld our view on first amendment and antitrust grounds and, most prominently, because it felt the FCC had exceeded its regulatory jurisdiction.[15]

Another source of regulatory strangulation could be the local franchising process. A cable-television system is typically required to obtain a franchise from the municipality before it is authorized to use city streets and rights of way. As pay television and additional services render the cable-television business more profitable, a frenzy of competitive franchise bidding results. To the extent the competitive proposals are realistic and the municipalities are not greedy, the process will produce innovation. But if cable companies become willing to exceed financial and technological realities in their promises in order to obtain franchises and city councils encourage excessive bidding, some of the most promising new franchise areas will become graveyards for over-extended companies and unfulfilled promises. It is particularly important to realize that one of the parties to a franchise is the government and that commitments regarding communications services and content involve important first amendment concerns.

A technology as fertile as cable television necessarily challenges the existing economic and power structures in many areas. As its potential is realized, cable television will effect fundamental changes in industries such as film distribution, data and information delivery, and communications. We can expect that the present powers in those areas that have the most to lose by any restructuring will mount political, legal, and economic challenges to the cable-television industry, as the commercial networks already have.

Will hard wiring itself become obsolete and eventually be replaced by wireless transmission? While there is a certain appeal to thinking that it will be, the capacities of a wire or fiber in terms of security, two-way communications, and multiple channels, particularly when combined with the expected increased demand for other uses of the airwaves and concerns about microwave saturation of the atmosphere, suggest that hard wiring will be the likely and most efficient means of fixed-point to fixed-point and fixed-point to multifixed-point communications in the foreseeable future, leaving wireless transmission for mobile and long-distance communications.

But the ultimate question is whether cable television will meet the challenge of the future and develop the programming and services which take advantage of its technological capacities. The industry is rapidly approaching the critical mass of subscribers for significant experimentation and innovation, for it will be the consumer who judges the value—and thus the viability—of the services. If cable television provides nothing more than enhanced broadcast signals and a handful of entertainment-program services, there is little reason to doubt that other technologies, perhaps STV and DBS, will remain quite competitive.

If, however, cable-television systems do have the imagination and commitment to realize their potential, and a full range of valuable services is offered to subscribers, no single-channel delivery systems, whether over-the-air commercial-broadcast stations, STV stations, DBS, or MDS, will make long-range sense. As the services on the wire become part of the essential communications of this nation, more cable systems will be built and interconnected. If this occurs, a programmer desiring to reach a television audience in a wired area will have no reason to broadcast; he will merely have his signal carried, along with all the others, on a wire. And any well-financed enterprise will have as great an opportunity to reach viewers, utilizing a range of financial formats, as would one of the present commercial networks.

Whether this or a different version of the future is the correct one, then, will finally depend on whether the challenge is met.

Notes

1. *See, e.g.*, A. Pearce, *supra* at 3.

2. *See generally* O. Chase, *supra* at 137.

3. For discussions of the economics of cable system operation, see Report, Docket No. 21284, 71 F.C.C.2d 632, 661-73 (1979); R. Noll, M. Peck & J. McGowan, Economic Aspects of Television Regulation 151-207 (1973).

4. This has been partly a matter of timing. The technology for direct payment existed in cable television in the early 1970s when pay cable emerged. The technology for direct payment now exists for over-the-air broadcasting (STV), but the commercial-broadcast industry formed prior to the time this technology became feasible.

5. *See* Broadcasting Yearbook 1979, at B-1 to B-76.

6. *See* J. Beebe & B. Owen, Alternative Structures for Television (Office of Telecommunications Policy Staff Research Paper OTP-SP-10) (1972), *reprinted in* D. Ginsburg, Regulation of Broadcasting 323-30 (1979) (excerpt).

7. An example of the first amendment implications is HBO's carriage of the George Carlin "Seven Dirty Words" routine. Mr. Carlin's routine, when broadcast on FM radio was the subject of FCC v. Pacifica Foundation, 438 U.S. 726 (1978). Because of the differences between broadcasting and pay television (including the latter's multiple-channel capacity and limited access), the rationale of *Pacifica* would not seem to apply to pay cable.

8. *See e.g.,* Boyle, *Light-Wave Communications*, Sci. Am., Aug. 1977, at 40-48

9. *Id*. at 40.

10. *See* Broadcasting, July 31, 1978, at 27-31.

11. *See* Broadcasting, May 14, 1979, at 24.

12. Broadcasting, Aug. 20, 1979, at 30-36.

13. *See* A. Horowitz, *infra* at 181.

14. First Report and Order, Dockets Nos. 19554 & 18893, 52 F.C.C.2d 1 (1975).

15. Home Box Office, Inc. v. FCC, 567 F.2d 9 (D.C. Cir.), *cert. denied*, 434 U.S. 829 (1977).

21 Satellite-to-Home Broadcasting

Andrew Horowitz

Introduction

One of the new technologies that may bring extensive changes to the system of broadcasting is satellite communications.[1] Satellites have in fact revised to a large extent the entire economic prospect for cable, and in particular for pay cable.

This chapter will deal with the prospect of direct-to-home satellite broadcasting. To give the reader some idea of the nature of these prospects, I will first attempt to explain what satellite-to-home broadcasting is, and will then at least touch on such issues as: (1) what the technology is; (2) how it differs from the technology of satellites that we know today; (3) where these developments are taking place around the world (most are taking place outside the United States); and (4) what the status of this technology is in the United States. I will also discuss some of the key political decisions that will have to be made, and the arenas, domestic and international, in which these political decisions will have to be made in the next few years—decisions that will greatly affect how soon we will see satellite-to-home broadcasting in this country as well as worldwide.

Lest this topic appear to be relevant only to the remote future, one should consider an article that appeared in *TV Guide* in October of 1978.[2] It concerns a gentleman in a rural community outside of Oklahoma City who has constructed a twenty-foot-diameter satellite receiving antenna in his back yard and is receiving thirty-six channels of television programming. He is receiving live soccer from Argentina, bullfights from Mexico, and programs in French from Montreal. He gets many sports programs, including live events from Madison Square Garden in New York. And he is also able to view programs such as Home Box Office and Showtime that are normally available only to those who have cable or pay-television services. Of course all this could come about only through evasions of certain regulatory practices; but it is happening today, twenty miles outside of Oklahoma City. The future is here.

Definition of Direct Satellite Broadcasting

First, let us consider what direct-broadcast satellite (DBS) broadcasting is. The whole notion of DBS is something that has been largely fashioned and

181

pioneered outside of the United States. Those who are familiar with it realize that it has been a hotly debated issue internationally for some time, both in the General Assembly of the United Nations and in various United Nations-affiliated bodies.[3]

Basically there are two distinct types of DBS service. The obvious one is implied in the name itself: A signal is sent directly from a satellite to a home receiver, augmented by a receiving device and a small antenna placed on top of the roof. This is known as *individual reception*. In the second type of DBS service, known as *community reception*, a signal is sent via satellite directly to a school or other community center, where various members of the community can then gather. Satellites have been used in this way in countries like India and Brazil, largely in an educational context.[4] Those countries lack the home-distribution systems that we have here, so that people would not normally purchase this kind of facility on their own; but they share community reception, hence the use of that term.

The Technology of DBS

The technology required to operate these kinds of systems is somewhat different from the technology that operates today domestically and internationally in commercial satellite systems. The kinds of satellites in orbit now are basically low-powered ones; for various reasons, they transmit little power down to earth. The satellite technology for DBS, however, utilizes much higher power, so that the equipment on the ground can be less sensitive and thus much smaller.[5]

Experimentation for this type of high-powered satellite, low-powered ground receiver is now being conducted by the Japanese, who intend to implement in the very near future an operational DBS system of their own with one of these high-powered satellites.[6] Work in this area is also taking place in Canada (some of it in conjunction with the United States),[7] and to some extent in Western Europe.[8] The West Germans and French in particular are looking forward to a great boom in this technology in the third world and are gearing up their electronics industries to service that market.

Although the main impetus for DBS has come from other countries, the United States has shown interest in this technology in both the public and private sectors. Both the FCC and the National Aeronautics and Space Administration (NASA) have participated in experimentation and undertaken research in this area,[9] and, of course, direct-to-home satellite program distribution is on the agenda of the Network Inquiry Special Staff.[10]

Several manufacturers have taken an active interest in direct-to-home equipment. For example, Hughes Aircraft Company, which is already in the business of building communications satellites,[11] is presently under contract with NASA to develop a 1-meter dish antenna as a prototype for direct-to-home satellite broadcasting.[12] It is likely that the principal short-term markets for that device will be outside the United States, however. Another company, Scientific-Atlanta, is offering 5-meter earth stations to consumers, at least to those who are willing and able to pay $20,000 for them and who have a suitable site on which to install this rather large unit.[13] Presumably those who purchase antennas from Scientific-Atlanta would be primarily interested in intercepting signals presently transmitted via satellite, much as Mr. Cooper of Oklahoma City is doing.[14] In response to the Scientific-Atlanta development, a St. Louis television station has asked the Commission to investigate and evaluate the impact of consumer-owned earth stations on the existing system of local broadcasting stations.[15]

There have also been suggestions that NASA get back into the research-and-development area of satellite development and begin building what are known as large space structures.[16] This prospect will become feasible once the space shuttle is in operation. That will allow us to put much more weight in space than is now possible. These large structures would have a multitude of small beams, each of which would be able to focus on a fairly small area of the earth's surface. Various NASA technical studies talk about there being as many as 100 beams on a single satellite,[17] so that conceivably each of these 100 beams could be focused on a different part of the earth's surface. Hence each beam would have a different channel from its neighboring beams, and there would be multiple-channel capacity without interference. By being able to launch several of these satellites, the United States could certainly be divided up into many sectors, each of which could get multiple channels.

The most significant move toward implementation of direct-to-home satellite broadcasting to date, however, was the surprise announcement by Comsat in August of 1979 that it plans to offer up to six channels of DBS service nationwide by 1983. Under Comsat's plan, viewers would pay a monthly charge that would include the use of a small rooftop antenna.[18] A host of legal and regulatory questions—both domestic and international—must be resolved before Comsat's plan can become a reality, and it will undoubtedly face strong opposition from many quarters.

The Politics of DBS

Domestic

For obvious reasons, the use of DBS has been strongly resisted by the present owners and operators of conventional broadcasting facilities. Through their trade association, the National Association of Broadcasters, local stations have mounted a vigorous and quite effective campaign to stem the development of this type of technology. Their argument is that it would render obsolete their own systems and jeopardize the notion of local control of broadcast facilities. While some would argue that many local broadcasters pay little heed to that principle anyway,[19] broadcasters are nonetheless expressing their concern that this technology would totally eliminate and destroy that principle.[20] On the other hand, many people in the fields of education, consumer information, and medicine see this type of technology as potentially beneficial—particularly in such applications as continuing professional education and provision of consumer information nationwide.[21] DBS is a very inexpensive way of getting a signal directly into people's homes.

As is well known, however, the educational, medical, and public-service constituency does not exactly have as much power in Washington as do commercial broadcasters. Hence the status of direct-to-home satellite broadcasting is somewhat suspect.

International

One of the critical political and regulatory arenas in which the future of DBS technology is being determined is the International Telecommunication Union (ITU), the United Nations agency that deals with the use of telecommunications. At the ITU's 1979 General World Administrative Radio Conference (WARC) in Geneva in the fall of 1979 the principal order of business is to consider changes in and additions to the assignments of frequencies to the various types of uses of the electromagnetic spectrum.[22] Since the successful development of new communications technologies— like DBS—depends on clearance to use the scarce spectrum resource, the actions taken at Geneva will obviously be of critical importance.

With the constantly expanding utilization of the spectrum by both existing and newly developing technologies, newer bands of frequencies must be opened up. This is particularly true in the satellite area. As a matter of fact, the kind of high-powered satellites needed for DBS can operate most effectively only in a band of frequencies dedicated exclusively to satellite use. It would be impossible for the technology to share frequencies with other services on the ground, such as microwave stations or radio or television stations; there must be a band of frequencies that will allow this high-powered signal to come in without interfering with anything else that is operating.[23]

Another problem that must be dealt with in establishing DBS service arises from the fact that these satellites must be placed in geostationary orbit some 22,300 miles above the equator. Only in that orbit can they constantly remain in the same position with respect to the earth's surface, so that earth stations can stay aimed at a satellite without having to "track" it across the sky.[24] Since only a single geostationary orbit exists, and since satellites in that orbit must be spaced sufficiently apart (about 4° of arc) to avoid interfering with each other, the total number of such satellites capable of covering the entire United States is very limited.[25] Accordingly, the potential extent of DBS service depends primarily on the amount of spectrum space set aside for that purpose.

The decisions about some new frequencies in the spectrum that will be opened up after the 1979 WARC conference are being hotly debated. While there is little enthusiasm in this country for maximizing the number of frequencies open for this purpose, the WARC is a one-country-one-vote forum. In the third world there is great interest in DBS technology, and additional frequencies will undoubtedly continue to be opened up internationally for this high-powered satellite broadcasting. The United States, in preparing for this conference, has taken a position that would retard the development of this technology; but it will probably be outvoted as it has been at other international forums in the past few years and will find itself once again in a minority of one.

The United States has no preexisting policy in opposition to the use of high-powered satellites such as those needed for DBS. Thus the position taken by American WARC planners must be the result of lobbying by the networks and others in the broadcasting industry.

A second international meeting that will play a major part in setting the course of DBS is the Region 2—North and South America—World Broadcasting-Satellite Conference scheduled for the spring of 1983.[26] This will be the Americas' counterpart to the 1977 World Broadcasting-Satellite Conference in Geneva, which established a plan for DBS service in the rest of the world. The plan provides for several direct-to-home channels for each nation (or for each region of nations with large population and great territorial expanse).[27]

The 1977 plan contemplates the implementation at the 1983 conference of a similar system for the Western Hemisphere.[28] The United States, however, consistent with its position at the 1977 World Broadcasting-Satellite Conference, seems to be resisting this concept. Instead, it is exploring the possibility of adopting a system of community reception that would allow many more channels than the individual-reception scheme.[29] Of course, the community-reception approach would also spare the existing networks and their affiliates from the potential competition that direct-to-home satellite transmission would offer. It is thus not surprising, given the broadcasters' power, that the United States is actively pursuing the community-reception approach to DBS.

No discussion of the international political ramifications of DBS would be complete without mention of a long-standing dispute between the United States and, principally, the USSR. The United States has long advocated the principle that there should be no international restrictions on the free flow of information throughout the world.[30] Thus any state (or its nationals) should, in the view of the United States, be free to broadcast via DBS even though the satellite signal could be received at antennae in another nation. The USSR, backed by most other nations, would regard such broadcasts as violations of the sovereignty of the receiving nation unless the latter had consented.[31] The Soviet Union and others (even including Canada) are concerned that DBS could be used as a form of "cultural imperialism" whereby the transmitting state could directly propagandize citizens of other countries with material that those countries would consider culturally or politically offensive.[32]

So far the United States has been singularly unsuccessful in advancing its view, and the 1977 Broadcasting-Satellite Plan is designed to conform to the Soviet position. It is engineered so as to provide each nation with four or more beams designed to intersect other nations' territory to the least extent practicable.[33] As previously noted, the same approach is contemplated for the Western Hemisphere.[34]

Conclusion

Although one may question the likelihood of the realization of direct-to-home satellite broadcasting in the United States within the next four or five years, as projected by Comsat,[35] we will undoubtedly have such a system in this country eventually—perhaps ten years from now. This will come about not so much because of domestic initiatives like Comsat's, but because such systems will be operational in Canada, Japan, and parts of Latin America and Western Europe. When that happens, it is inevitable that we will have it too, notwithstanding the battle that entrenched interests—broadcasters and cable operators, among others—are sure to wage.

Notes

1. P. Gross, *supra* at 175-76.
2. Cooper, *Get the Johnny Carson Show Before It's Bleeped*, TV Guide, Oct. 21, 1978, at 33 (N.Y. Metro. ed.).
3. Smith, *Direct Broadcasting: Sixteen Years of Debate*, Satellite Communications, March 1979, at 20. *See generally* K. Queeney, Direct Broadcast Satellites and the United Nations (1978).

4. *See, e.g.*, D. Smith, Teleservices Via Satellite 120-45 (1978); K. Queeney, *supra* note 3, at 204-06.

5. I. Galane, FCC Participation in the Joint U.S.-Canadian Communications Technology Satellite Experiment 12-15 (1979) (FCC RS 79-02). For a general discussion of the technical aspects of DBS, see A. Belendiuk & S. Robb, Broadcasting Via Satellite 44-68 (1979).

6. *See* Smith & Weigend, *Yuri: The First Dedicated Broadcast Satellite in Japan*, Satellite Communications, July 1978, at 23.

7. *See generally* I. Galane, *supra* note 5.

8. *See, e.g.*, LeDuc, *Direct Broadcast Satellite Services for Western Europe: A Hidden Barrier*, Satellite Communications, Feb. 1978, at 34; Broadcasting, June 11, 1979, at 56-57.

9. *See e.g.*, I. Galane, *supra* note 5; P. Sawitz & S. Hrin, On the Use of the 12 GHz Frequency Band by the Broadcasting-Satellite Service (ORI Technical Report 1507, NASA Contract NAS5-24393) (undated). *See also* Office of Science and Technology Policy, Executive Office of the President, Summary of Survey on the Federal Role in Satellite Communications Research and Development (1978).

10. Further Notice of Inquiry, Docket No. 21049, 69 F.C.C.2d 1524, 1536 (1978). (The editors of this book are studying direct-to-home satellite broadcasting as consultants to the Network Inquiry.)

11. *See, e.g.*, Broadcasting, April 23, 1979, at 66.

12. I. Galane, *supra* note 5, at 34 n. 82.

13. *See* Broadcasting, April 30, 1979, at 51; Wall Street Journal, April 19, 1979, at 13, col. 2 (Eastern ed.).

14. *See* note 2 *supra*.

15. Petition for Rulemaking (RM-3377), filed by 220 Television, Inc. (May 7, 1979).

16. *E.g.*, Space Applications Board of the National Research Council, National Academy of Sciences, Federal Research and Development for Satellite Communications (1977); Office of Science and Technology Policy, Executive Office of the President, Summary of Survey on the Federal Role in Satellite Communications Research and Development (1978).

17. *E.g.*, N. Reilly & J. Smith, Application of a Large Space Antenna to Public Service Communications (1977) (Jet Propulsion Laboratory, California Institute of Technology).

18. *See* Broadcasting, Aug. 6, 1979, at 27; Broadcasting, Aug. 13, 1979, at 55.

19. *See, e.g.,* S. Robb, *supra* at 76-79, 83-86.

20. Broadcasting, Aug. 20, 1979, at 5. *See also* Broadcasting, Aug. 6, 1979, at 27-28.

21. *See* I. Galane, *supra* note 5, at 16-17.

22. A. Rutkowski, *International Data Transfer, Satellite Communica-*

tions and the 1979 World Administrative Radio Conference in The New World Information Order: Issues in the World Administrative Radio Conference and Transborder Data Flow 3 (1979); Broadcasting, Sept. 17, 1979, at 35-45.

23. *See* Frost & Sullivan, Inc., The Commercial Satellite Communications Market in North America 58-60 (1979).

24. A Chayes, J. Fawcett, M. Ito, A. Kiss et al., Satellite Broadcasting 1-2 (1973); A. Belendiuk & S. Robb, *supra* note 5, at 51; Frost & Sullivan, Inc., *supra* note 23, at 29-34.

25. A. Belendiuk & S. Robb, *supra* note 5, at 50-51; Frost & Sullivan, Inc., *supra* note 23, at 55-56.

26. P. Sawitz & S. Hrin, *supra* note 9, at 2.

27. International Telecommunication Union, Final Acts, World Broadcasting-Satellite Administrative Radio Conference, Geneva, 1977 [hereinafter cited as Final Acts].

28. *Id.* at 73-74 (Art. 12), 145-56 (Recommendation No. Sat-8).

29. Frost & Sullivan, Inc., *supra* note 23, at 62; P. Sawitz & S. Hrin, *supra* note 9 at 45, 60.

30. K. Queeney, *supra* note 3, at 106-07, 161-64; G. Skall & K. Schaefer, Direct International and Domestic Television Broadcasting by Satellite—A Myth or Potential Reality 3 (1978); Note, *Legal Implications of Direct Satellite Broadcasting—The U.N. Working Group*, 6 Ga. J. Int'l & Comp. L. 564, 568-69 (1976).

31. K. Queeney, *supra* note 3, at 95-108.

32. *Id.* at 109-12; Pool, *Direct Broadcast Satellites and the Integrity of National Cultures* in National Sovereignty and International Communication 120-53 (K. Nordenstreng & H. Schiller eds. 1979).

33. Final Acts, *supra* note 27, at 32-72 (table of assigned frequencies). *See* K. Queeney, *supra* note 3, at 212.

34. Final Acts, *supra* note 27, at 73-74 (Art. 12), 145-46 (Recommendation No. Sat-8).

35. *See* Broadcasting, Aug. 6, 1979, at 27; Broadcasting, Aug. 13, 1979, at 55.

Part VII
Quo Vadimus?

22 Network Television as a Medium of Communication

David M. Rice

Introduction

In discussing television, particularly network television, it is important to recognize that it serves both as an advertising medium and as a medium of communication. This dichotomy of function lies at the heart of the controversy that has surrounded the networks from the heyday of radio to the present time. Indeed, much of the discussion at the conference on "Network Television and the Public Interest" focused on the conflicts inherent in network television's twofold role.

The overall picture of network television that emerged from the conference and is presented in this book is that of a politically and economically powerful industry over which the government exercises little control insofar as programming content is concerned. Programming decisions are not made in response to Mr. Justice Black's observation in the *Associated Press* case that "the widest possible dissemination of information from diverse and antagonistic sources is essential to the welfare of the public. . . ."[1] Instead, the primary concern is the desire of product advertisers to deliver their sales pitches to as large and demographically desirable an audience as possible—and their willingness to pay handsomely for the privilege.

The operation of the networks in this manner has naturally met with the favor of product advertisers. It has also been highly profitable for both the networks and their affiliates. But not everyone is satisfied with the networks' performance.

A wide variety of interest groups, including some segments of the business community, have expressed concern over what they regard as shortcomings in network television's functioning as a medium of communication. Some of these groups have criticized the networks' programming efforts, particularly in the areas of informational and cultural programming, and some have sought access to network television in order to communicate their views directly to national audiences. These and other criticisms have resulted in periodic examinations by the FCC, the Congress, and the courts of the power and performance of the networks.

Network Television in American Society

To understand the intensity of feeling underlying the attacks on the networks, it is necessary to appreciate the unique role network television plays in our society. Television is at once our principal source both of entertainment and of information. Most Americans spend as much as a thousand hours each year in front of their television sets[2]—more time than we spend attending theaters, concerts, or sporting events or reading books. And in an age of fewer and fewer multinewspaper towns, television has come to be the main supplier of news and information for most Americans, and the sole supplier for many.[3]

Television thus has become the *lingua franca* of America. Friends and neighbors can share a laugh over Archie Bunker's malapropisms and Johnny Carson's monologue of the night before without even having to retell the jokes. We expect each other to know "the way it was" according to Walter Cronkite; and if he and his counterparts at NBC and ABC do not cover an event, it may as well not have taken place as far as most Americans are concerned. As future generations of "television babies" reach adulthood and join the first such generation, which is now in its late twenties and early thirties—an age group heavily targeted by advertisers—the dominant role of television may be expected to increase still further.[4]

To an even greater extent than that to which television dominates our society, the three networks dominate television. Both as station owners and through their affiliates, the networks supply not only most entertainment programs,[5] but also much news coverage—indeed, nearly all the coverage of national and international news.[6] The network-owned stations reach about one-third of the population of the United States, and affiliated stations blanket the rest of the country.[7] Only in the larger markets is it possible to receive an unaffiliated commercial VHF station,[8] and those stations present largely warmed-over network programming of earlier years.

For the major portion of the program day, each network feeds programming to its owned and affiliated stations across the country. Virtually all of this programming is carried on owned stations, and most of it is cleared for showing by the affiliates since this is an effortless and risk-free source of profits.[9] Thus viewers in Little Rock and Peoria as well as those in New York and Los Angeles are all offered the same bill of fare most of the time, with a varying selection of side dishes from public television or from independent stations in the larger markets. As NBC President Fred Silverman recently remarked, network television "is the only medium capable of reaching the whole country at one time, the only medium that can communicate a shared experience to all levels of society."[10]

Network Television as an Advertising Medium

Since its earliest days, network television has been dominated by advertisers. At first advertisers were the principal producers of television programming, with each program being identified with its "sponsor," just as had been done on network radio.[11] Around 1960, however, a dramatic reversal took place: The networks assumed the responsibility for most program production, and advertisers purchased one-minute (later, thirty-second) commercial "spots" rather than entire programs.[12]

This shift in the advertiser's role was beneficial to both the networks and the advertisers. It enabled the networks to safeguard themselves against a repetition of the quiz-show scandals that had just rocked the country, by giving them control over their own programming schedules for the first time, and brought them increased profits from their participation in program production.[13] The new system relieved advertisers of the need to bear the high costs—and the risks—of program development and production, and allowed them to spread their advertising budgets over many time periods on all three networks.[14] Although the benefits of viewer loyalty and gratitude that were supposed to flow from program sponsorship were gone, each advertiser's message was being delivered to the public in a far more pervasive manner than before.

Naturally, once the networks had taken over the program-production function, advertisers no longer enjoyed the sort of direct control over program content that they had exercised as program producers and sponsors. But this is not to say that the advertiser was no longer influential in determining network programming. Indeed, the networks' goal in producing and scheduling their programs was to provide suitable surroundings for advertisers' commercial messages. As CBS President Frank Stanton stated in 1960: "Since we are advertiser supported we must take into account the general objectives and general desires of advertisers as a whole. . . . [I]t seems to be perfectly obvious that advertisers cannot and should not be forced into programs incompatible with their objectives."[15]

The nature of network programming and its dominance of most stations' offerings are the natural consequences of the economic foundation on which the networks are built—their ability to deliver mass audiences to advertisers. Since the rates those advertisers will pay are proportional to the size of the audience, the networks are economically motivated to offer programming that will attract as large an audience as possible. Once advertising revenues surpass the substantial but fixed program-production costs, increases in audience size—and hence in revenues—translate almost directly into profit.[16] Thus a change of only 1 or 2 percent in audience share can mean many millions of dollars in network profits.[17] Moreover, since the affiliated stations also sell advertising time within network programs,[18] their profits are also dependent on the size of the audiences those programs attract.

Given this economic structure, the programming objectives of the networks are easily understood. Programs are chosen on the basis of their hoped-for ability to draw a large audience share at the expense of competing programs on the other networks. A weak program inflicts both direct and indirect losses on the network that carries it. Its low ratings not only will result in the loss of millions of dollars in potential profits during its own time slot, but also may cut into the ratings of programs in adjacent time periods, perhaps affecting the entire evening on which it is shown.[19] It is thus not surprising that the networks are reluctant to carry public-affairs programming in prime time and that cultural and educational programs are likewise in disfavor with the networks.[20] And, of course, network programs must not be "incompatible" with advertisers' objectives; popular success is useful only if it can be translated into advertising revenue.

These economic realities have produced prime-time network-programming lineups dominated by situation comedies and adventure shows, interspersed with feature films (some of which are produced expressly for television), variety shows, sports events, and occasional "specials." Daytime network programming consists mostly of soap operas and game shows, while the weekends are taken up predominantly with sports. All of these are designed to appeal to mass audiences and hence to maximize advertising revenues. This system has the virtue of giving a large portion of the television audience the sort of fare it indicates—through the ratings—that it likes. Also, since large audiences mean large revenues, production budgets for network programs can be much larger than are possible for most non-network shows. While production cost is surely not the appropriate measure of program's quality, few would dispute that the independent productions being carried in the prime-time access period are generally of a lower quality than prime-time network shows.[21]

The system of mass-appeal programming has serious drawbacks, however. The program mix it produces tends to neglect minority tastes and interests—not only those of ethnic and racial minorities but also the interests of the elderly and of children.[22] Viewers whose tastes run to opera, Shakespeare, and other "high-culture" programming fare even worse. A degree of program diversity is produced by counterprogramming—the scheduling of a program aimed at viewers other than those to whom the competing offerings primarily appeal. But even then the various targeted groups are all part of the same mass audience for which all three networks are competing. A popular situation comedy on one network will thus be countered with an action-adventure show or a made-for-TV movie, not with an opera, a discussion of important public issues, or a program aimed at black or Hispanic audiences.[23] As Dean Roscoe L. Barrow, who directed the FCC's Network Study in the mid-1950s, observed:

The influence of the advertising function has been to bring about a serious imbalance in television programming. Gresham's law operates in television to drive out programs of interest to substantial minority audiences and to bring in those attracting a maximum number of viewers. . . .

Since television is supported by the advertising dollar, it is an economic fact of life that diversity in programming cannot be substantially greater than the diversity of commercial interest in reaching a limited audience.[24]

Network Television as a Medium of Communication

Network television is, of course, more than a string of adventure shows, situation comedies, variety shows, game shows, and movies interspersed with product commercials. It plays an important role in our society as a medium for the communication of ideas and information. This communicative function is pervasive in every aspect of television, not only in newscasts and documentaries but also in entertainment programming and advertising.

Entertainment Programming and Advertising

Entertainment programs like "Lou Grant," "M*A*S*H," and "All in the Family" are relatively overt in offering commentary on significant contemporary issues, but as Jencks points out, virtually every show carries some "message" to its audience.[25] Unfortunately, most network programming draws its communicative content from a relatively small and stereotyped set of ideas and patterns. Ben Stein attributes this to the insularity and homogeneity of the Hollywood-based television-production community;[26] Erik Barnouw contends that it is yet another consequence of advertiser domination of television.[27] Whichever thesis is correct (and there is surely some truth in each), network entertainment programming presents a far narrower cross-section of ideas and program forms than one might expect, given the thousands of hours of prime-time programming the networks present each year.

Advertising, which occupies more television time than anything but entertainment programming, is clearly designed to convey the advertiser's message to viewers. The message conveyed often goes beyond extolling a particular product; for example, it may be aimed at bolstering the advertiser's corporate image. As Barnouw observes, "a network commercial is likely to promote not only a product but a way of life, a view of the world, a philosophy."[28] Not surprisingly, that philosophy is nearly always one of conspicuous consumption.

The networks naturally are delighted to carry advertising, since that is the source of their profits. But not all advertisements are welcomed by the networks; their policy is to refuse to carry advertising that they perceive as controversial. This policy has its roots in economics.

Since profits depend upon maintaining high ratings, the networks are fearful of presenting anything—whether a program or an advertisement—which might offend or alienate the audience, perhaps causing some viewers to turn to another channel. This attitude is exemplified by Jencks's hypothetical example of right-to-life groups purchasing time during "The Waltons" to convey their antiabortion message, replete with photographs of dead fetuses.[29]

The networks also fear that if they carry controversial advertising, they will be obligated by the fairness doctrine to devote time to the presentation of opposing viewpoints.[30] This would necessitate the kind of programming which is least desirable from an economic point of view. Or worse yet, they say, they might be required to give away valuable advertising time to advocates of such opposing viewpoints.

Thus, for over three-quarters of the broadcast day,[31] the messages being transmitted by the networks and their affiliates are the noncontroversial ones contained in product advertisements and in the surrounding entertainment programs. These messages are delivered quite effectively both because of their constant repetition and because considerable resources are devoted to their production; network shows generally cost several hundred-thousand dollars per half-hour,[32] and a thirty-second advertisement will cost from $20,000 to $200,000 or more.[33] The result is an almost uninterrupted barrage of slickly produced but tame reiterations of the same themes, with the principal watchwords being "consume" and "buy."

News, Public Affairs, and Other Informational Programming

Despite the fact that the greatest share of television time and production resources is devoted to entertainment and advertising, it is usually news, public-affairs, and other informational programming that comes to mind when we speak of television as a communication medium. Although all such programs (including such program categories as public-service, educational, and agricultural) occupy only about as much time as advertising alone,[34] they have drawn the lion's share of the attention of legislators, regulators, and media critics.

This preoccupation with television as a communicator of news and information is largely based on the importance our society attaches to the role of the press. Since colonial times we have regarded the press as an essential watchdog over the government, on which the electorate relies to make informed use of its franchise.[35] As applied to network television, this outlook creates a dilemma. On the one hand, it is obviously important to avoid or minimize government interference in television's news and information function. There is little value in a watchdog that is controlled by, or which fears, that from which it is supposed to protect us. On the other hand, given the concentration of national television-news production in the hands of only three entities—the networks—which are economically motivated to program so as to maximize audience size, and given the further fact that most Americans rely on television as their primary source of news,[36] there is ample cause for concern over how effectively the watchdog function can be performed by, and how safely it can be entrusted to, the three commercial networks.

It is thus not surprising that the FCC has sought to pressure broadcasters to carry substantial amounts of news, public-affairs, and other informational programming, without mandating that any specific amount of such programs be broadcast or attempting to dictate or influence their content.[37] Under this policy, however, only a small proportion of television programming is devoted to news coverage and still less to public affairs.[38] Indeed, in the absence of FCC pressures, economic forces might reduce such programming to even lower levels, perhaps eliminating it from some stations altogether.[39]

Perhaps even more significant than the amount of time the networks devote to news and public affairs is their insistence on maintaining virtually complete control over the production of such programs,[40] thus making nationwide dissemination of the views of "diverse and antagonistic sources"[41] available only when, and to the limited extent, the networks see fit. The networks' policy of in-house production of all news and public-affairs programming has been challenged by a number of independent producers of documentaries who have been denied network exposure for their films.[42]

Network decision making with respect to news, public-affairs, and other informational programming is subject to the same economic pressures that affect entertainment programming—concern with maximizing ratings and avoiding program material that advertisers might perceive as potentially offensive to viewers. Thus competition among the networks for high ratings is as fierce for newscasts as for entertainment programming,[43] and nearly as much attention is paid to the image projected by the newscasters and the sets from which they broadcast as to the content of their news reports. The interplay between the informational and advertising function of television is illustrated by the broadcasters' delegation of the selection of public-service announcements (PSAs) to such groups as the Advertising Council[44] and the National Football League.[45] This has the effect of assuring advertisers the safe environment they seek for their ads by favoring PSAs of established charities over those of more controversial and activist groups. This practice has been challenged as a violation of the fairness doctrine by a committee representing a number of these disfavored groups.[46] This charge is somewhat ironic, since it attacks as one-sided and controversial a practice adopted by the networks for the very purpose of avoiding controversy.

Political Broadcasting

Television's role as the primary source of news and information for most Americans makes it a significant factor in the political process, particularly in campaigns for public office. Indeed, a recent study found candidates' television images to have the most significant influence on undecided voters.[47] That candidates recognize this is clear from the vast sums they spend for the purchase of television time; this has become the largest of all types of campaign expenditures.[48]

Congress has also recognized the importance and sensitivity of television's role in the political process by requiring stations to afford "equal opportunities" to all legally qualified candidates.[49] In addition, under a 1972 amendment to the Communications Act, stations must "allow reasonable access to or . . . permit purchase of reasonable amounts of time" for candidates for federal elective office.[50] Since most campaigns are confined to a local geographical area, the principal impact of these legislative provisions does not fall on the networks. In presidential races, however, access to the nationwide audiences that the networks alone can offer is essential to candidates for that office.

The networks have been unwilling to give time away to the major parties' presidential candidates under circumstances that would force them to give equal opportunities to numerous minor-party candidates. Thus in 1960 an act of Congress[51] suspending the equal-opportunities doctrine was necessary to bring about the Kennedy-Nixon debates.[52] And in 1976 the Ford-Carter debates were possible only because of an FCC decision that they came within the statutory exemption of "on-the-spot coverage of bona fide news events"[53] from the equal-opportunities requirement.[54] Still more recently, CBS advanced the broadcast date of a news documentary on Senator Edward M. Kennedy to a date preceding the senator's formal announcement of his candidacy for the Democratic presidential nomination in order to avoid equal-opportunities obligations.[55]

The networks are not only averse to giving time away, but also are not always willing even to sell time to presidential candidates. When several candidates for the 1980 Republican and Democratic presidential nominations sought to purchase thirty-minute segments of prime time in the fall of 1979, the networks refused to make that time available. They contended that it was too early in the campaign to warrant the sale of such large segments of time. An NBC vice-president stated that "the decision . . . is based to a large extent on our sense of whether the public is ready for political campaigning."[56] This explanation, as the Commission pointed out in upholding a complaint filed by President Carter's campaign committee, is incongruous in light of the substantial news coverage that the networks were already giving to the campaign.[57] A more plausible explanation of the networks' position is that the candidates were seeking to purchase time during a period in which the networks were engaged in intense competition for audience ratings. During the fall the networks are battling to establish audience acceptance of their new program lineups, and the disruption caused by half-hour political broadcasts could interfere with that process. Moreover, November ratings are particularly important to the networks since this "sweep" period is used to establish the advertising rates of their owned and affiliated stations.[58] The networks' treatment of the presidential candidates' requests once again demonstrates the subordination of television's communicative function to the maximization of advertising revenues.

Opposition to Network Dominance

The operation of television primarily as an adverstising medium dominated by the three television networks has aggrieved a wide variety of groups and individuals who use—or wish to use—television to communicate with the American public. Moreover, this concentration of control over content is seen by many as running counter to the public's interest in receiving a wide diversity of informational and entertainment programming. In the 1969 *Red Lion* case,[59] the Supreme Court recognized the importance of the public's right to have the broadcast media provide that diversity:

> [T]he people as a whole retain their interest in free speech by radio and their collective right to have the medium function consistently with the ends and purposes of the First Amendment. It is the right of the viewers and listeners, not the right of the broadcasters, which is paramount. . . . It is the right of the public to receive suitable access to social, political, esthetic, moral, and other ideas and experiences which is crucial here. That right may not constitutionally be abridged either by Congress or by the FCC.[60]

Network control over programming naturally affects the other participants in the television industry. Thus affiliated stations complain that the networks' economic power is used to impose network programming selections and schedules on individual licensees.[61] Entertainment-program producers, and the creative talent they employ, object to having to conform to network-imposed content standards,[62] and documentary-film producers are almost totally excluded from network television.[63]

Although the concern of affiliates and producers over limitations on their freedom to communicate via television is substantial, their complaints against the networks have focused primarily on economic concerns. Thus, the program producers have complained that the oligopsonistic market for television programming deprives them of their rightful share of industry profits,[64] a charge echoed in the Justice Department's antitrust suits against the networks.[65] Owners of network-affiliated stations also have contended that the networks retain an undue share of profits,[66] and have sought curbs on network power primarily to enhance their own stations' profitability. Even a cursory glance at most affiliates' programming during the prime-time access period confirms this; few stations have used this time segment for the kinds of specialized and local programming that the Commission sought to encourage when it adopted PTAR.[67]

Those groups and individuals who do not earn their livelihood in the television and related industries are, not surprisingly, concerned less with the economic aspects of network dominance and more with their own needs for access to the television audience. Attempts to establish a right of access, however, have been singularly unsuccessful.[68] Although the fairness doctrine requires broadcasters to present opposing opinions on controversial issues of public importance, it leaves the manner of achieving the necessary "fairness" to the licensees' discretion and does not entitle any particular advocate or spokesperson to air time.[69] This gives the network news departments nearly total control over who will have the opportunity to express views on public issues to national audiences and over the manner in which those views will be presented.

Only in the area of political broadcasting has any significant right of access been established.[70] As previously noted, the Communications Act itself confers some access rights on candidates for office.[71] In addition, the Commission's fairness doctrine regulations grant reply time to candidates who have been opposed, or whose opponents have been endorsed, in station editorials.[72] Both the Commission[73] and the courts[74] have refused to extend the right of reply beyond election campaigns. Thus, while the president is nearly always able to secure live three-network coverage of news conferences and major addresses, his political opponents are not assured of reply time.[75] Moreover, the Supreme Court has held, in *CBS Inc.* v. *Democratic National Committee*, that broadcasters are not required to sell time to political parties or other organizations for "editorial advertisements."[76] This leaves political groups and office holders, like other issue partisans, entirely dependent on network decision makers for access to national television audiences. Where that access is not forthcoming, such groups may find it necessary to resort to rallies, demonstrations, or similar events, organized for the express purpose of attracting television-news coverage so as to publicize their views.

The Business Community and the Networks

Product Advertising

The American business community is naturally highly interested in both the advertising and communicative aspects of network television. The primary interest of most companies is in product advertising, and since their advertising dollars support the television industry they are well cared for by broadcasters and the networks. Virtually every aspect of network television is designed to attract and please national advertisers, and local stations are similarly accommodating to both national and local advertisers.

Broadcasters do not have an entirely free hand in formulating their advertising practices. The networks and most stations subscribe to the NAB Television Code,[77] which prescribes standards for television advertisements[78] and limits the amount of time that network affiliates[79] and other stations[80] may devote to advertising and promotional matter. The Commission has always considered excessive commercialization to be inconsistent with a licensee's obligation to serve the public interest,[81] but it has declined to adopt specific rules limiting commercial time.[82] Instead the FCC has made use of a processing guideline, the practical effect of which is to leave the matter to industry self-regulation via the NAB Code.[83]

This approach has recently come under attack from two very different perspectives. In June of 1979 the Justice Department filed a civil antitrust suit against the NAB, charging that its Television Code artificially limits the availability of advertising time, thereby driving up advertising costs and restraining competition.[84] The suit produced an unusual phenomenon: broadcasters, advertisers, public-interest groups, and the FCC in agreement—in opposition to the suit.[85] One citizens group, the National Citizens Committee for Broadcasting, did more than express its opposition to eliminating limits on advertising time: It petitioned the Commission to adopt rules imposing more stringent limitations on advertising time than those contained in the NAB Code.[86]

Some product advertisers have encountered regulatory problems because of the nature of their products or the audience to which their advertisements are addressed. Advertising aimed at children, for example, has been the subject of intense scrutiny by both the FCC and the FTC. So far the FCC has not adopted special rules governing such advertising,[87] but it is presently considering a wide variety of regulatory options.[88] The FTC has been considering adoption of a trade-regulation rule on television advertising directed at children since early 1978.[89] The proceeding has been the subject of an intense industry lobbying campaign in Congress,[90] and its continued vitality is very much in doubt.[91]

As early as 1946 the FCC intimated that product advertising could raise controversial issues that would trigger fairness doctrine obligations.[92] It was not until more than twenty years later, however, that the Commission held that advertisements for a product—cigarettes—required broadcasters to carry opposing, that is, antismoking, viewpoints.[93] After it became clear that this interpretation of the fairness doctrine would have far-reaching effects,[94] the Commission concluded that it had been unwise in regarding the mere broadcasting of product commercials as raising issues to which the fairness doctrine might appply.[95] Thus, broadcasters need no longer fear that acceptance of product advertisements will obligate them to make air time available for opposing viewpoints.

Image Advertising

In recent years an increasing number of businesses have come to recognize the desirability of access to network television not only to advertise their products, but also to communicate with their consumer constituencies.[96] Indeed, a recent *U.S. News & World Report* survey of consumer views on business showed that business was perceived as weak in communicating with customers,[97] a perception many companies wish to change. Network television is the most natural and cost-effective medium for upgrading a corporate image. The use of network television for communicating corporate-image messages may be particularly appropriate in overcoming what many consider a negative image of business presented in network programming. Ben Stein recently observed that "the murderous, duplicitous, cynical businessman is about the only kind of businessman there is on TV adventure shows, just as the cunning, trickster businessman shares the stage with the pompous buffoon businessman in situation comedies."[98] The business community is also unhappy with what it perceives to be an antibusiness bias in television news broadcasts.[99]

Image advertising is often used on a large scale by companies that have received considerable adverse publicity. A case in point is the International Telephone and Telegraph Company, better known as ITT. In the early 1970s ITT's reputation suffered greatly from revelations about a favorable antitrust settlement it obtained soon after offering $400,000 to help underwrite the 1972 Republican National Convention, and about its activities during the period leading up to the overthrow of the Allende regime in Chile.[100] In 1974 and 1975 ITT conducted a large-scale television campaign involving sponsorship of a children's series, "The Big Blue Marble" (which featured themes of international understanding) and the use of image advertisements in prime time.[101] Studies of public attitudes toward ITT confirmed the success of the campaign. The public increasingly perceived ITT as caring about the general public and being a socially responsible company; favorable responses more than doubled in a single year.[102]

Unlike product advertising,[103] "image" or "institutional" advertising is not free from fairness doctrine implications. While the Commission recognizes that such advertising "ordinarily does not involve debate on public issues,"[104] where the advertisement does "play an obvious and meaningful role in public debate. . . .the fairness doctrine . . . applies."[105] The Commission thus requires licensees to make judgments as to whether particular institutional advertisements meet this test. Only "a reasonable, common sense judgment . . . tak[ing] into account [the licensee's] general knowledge of the issues and arguments in the ongoing public debate" is required, however.[106] Only where a licensee fails to exercise good faith will the fairness doctrine be violated.[107]

Issue Advertising

Corporations are becoming increasingly desirous of participating in public debate on important issues, particularly those that affect their businesses.[108] Thus a group of banks and business corporations fought a successful battle all the way to the U.S. Supreme Court to establish the right of corporations to expend funds to publicize their views on referendum proposals. In its 1978 decision in *First National Bank of Boston* v. *Bellotti*, the Court held in a 5-4 decision that speech otherwise protected by the first amendment did not lose that protection merely because it was expressed by a corporation and did not pertain directly to the company's business interests.[109] Participation in debate relating to a referendum issue "is at the heart of the First Amendment's protection"[110] and so a state can not constitutionally forbid corporations from expending their funds to influence votes by speaking out on the issue. However, the Court stopped short of declaring that corporate speech is protected by the first amendment to the same extent as that of individuals, leaving that issue unresolved.[111]

The *Bellotti* case, of course, does not assure corporations access to the television medium to express their views. And since commentary of the sort involved there is almost by definition "controversial," the fairness doctrine is fully applicable.[112] This means that neither the networks nor most individual stations will be willing to sell advertising time for this purpose, lest they have to extend an opportunity for opposing views to be heard, and perhaps even to give time away to opposing advocates.[113]

This network policy has led to confrontations with such companies as Mobil, which spent about $3.5 million of a $21 million public-relations budget in 1978 on advocacy advertising,[114] and Kaiser Aluminum. In mid-1979 Kaiser tried to get the networks to carry three issue-oriented commercials dealing with free enterprise, government red tape, and the energy situation; but all three networks refused to run the ads.[115] In justifying their refusals, the networks noted that the fairness doctrine would apply if the ads were run and expressed fear that allowing advertisers to purchase time for such advertising would allow the wealthy "to speak the loudest."[116] Kaiser responded by purchasing full-page advertisements in several major newspapers, taking the networks to task for refusing to carry their issue advertisements.[117] The networks were not intimidated, however, and stuck by their policy of refusing issue advertising.[118]

Given the networks' firm adherence to a policy of rejecting any advertising that would create fairness doctrine obligations, corporations like Mobil and Kaiser have no choice but to confine their issue advertising to other media that are not subject to the doctrine, or to seek out individual broadcasters who do not follow the same policy as the networks. The latter option, however, is simply not cost-effective and could well involve producing different versions of the commercials for different stations.

While the networks justify their policy in terms of journalistic principles, it is difficult to believe that it is not motivated, at least in part, by economic considerations. As long as the networks perceive the advertising community as preferring a bland, noncontroversial environment for its product commercials, they will prefer to exclude all debate on controversial issues rather than to permit opposing views to be heard. It is thus unfair to blame the fairness doctrine for the exclusion of issue advertising; even if the doctrine were repealed the networks would prefer to sell their advertising time to Proctor and Gamble or General Motors rather than to companies that will make viewers sit up and listen, and perhaps even think.

Notes

1. Associated Press v. United States, 326 U.S. 1, 20 (1945).
2. The Roper Organization, Inc., Public Perceptions of Television and Other Mass Media: A Twenty-Year Review 1959-1978, at 4-5 (1979).
3. *Id.* at 2-4.
4. L. Brown, Keeping Your Eye On Television 12 (1979).
5. *See* S. Robb, *supra* at 83; Petition for Inquiry, Rule Making and Immediate Temporary Relief (RM-2749), filed by Westinghouse Broadcasting Company, Inc. (Sept. 3, 1976), at 11-15 [hereinafter cited as Westinghouse Petition].
6. For a discussion of the operation of the network news departments, see S. Robb, Television/Radio Age Communications Coursebook 2-38 to 2-41 (1978).
7. *See* Broadcasting Yearbook 1979, at B-1 to B-84.

8. *See id.*

9. Carnegie Commission on the Future of Public Broadcasting, A Public Trust 151 (Bantam ed. 1979) [hereinafter cited as Carnegie II Report]; S. Robb, *supra* at 81, 90.

10. Broadcasting, Sept. 24, 1979, at 27.

11. B. Owen, J. Beebe & W. Manning, Television Economics 23 (1974).

12. E. Barnouw, The Image Empire 150 (1970).

13. *See id.* at 150-51.

14. *See* Network Inquiry Special Staff, FCC, The Historical Evolution of the Commercial Network Broadcast System 113-15 (1979) (preliminary draft).

15. House Comm. on Interstate and Foreign Commerce, Television Network Program Procurement, H.R. Rep. No. 281, 88th Cong., 1st Sess. 335 (1963).

16. *See* A. Pearce, *supra* at 9-11.

17. *See* L. Brown, Keeping Your Eye on Television 23-27 (1979).

18. Network Inquiry Special Staff, FCC, An Analysis of the Network-Affiliate Relationship in Television III-1 to III-2 (1979) (preliminary draft).

19. *See* R. Jencks, *supra* at 46.

20. Carnegie II Report, *supra* note 9, at 26.

21. *See, e.g.*, R. Wiley, *supra* at 112-13.

22. I Office of Plans and Policy, FCC, Television Programming for Children: A Report of the Children's Television Task Force 31-38 (1979).

23. For an explanation of why this is so, *see* R. Noll, M. Peck, & J. McGowan, Economic Aspects of Television Regulation 49-53 (1973).

24. Barrow, *The Attainment of Balanced Program Service in Television*, 52 Va. L. Rev. 633, 635, 638 (1966).

25. R. Jencks, *supra* at 42-43.

26. B. Stein, The View from Hollywood Boulevard (1979).

27. E. Barnouw, The Sponsor: Notes on a Modern Potentate 101-21 (1978).

28. *Id.* at 79.

29. R. Jencks, *supra* at 51.

30. *Id.* at 50-52.

31. *See* FCC, Television Broadcast Programming Data, 1978, Release No. 19247 (July 20, 1978).

32. A. Pearce, *supra* at 10-12.

33. E. Barnouw, The Sponsor: Notes on a Modern Potentate 81 (1978).

34. *Compare* FCC, Television Broadcast Programming Data, 1978, Release No. 19247 (July 20, 1978), *with* National Association of Broadcasters, Television Code (20th ed. 1978).

35. Blasi, *The Checking Value in First Amendment Theory*, 1977 Am. Bar Foundation Research J. 521, 532-44.

36. *See* note 3, *supra*.

37. Under the Commission's "processing guidelines," only those television renewal applications which propose at least 5 percent of news and public-affairs programming may be approved by the staff under delegated authority. 47 C.F.R. §0.281(a)(8) (1979). In order to avoid having renewals referred to the Commission *en banc*, and perhaps designated for hearings, broadcasters invariably comply with the guideline percentage.

38. *See* FCC, Television Broadcast Programming Data 1978, Release No. 19247 (July 20, 1979).

39. The FCC has recently begun to question whether such pressures are in fact responsible for increasing news and public-affairs programming over what unregulated marketplace forces would produce. *Cf.* Notice of Inquiry and Proposed Rule Making in BC Docket No. 79-219, 73 F.C.C.2d 457 (1979)(deregulation of radio).

40. *See* Neubauer, *The Networks' Policy Against Freelance Documentaries: A Proposal for Commission Action*, 30 Fed. Com. L. J. 117 (1978).

41. *See* note 1, *supra*.

42. Broadcasting, Sept. 18, 1978, at 78-80.

43. *See* Carnegie II Report, *supra* note 9, at 27.

44. E. Barnouw, The Sponsor: Notes on a Modern Potentate 140-46 (1978).

45. *See* N.Y. Times, Nov. 13, 1979, at B12, col. 3.

46. *Id.*

47. Lucas & Adams, *Talking, Television and Voter Indecision*, J. Com., Autumn 1978, at 120-31.

48. H. Alexander, Financing the 1968 Election 93 (1971).

49. 47 U.S.C. §315(a) (1976).

50. 47 U.S.C. §312(a)(7) (1976).

51. Act of Aug. 24, 1960, Pub. L. No. 86-677, 74 Stat. 554.

52. *See* E. Barnouw, The Image Empire 161-62 (1970).

53. 47 U.S.C. §315(a)(4) (1976).

54. Aspen Institute, 55 F.C.C.2d 697 (1975), *aff'd sub nom.* Chisholm v. FCC, 538 F.2d 349 (D.C. Cir.), *cert. denied*, 429 U.S. 890 (1976).

55. Brown, *'Teddy' on CBS Sunday*, N.Y. Times, Nov. 1, 1979, at C19, col. 1.

56. Brown, *Networks Opposing Political Ads Now*, N.Y. Times, Oct. 14, 1979, §1, at 32, col. 1.

57. Carter-Mondale Presidential Committee, Inc., 74 F.C.C.2d 631, 646, *reconsideration denied*, 74 F.C.C.2d 657 (1979), *petition for rev. filed sub nom.* CBS Inc. v. FCC, No. 79-2403 (D.C. Cir. Nov. 28, 1979).

58. *See* Brown, *supra* note 57; Duscha, *No Time for Candidates on TV*, Newsday, Nov. 6, 1979.

59. Red Lion Broadcasting Co. v. FCC, 395 U.S. 367 (1969).

60. *Id.* at 390.

61. *E.g.,* Washington Petition, *supra* note 5, at 23.

62. *See, e.g.,* Writers Guild of America, West, Inc. v. FCC, 423 F. Supp. 1064, 1125-27 (C.D. Cal. 1976), *rev'd sub nom.* Writers Guild of America, West, Inc. v. ABC, 609 F.2d 355 (9th Cir. 1979), *petition for cert. filed,* 48 U.S.L.W. 3736 (U.S. April 29, 1980) (No. 79-1717).

63. *See* Neubauer, *supra* note 40.

64. *See, e.g.,* Report and Order, Docket No. 12782, 23 F.C.C.2d 382, 394, *on reconsideration,* 25 F.C.C.2d 318, 321-24 (1970).

65. United States v. ABC, Civ. No. 74-3600-RJK (C.D. Cal., complaint filed Dec. 10, 1974); United States v. CBS Inc., Civ. No. 74-3599-RJK (C.D. Cal., complaint filed Dec. 10, 1974); United States v. NBC, Civ. No. 74-3601-RJK (C.D. Cal., complaint filed Dec. 10, 1974).

66. *E.g.,* Westinghouse Petition, *supra* note 5, at 30-40.

67. *See* National Ass'n of Independent Television Producers & Distribs. v. FCC, 516 F.2d 526, 533-34 (2d Cir. 1975).

68. *See* O. Chase, *supra* at 142-44.

69. Fairness Report, 48 F.C.C.2d 1, 10-17 (1974), *reconsideration denied,* 58 F.C.C.2d 691 (1976), *aff'd in part and rev'd in part on other grounds sub nom.* National Citizens Committee for Broadcasting v. FCC, 567 F.2d 1095 (D.C. Cir. 1977), *cert. denied,* 436 U.S. 926 (1978).

70. Individuals whose personal integrity has been attacked on the air are also granted a right of reply. 47 C.F.R. §73.679(a) (1979).

71. *See* notes 49-50 *supra* and accompanying text.

72. 47 C.F.R. §73.679(c) (1979).

73. *E.g.,* First Report—Handling of Political Broadcast, Docket No. 19260, 36 F.C.C.2d 40, 46-48 (1972).

74. *E.g.,* Democratic National Committee v. FCC, 481 F.2d 543 (D.C. Cir. 1973).

75. *Id.* The networks, on a voluntary basis, have carried such replies on numerous occasions. *See, e.g.,* Committee for the Fair Broadcasting of Controversial Issues, 25 F.C.C.2d 283, 296 n.22, 299-300 (1970), *rev'd sub nom.* CBS Inc. v. FCC, 454 F.2d 1018 (D.C. Cir. 1971).

76. CBS Inc. v. Democratic National Committee, 412 U.S. 94 (1973).

77. National Association of Broadcasters, Television Code (20th ed. 1978).

78. *Id.,* §§IX-XIII.

79. *Id.,* §XIV.

80. *Id.,* §XV.

81. *E.g.,* FCC, Public Service Responsibility of Broadcast Licensees 29-57, 73-89 (1946); Programming Policy Statement, 44 F.C.C. 2303, 2313 (1960).

82. Report and Order, Docket No. 15083, 36 F.C.C. 45 (1964).

83. 47 C.F.R. §0.281(a)(7)(iv) (1979).

84. United States v. National Ass'n of Broadcasters, Civ. No. 79-1549 (D.D.C., complaint filed June 14, 1979).

85. Brown, *Antitrust Action on TV Commercials: Industry and Admen Fear an Exercise in Futility*, N.Y. Times, June 16, 1979, at 46, col. 1; National Association of Broadcasters, Broadcasting and Government: A Review of 1979 and a Preview of 1980, at 32 (1980).

86. Broadcasting, Aug. 13, 1979, at 26.

87. Children's Television Report and Policy Statement, Docket No. 19142, 50 F.C.C.2d 1, 8-18 (1974), *reconsideration denied*, 55 F.C.C.2d 691 (1975), *aff'd sub nom.* Action for Children's Television v. FCC, 564 F.2d 458 (D.C. Cir. 1977).

88. Notice of Proposed Rule Making, Docket No. 19142, 75 F.C.C.2d 138 (1979).

89. Notice of Proposed Rulemaking, FTC File No. 215-60, 43 Fed. Reg. 17967 (1978).

90. *See* A. Pearce, *supra* at 19-20.

91. *See, e.g.*, Broadcasting, Dec. 3, 1979, at 53-54.

92. Sam Morris, 11 F.C.C. 197 (1946).

93. WCBS-TV, 8 F.C.C.2d 381, *on reconsideration*, 9 F.C.C.2d 921 (1967), *aff'd sub nom.* Banzhaf v. FCC, 405 F.2d 1082 (D.C. Cir. 1968), *cert. denied*, 396 U.S. 842 (1969).

94. *See, e.g.*, Retail Store Employees Union, Local 880 v. FCC, 436 F.2d 248 (D.C. Cir. 1970); Friends of the Earth v. FCC, 449 F.2d 1164 (D.C. Cir. 1971).

95. Fairness Report, 48 F.C.C.2d 1, 24-28 (1974), *reconsideration denied*, 58 F.C.C.2d 691, 697-99 (1976), *aff'd in part and rev'd in part sub nom.* National Citizens Committee for Broadcasting v. FCC, 567 F.2d 1095 (D.C. Cir. 1977), *cert. denied*, 436 U.S. 926 (1978).

96. *See, e.g.*, Broadcasting, Sept. 20, 1976, at 54-58.

97. *See* Kaiser Aluminum & Chemical Corporation, At Issue: The Controversy Over Concentrated Industries 31 (1978).

98. B. Stein, The View From Sunset Boulevard 18-19 (1979).

99. Dougherty, *TV Critics of Business Criticized*, N.Y. Times, Nov. 15, 1979, at D18, col. 3.

100. E. Barnouw, The Sponsor: Notes on a Modern Potentate 85 (1978).

101. *Id.* at 85-86.

102. *Id.* at 86.

103. *See* text accompanying note 95, *supra*.

104. Fairness Report, *supra* note 95, 48 F.C.C. 2d at 23.

105. *Id.*

106. *Id.*

107. *Id.* at 24.

108. McDowell, *Bridging the Communications Gap*, Saturday Review, Sept. 29, 1979, at 16-20.

109. 435 U.S. 765 (1978).

110. *Id.* at 776.

111. *Id.* at 777-78.

112. Fairness Report, *supra* note 95, 48 F.C.C.2d at 22.

113. *See* Cullman Broadcasting Co., 40 F.C.C. 576 (1963).

114. McDowell, *supra* note 108, at 17.

115. N.Y. Times, June 20, 1979, at C22, col. 1.

116. *Id.*

117. *E.g.*, N.Y. Times, June 19, 1979, at B7.

118. Broadcasting, June 25, 1979, at 72-73.

119. *Id.* at 72.

Index

About the Contributors

Eugene Aleinikoff is a member of the New York Bar.

Rene Anselmo is president of the Spanish International Network.

George L. Back is the principal of George Back & Associates, consultants. Prior to forming his own firm he served as chief executive of the Hughes Television Network.

David Blank is vice-president of CBS Inc.

Oscar G. Chase is a professor of law at New York University School of Law. Before entering the academic world, he spent almost a decade in state and federal test-case constitutional litigation as associate director of Community Action for Legal Services, the umbrella legal-services operation in New York City. He has written numerous articles on questions of constitutional law and did pioneering work on the first amendment status of public broadcasting. He also has been intensively involved in litigation challenging the Public Broadcasting Service's powers of censorship and program-content control.

Howard Eaton is a consultant with Olgilvy and Mather, Inc., in New York City.

Peter A. Gross is general counsel for Home Box Office, Inc.

Andrew Horowitz is managing director of Telecommunications Cooperative Network, Inc.

Richard W. Jencks is a broadcast consultant in Stinson Beach, California. He spent a number of years at CBS Inc., serving as general counsel and later as president of the CBS Broadcast Group. Mr. Jencks is an active lecturer and essayist.

Paul B. Jones was assistant general counsel for the Federal Communications Commission at the time of the Network Television Conference. He is now an attorney in the owned-stations division of American Broadcasting Companies, Inc.

Aaron Kahn is a member of the District of Columbia Bar.

Heather Kirkwood is senior staff attorney for the Media Project of the Federal Trade Commission.

Earle K. Moore is a partner in the law firm of Moore, Berson, Lifflander & Mewhinney in New York City.

James C.N. Paul is a professor of law at Rutgers Law School in Newark.

Alan Pearce is a consulting economist in Washington, D.C. Dr. Pearce was educated at the London School of Economics and Indiana University, and he served on the staffs of Chairman Dean Burch and Chairman Richard Wiley at the Federal Communications Commission. He also worked as staff economist for the House Subcommittee on Communications, as a telecommunications policy advisor in the Executive Office of the President, and as a consultant to the National Telecommunications and Information Administration. Dr. Pearce has published numerous articles on the economics of broadcast and cable television, including a seminal study of the economics of network television.

Alan Reitman is associate director of the American Civil Liberties Union.

Scott H. Robb is a partner in Robb & Kuhns, a communications law firm in New York City that represents a number of network-affiliated stations. Before joining the firm, he was a senior attorney at the National Broadcasting Company, involved primarily with regulatory issues before the Federal Communications Commission. He has published numerous articles and a book, *Communications Coursebook*.

David M. Rubin is a professor at New York University School of Journalism.

Andrew Jay Schwartzman is executive director of the Media Access Project in Washington, D.C.

Melvin Simensky is a partner in the law firm of Gersten, Scherer & Kaplowitz in New York City.

Richard E. Wiley is a senior partner in the Washington- and Chicago-based law firm of Kirkland & Ellis. From 1971 to 1977 he served as general counsel, then a commissioner, and then chairman of the Federal Communications Commission. He is currently an adjunct professor at a number of law schools and writes regular columns on communications law for a variety of publications.

About the Editors

Michael Botein is a professor of law at New York Law School and director of its Communications Media Center. He has published a number of scholarly books, monographs, and articles on wide-ranging issues in regulation of the communications media, including cable television, copyright, broadcast-licensing procedures, and emerging technologies. He has served as a consultant to the Administrative Conference of the United States, the Federal Communications Commission, and the RAND Corporation.

David M. Rice is a professor of law at New York Law School and associate director of its Communications Media Center. After a number of years of legal practice in New York City, he joined the faculty of the Brooklyn Law School and then later the New York Law School. He has represented numerous groups in cases before the Federal Communications Commission and the federal courts involving a variety of communications issues, and has served as a consultant to the Commission. Professor Rice is chairperson of the Section on Mass Communications Law of the Association of American Law Schools.